Citizen Relationship Management

T0316873

European University Studies

Europäische Hochschulschriften
Publications Universitaires Européennes

Series XXXI
Politics

Reihe XXXI Série XXXI
Politik
Politics

Vol./Bd. 560

PETER LANG

Frankfurt am Main · Berlin · Bern · Bruxelles · New York · Oxford · Wien

Alexander Schellong

Citizen Relationship Management

A Study of CRM in Government

PETER LANG
Internationaler Verlag der Wissenschaften

Bibliographic Information published by the Deutsche Nationalbibliothek
The Deutsche Nationalbibliothek lists this publication in the Deutsche Nationalbibliografie; detailed bibliographic data is available in the internet at <http://www.d-nb.de>.

Zugl.: Frankfurt (Main), Univ., Diss., 2008

D 30
ISSN 0721-3654
ISBN 978-3-631-57844-5

© Peter Lang GmbH
Internationaler Verlag der Wissenschaften
Frankfurt am Main 2008
All rights reserved.

All parts of this publication are protected by copyright. Any utilisation outside the strict limits of the copyright law, without the permission of the publisher, is forbidden and liable to prosecution. This applies in particular to reproductions, translations, microfilming, and storage and processing in electronic retrieval systems.

Printed in Germany 1 2 3 4 5   7

www.peterlang.de

To my parents

Zita and Priv. Doz. Dr. med. Hubertus Schellong

Which government is the best? The one that teaches us to govern ourselves

Johann Wolfgang Goethe (1749-1832)

Everything that can be counted does not necessarily count, everything that counts cannot necessarily be counted

Albert Einstein (1879-1955)

Acknowledgements

Noticing that around the world there is still a major gap between the promise and execution of citizen-orientation in government, I began this endeavour to understand whether a private-sector management practice called Customer Relationship Management (CRM) could work in government. Over time I realized that certain aspects of CRM were in fact not new to government. This study should allow researchers and practitioners alike to better understand, apply or discuss Citizen Relationship Management (CiRM) as well as 311 type initiatives.

The completion of this dissertation closes an exciting as well as challenging period in my life. This dissertation journey allowed me to spend some time behind the ivy-covered walls of Harvard and at The University of Tokyo in one of the world's most vivid mega cities. It is impossible to adequately thank those who made their contribution to this dissertation in one way or another.

First and foremost, I would like to extend my deep thanks and appreciation to Professor Dieter Mans, my advisor, for having faith and confidence in me. His openness to and support of many of my ideas have been a critical success factor of this dissertation. He listened and questioned where necessary but allowed me to find my own way. In addition, I would like to thank Professor Josef Esser, my second advisor and the members of my defense committee, Professor Klaus Allerbeck, Professor Tanja Brühl and Professor Andreas Nölke.

I am especially grateful to Professor Jane Fountain and Professor David Lazer, who invited me to the National Center for Digital Government, and its successor, the Program on Networked Government at Harvard's Kennedy School of Government. They profoundly influenced my development as a researcher and the structure of this study. I could not have realized the dissertation in its present state without their support and the available resources of an institution such as Harvard. Moreover, David introduced me to the interesting fields of social networks and complexity. At the end of the day, everything turns out to be connected.

I owe a special debt of gratitude to those who participated in my interviews. Nobody who was approached refused my request for help. To the contrary, I received more support than I had ever expected. The participants allowed me to observe, interact, ask any kind of question and gain deep insights into related and unrelated matter of this research. I became aware of the numerous challenges in creating public value. I deeply respect those that find their calling in public service. Unfortunately, my commitment to provide them with anonymity prevents me from mentioning many of their names. For Miami-Dade County, I am especially grateful for the support and sponsorship of Judi Zito and her family. Her leadership style, innovativeness and far-sightedness are a true inspiration. Quería darle las gracias a Mary Trujillo por su cuidado de corazón. In addition, I would like to thank County Manager George Burgess, Becky Jo Glover and Loretta Cronk. Elliot Schlanger made it possible to do research in the City of Baltimore and to participate in a CitiStat meeting. Ted O'Keefe gave me access to the City of Chicago. Jason Resa patiently responded to all of my inquiries and perfectly arranged my interviews. Gino Menchini, Dean Schloyer and Lawrence Knafo provided insights into the complex nature of public management in a place such as the City of New York. Moreover, I would like to thank John Kost from Gartner, Jeff Winbourne from Winbourne & Costas and Mark Howard from Accenture for openly sharing their knowledge and network in support of this research.

私は奥村裕一氏に感謝申し上げたい。奥村氏は私の日本文化に対する理解を深めさせて下さり、日本での研究活動を行うにあたって様々な援助をして下さった。政府における新しい計画と手法、また文化的相違について、日々交わした会話は大変貴重なものであった。東京大学法学政治学研究科の城山英明教授にも感謝申し上げたい。日本にお招き頂いたことにより、研究視野を広げることができた。そして、あらゆる面でサポートしてくれた佐藤邦子さん、毛利美都代さん、藤井秀之さんにも感謝の意を述べたい。

I have benefited greatly from the interactions and reflections with my colleagues and the faculty I met throughout this journey. My colleagues at Harvard—Bernie Cahill, Thomas Langenberg, Curt Ziniel, Jeff Boase, Jeanne Mengis, Birgit Rabl and Andrew Feldman (FW2)—remain friends. In particular, I would like to thank Dr. Ines Mergel. Discussions with the faculty of the Kennedy School have much improved the structure of my thoughts and enabled me to identify new approaches to my research. Professor Bob Behn taught me a lot about performance management and CitiStat. Professor Jerry Mechling gave me access to his executive education programs, "Leadership in a Networked World," and made me aware of the challenges of cross-boundary collaboration and ICT. Professor Philipp Müller was an invaluable mentor for many aspects of my academic and non-academic life. He truly believes in people.

The Johann Wolfgang Goethe-University Graduate Scholarship and a Siemens AG Doctoral Fellowship provided funding during the conduct of this research. In this regard, I would like to thank Gerda Jung, Karl Klug, Dr. Thomas Deil and Alexander von Erdmannsdorff.

Finally, I would like to express my deepest gratitude for the support of my friends and family. In particular, my parents have been the foundation of what I am today and what I have accomplished with this work. Thank you.

Table of Contents

List of Figures

List of Tables

List of Abbreviations

115	German federally reserved number for non-emergency services
211	U.S. federally reserved number for social- and health related services
311	U.S. federally reserved number for non-emergency services
411	U.S. federally reserved number for directory assistance
511	U.S. federally reserved number for traffic information
911	U.S. federal reserved number for emergency services
B2C	Business to Consumer
B2G	Business to Government
BmI	Bundesministerium des Innern
BPA	Business Process Analysis
BPR	Business Process Re-engineering
CAS	Computer Automated Selling
C	Citizen
C2C	Consumer to Consumer
CIO	Chief Information Officer
CiRM	Citizen Relationship Management
CitiStat	Performance Management System
CitiTrack	Customer Service Request (CSR) software system
CLI	Caller Line Identification
CLV	Customer Lifetime Value
CiLV	Citizen Lifetime Value
CRM	Customer Relationship Management
CSA	Customer Service Advocate
CSR	Customer Service Representative (call taker)
CTI	Computer Telephony Integration
CompStat	Policing Performance Management Concept developed by the NYPD
DMV	Department of Motor Vehicles
DOD	Department of Defense
DOB	Department of Buildings
DoITT	Department of Information Technology and Telecommunications
DOS	Department of Sanitation
EA	Enterprise Architecture
eGov	Electronic Government
EO	Elected Official
ERP	Enterprise Resource Planning
FCC	Federal Communications Commission
G2C	Government to Citizen
GIC	Government Information Center (Miami-Dade County)
GIS	Geographic Information System
ICT	Information and Communication Technology

IRS	Internal Revenue Service
IVR	Integrated Voice Response
KGSt	Kommunale Gemeinschaftsstelle für Verwaltungsvereinfachung
MBO	Management by Objective
NAO	National Audit Office
NPM	New Public Management
NPR	National Performance Review
NSM	Neues Steuerungsmodell
NYPD	New York Police Department
OLAP	Online Analytical Processing
PA	Public Administration
PPP	Public Private Partnership
RM	Relationship Marketing
SEM	Structural Equation Modelling
SES	Socio-Economic Status
SOA	Service-Oriented Architecture
SR	Service Request
TQM	Total Quality Management
VoIP	Voice over IP
ZBO	Zero-Based Budgeting

1 Introduction

Government, and especially public administration, plays a key role in the lives of citizens. The economic stagnation faced by many democracies in the early 1980s and its association with overregulation, poor bureaucratic responsiveness and simultaneous erosion of trust, forced governments to rethink their models of governance for the first time in fifty years (Frederickson/Smith 2003: 214-215). All these elements resulted in a global push to reshape the formal and informal ties between government and society. One of the common objectives, therefore, was a more citizen-oriented government and public services. Subsequently, governments around the globe viewed the Internet as a powerful force that could increase their responsiveness to citizens or as a means to further empower the state (Fountain 2001a).

Facing the effects of competition and globalization, the business world also recognized the importance of focusing on its customers instead of on transactions or their products. Thereafter, progressively more sophisticated consumers and advances in academic research made private businesses realize that customers were individuals with distinctive attributes and that customer relationships were an important type of organisational asset. In fact, customer relationships were seen as a potential source of competitive advantage in the 1990s (Porter 1985). The rise of the Internet further strengthened the role of the customer and opportunities for businesses to tap into customer resources such as labour, knowledge or social capital. However, in order to do this, organisations needed to move from narrow product-focused strategies towards customer-focused strategies. Moreover, enterprises had to radically transform into customer-centric organisations and continuously improve the customer relationship. These strategies eventually led to Customer Relationship Management (CRM).

CRM is the acronym and term used for a body of management philosophies, practices and technology utilizations. CRM is interpreted and implemented in different ways, and its impact remains to be completely understood. Many believe that CRM has generic validity which when applied to government improves customer service, citizen-orientation and efficiency. In short, CRM can dramatically improve the citizen–government relationship and public services.

This study essentially addresses the following questions:

How is CRM understood and implemented in U.S. government? What is the impact of CRM initiatives? What is the contribution of CRM to currently active reform movements that aim at improving citizen-orientation? The answers to these questions should support two additional objectives of this study. First, answering the fundamental question of whether there is a difference between private and public CRM, and second, conceptualizing Citizen Relationship Management.

1.1 Background and scope of the problem

Public administration is often neglected in the discussion about the citizen–government relationship, although it plays a vital role in the way government exerts its role in society. Citizens experience policies and the structure of the state through their interactions with public administration such as law enforcement and public service agencies. Administrative practices and capabilities are usually subsumed within the general discussions of government and governmental obligations to citizens. In fact, philosophical foundations of the administrative component of government are seldom discussed at all (Waldo 1984; Rohr 1986). Yet citizen-initiated contacts with administrative officials to request or complain about a service are a critically important mode of public participation in the urban political system (Coulter 1988). Those interactions represent a pure form of Hirschman's (1970) "voice" option, because the subject matter is automatically important and salient for the citizen (Coulter 1988: 1). Opinions offer policy makers information to "(1) understand and establish public needs; (2) develop, communicate and distribute public services and; (3) assess the degree of public service satisfaction" (Vigoda 2000: 167).

On average, citizens have more contacts throughout their lifetime with non-elected public servants on the municipal level than with their other elected representatives. According to Naschhold, Watt and Arnkill (1996: 131), "[L]ocal government has entered the political arena as a central actor." Administrators are already to a very large extent involved in the means and ends formulation of policies at the political level (Hansen/Ejersbo 2002). Citizens also tend to have the greatest interest in their local community (Steyaert 2000). Therefore, municipal administration can be considered an important factor for trust building in the overall citizen–government relationship (Phillips 1996).

Governments have been aware of becoming more effective and efficient for quite some time. Efforts to improve public services can be traced back to the beginning of the 20th century. Since the emergence of neo-economic New Public Management (NPM) and related approaches such as Total Quality Management (TQM) (Berman/West 1995), a "customer-driven" government has been on the agenda for public servants and academics (Osborne/Gaebler 1992; Swiss 1992; Gore 1993; Albrecht 1993; Kißler et al. 1997; Alkadry 2003 ;OECD 2003). However, while studies about the private-sector customer are plentiful, relatively few offer insights on the citizen as customer. Nevertheless, by its embrace of customer service, public administration committed itself to finding the value of its efforts in the satisfaction of its citizens. In addition, citizen demands were perceived as an agent of organisational change (Lowenthal 1994). NPM became a normative model, influencing the way of thinking about the role of public administrators, public services and their goals (Denhart/Denhart 2003). But as shown by Hood and Peters (2004), there was no common way of understanding and implementing NPM. Accompanying management reforms, such as contracting out or management decentralization, were a matter of detailed negotiation and interaction within the government system rather than a matter of public interest and visible benefit (Batley 2004). Hence, despite TQM, which is a set of management activities based on statistics that is aimed at continuous quality improvement through employee empowerment and customer consultation, NPM tended to have a single-sided, internal focus (Traunmüller/Lenk 2002).

The emergence of electronic government in the late 1990s added new momentum to NPM and the goal of finding ways of improving citizen-orientation through electronic information and service provision (Caldow 1999; Cook 2000; Hagen 2000; Fountain 2001a; Gisler/Spahni 2001; Ashford/Rowley/Slack 2002; Abramson/Morin 2003; West 2005a). Information and communication technology offered the opportunity to build the "virtual state", (Fountain 2001a) neutralizing the temporal, spatial and hierarchical limits of government and public services. In the context of eGovernment research, however, both practitioners and academic scholars argue that governments are not exploiting the potential benefits of ICT for citizen-orientation and participation Christensen/Verlinden/Westerman 2002). Instead of infusing organisational and institutional change, most eGovernment projects represent simple reproductions of existing institutional patterns and structural relations among agencies (United Nations 2003).

Concurrent with these developments, vendors and researchers showed interest in Citizen or Constituent Relationship Management (CiRM) (Kavanagh 2001; Janssen/ Wagenaar 2002; Trostmann/Lewy 2002). The term is derived from CRM, which was influenced by the study of relationship marketing (Berry 1983).

In the private sector, CRM is a widely-applied concept dealing with building stronger relationships between an enterprise and its customers (Peppers/Rogers 2004). At the core of CRM lies the goal to increase customer revenue over the lifetime of the customer relationship. Further benefits are believed to be the reduction of marketing costs, strengthening of customer loyalty or identification of opportunities for up- and cross-selling. Relationship development and management require significant resources, commitments and organisational changes. CRM typically builds on information technology to support and coordinate different types of exchanges that occur across multiple channels. Information about current and prospective customers is centrally stored, analysed and combined with additional data for management decisions and service operations. CRM definitions vary. Some scholars limit CRM to a series of customer-oriented technology solutions; others stress its holistic character, which requires a customer-centric business philosophy, business processes re-engineering and often dramatic cultural and organisational changes (Zablah/Bellenger/Johnston 2004). Evidence about the impact of CRM on a firm or evidence about customer perceptions of CRM efforts is still scarce. In fact, the literature reported that CRM projects often fail or pose many obstacles to successful implementation (Verhoef/Langerak 2003). For example, the effective management of customer relationships grows in complexity as the heterogeneity (preferences and needs) in a firm's customer base increases (Sawhney/Zabin 2002; Eriksson/Mattsson 2002). CRM has also been criticized for misunderstanding the fundamental nature of a human relationship and factors such as trust and intimacy (Fournier/Dobscha/Mick 1998). Companies struggle with creating and sustaining good customer relationships (Price/Arnould/Tierney 1995). In contrast to CRM, knowledge about Citizen Relationship Management is in its nascent stage.

Current initiatives are mostly technology-driven through the use of CRM software in contact centers. Some publicly-owned utility agencies (e.g. water, sewer or power) have actually been using CRM software to manage their customers. Deriving a conceptualization of CiRM from a holistic understanding of CRM leads to the question of the validity and applicability of the use of CRM in government. A large-scale introduction of CiRM wreaks havoc with the structure of traditional administration, federalism, accountability and privacy, and it changes the roles of political and administrative actors. Financial revenues used by government agencies come from a collective tax base and not from product and service-generated sales. On the other hand, many aspects of CRM are not sector-specific (e.g. providing services through a variety of channels) and can be translated into the context of government. Public servants in welfare already keep files with detailed information about their clients in order to offer personalized support. Advice and services can be offered through different channels (phone, in person, Internet) to those in need.

Finally, the concept of "customer", which was borrowed from the private sector, has flaws (Moore 1995). In this model, self-interest and the pursuit of maximizing individual utility are valued (Roberts 2004). As a resource, customers mostly supply information or capital (Mills/Chase 1983). Moreover, it is difficult to identify who the customers of a government agency are. Advocates of traditional public administration point out that agencies serve their clients but also owe accountability to the collective interests of citizens, not the aggregation of their preferences (Kelly 2005). Even if all customers are identified, government has another dilemma. Citizens seem to have different and competing interests (Denhart/Denhart 2003). Value creation and citizen satisfaction in one sector of the public market may also lead to dissatisfaction in another sector. Furthermore, agencies are in many cases in the business of imposing obligations, not providing services (Smith/Huntsman 1997).

In particular, the consumerist notion of deconstructing citizens as customers raised concerns among researchers (Barnes/Prior 1995; Hood 1995). A major objection was that the citizen–government relationship is redefined as a passive commercial transaction rather than democratic participation. According to Box (1999) and others (Walsh 1991; Brown 1992; Ryan 2001), the ideas underlying the term "customer" strengthen elitist politics and reduce a complex relationship to a simplistic, voluntary one. Findings from a study in Israel that tested the relationship between public administration performance and citizenship involvement support Box's critique. Vigoda (2002a) showed that citizens were less inclined to actively participate in political and community affairs as they became gradually more satisfied with performance. Furthermore, extensive customer orientation in government increases the probability of short-term politics at the expense of long-term political goals (Swiss 1992).

1.2 Definition of terms

In this study, the term "Customer Relationship Management" (CRM) is understood holistically. CRM is essentially a cluster of philosophies, strategies and practices facilitated by technology that are designed to build a customer-centric organisation. I use the term "Citizen Relationship Management" (CiRM) to clearly delineate CRM's application in government. "Understanding" refers to the iterative process whereby a person tries to conceptualize an abstract or physical object (Miyake 1986). The term "implementation" refers to the process or a series of events that aim at putting into practice a concept, policy or idea. Finally, "impact" refers to the effects a concept has at the intra- and inter-organisational level on organisational culture, governance and the relationship between politics, public administration and citizens.

1.3 Orientation of the research

This dissertation is based on interdisciplinary literature that seemed relevant to understanding the context of CRM. The literature included studies in political science, administrative science, business management and information science. Thus, the fundamental orientation of the research is similar to that of the policy sciences. The general approach of the policy sciences is problem-oriented, multidisciplinary, multimethod, empirical, intentionalist, process-oriented, value-committed rather than value-neutral or value-free (Brunner 1982; Torgerson 1985; deLeon 1997). The focus on a single academic discipline would lead to an overly narrow understanding of a complex phenomenon such as CiRM and eventually ill-defined policy recommendations (deLeon/Steelman 2001). Minsky (1986) also argued that in order to understand an issue, it is neccessary to understand it in more than one way.

The political science literature revealed a great deal about the characteristics of the setting in which CiRM is applied. It offered insights into the political context that surrounds policy making and implementation, the nature and behaviour of legislative institutions, and the philosophical ideas of citizenship. The administrative science literature supplied a rich, well-developed theory of public administration and public management in democracies. It also described important reform movements such as NPM and eGovernment, and discussed the differing roles of citizens. In addition, it provided empirical evidence on reform initiatives and their effects on public administration. The literature on business management, especially in the field of marketing, provided the frame of reference for CRM and its exploration in government. In addition, findings from research on CRM, consumer behaviour and customer satisfaction were considered when attempting to build a better understanding of the citizen as customer. The literature on information science, especially administrative information science, offered technical insights into CRM and eGovernment. The possibilities and limits of technology have a strong influence on the way it is enacted to facilitate CRM strategies and CRM operations.

1.4 Significance of the Study

The argument of advocates for CRM in government often focuses on the potential inefficiency and lack of customer service in public administration. However, advocates mostly present the concepts of CRM. Based on the few actual examples of CRM presented by authors, it becomes evident that there is no commonly-accepted framework that allows one to identify when CRM is taking place in government and when it is not. Moreover, even though most authors acknowledge that the citizen is more than just a customer, they do not review the literature of citizen-orientation in government or citizenship.

The present research is significant because it seeks to undertake the task of filling these gaps. This research ferrets out information from local and county governments that started CiRM initiatives. It provides information on what administrators think of CRM, how they implement it and how it affects the complex environment in government. This research involved key actors from the political level, administrative executive, administrative operative and external vendors, and therefore presents a more accurate assessment of real-life CiRM. Furthermore, this study challenges the conventional wisdom that public administration is not responsive and citizen-centric. It carefully looks across separate research streams on CRM, NPM, TQM, eGovernment and citizenship—derived from the existing literature in various academic fields—in order to identify commonalities and differences within the context of this study. While the results of the U.S. case studies allow for only tentative conclusions, the generalisability of those conclusions to others interested in moving forward with CiRM is anticipated to be high. Lessons drawn and a conceptualization of CiRM may guide both government actors and non-public actors, such as consultants or technology firms that may be interested in the subject matter. In addition, this study allows future research on CiRM to be more systematic through a grounded understanding of the context and a clear frame of reference. Indeed, there are other ramifications of CiRM which underline the importance of a thorough analysis. Lengnick-Hall (1996: 818) noted:

> *The relationship between customers as means and customers as ends must be carefully managed. There is a tremendous potential for customers to influence the system in either positive or negative ways. Miller (1990) described this as momentum. Traditional customers have the potential for perpetuating and amplifying their roles, contributions, and perspectives to the exclusion of other important stakeholders. In addition, the composite effects of customers as means and customers as ends should be considered. Participation studies suggest that if customers develop long-term, formal, influential relationships and become contributors to a process, they will be more likely to act on the outcomes and be satisfied with the results.*

Lengnick-Hall's comments above would support the need to manage citizen relationships and open new modes of citizen participation. However, as with eGovernment in general, CiRM increasingly demands that agencies act across jurisdictional boundaries and find new forms of governance. Such action would mark another step towards Networked Governance (Goldsmith/Eggers 2004), that is, the idea that the state is only one actor in a network designed to achieve certain goals. According to Kamarck (2002), compared to bureaucratic government, networked government has the advantage of being able to discover creative and innovative solutions to complex problems in a way that traditional, rule-bound, one-size-fits-all government cannot. Yet the limiting issue in these reforms is always human and legislative factors which can be studied in great detail through this research. In conclusion, this research enables public officials to think more clearly about the objectives, alternatives, consequences and uncertainties of CiRM. Furthermore, following an interdisciplinary approach, the study attempts in particular to make a contribution to administrative science by offering a framework for CiRM that is grounded in multiple case studies and a thorough literature review.

1.5   The empirical referent of the study

This dissertation examines the perceptions of CRM as well as the implementation and impact of CRM on the municipal level and in a multijurisdictional environment. It is important to realize that we are at a very early stage in the application of CRM in these contexts. The cases presented reflect the work of CiRM pioneers in government. These early adopters will continue to shape the philosophy and practices of CiRM in the coming years. Decision makers and outside actors in three cities—the City of Chicago, the City of Baltimore and the City of New York—offer insights from the municipal level. But in order to truly benefit from technology and CRM efforts, government entities have to collaborate closely across jurisdictional boundaries. The case of Miami-Dade County provides a unique opportunity to study CiRM in a multijurisdictional environment. In addition, due to the late starting date of its CiRM efforts, Miami-Dade County had the chance to either modify or follow existing models of CiRM, because Miami-Dade County analysed the implementations in Baltimore, Chicago, and New York. In general, all of the cases are similar. For instance, CiRM started in each case with initiatives to offer citizens a single, non-emergency telephone number for getting in contact with government—311. On the other hand, each case has its distinctive characteristics. The size, culture, complexity, leadership and the stages present in the CRM project differ in these cases. Therefore, the combination of single- and cross-case evidence should support conceptualizing CiRM. Although the explorative part of this study focuses broadly on a theoretical conceptualization of CiRM, the immediate empirical referent of the research is the 311 initiatives. Thus, the results also help us to convey the idea and challenges of 311 well. This study does not, however, explore citizen–administrative relationships.

1.6   Organisation of the dissertation

This dissertation is divided into two parts. The theoretical part reviews the literature and presents methodological foundations. The empirical part presents and discusses the data analysis and the results. The dissertation is organised as follows:

Chapter 1 provides an introduction to the guiding research question, the problem and a conceptual base for the research on CiRM.

Chapter 2 contains the interdisciplinary literature review. It conceptualises and presents CRM as a theoretical foundation for the research design and discussion. The theoretical background and empirical evidence of NPM, TQM and eGovernment are reviewed with regard to citizen-orientation. A foundational element in this chapter will be the discussion of the citizen–public administration relationship, especially the citizen as customer.

Chapter 3, the methodology section, discusses the research strategy used to examine CiRM in each of the cases considered in this study. The research method outlines the steps used in the development of research questions, selection of cases, collection of data, process of analysis and the handling of limitations. It also provides a brief overview of each case.

Research findings for each case study are outlined in **Chapter 4**. The case results are divided into three sections: Implementing CiRM, impact of CiRM and Understanding of CiRM This is followed by a discussion and Conceptualization of CiRM in **Chapter 5**.

Finally, **Chapter 6** provides conclusions and recommendations for future research. This chapter also considers the implications of the dissertation for theory and practice and public management.

A copy of the case study survey instrument and preparation material can be found in Appendix A, followed by the coding schema used in the grounded theory analysis (Appendix B). Appendix C provides material on TQM and Appendix D offers additional data collected during the case studies. Finally, the list of sources cited throughout this thesis can be found in References.

2 From Customer Relationship Management towards citizen-oriented government

Before embarking on a study of CiRM, it is important to review three areas of the literature. Each of these areas gives us a sense of what has been done to improve the citizen-orientation of government, how CiRM can be conceptualized and what its potential to affect society and polity might be. First, I explore CRM within the business management literature in Section 2.1. Second, I present an overview of different administrative reform approaches such as New Public Management (NPM) and eGovernment, which in one way or another are aimed at improving the citizen–government relationship (Section 2.2). Third, I present a brief summary of research on the relationship between citizens and public administration (Section 2.3). Moreover, I review the discourse on the role of the citizen in the state, in particular calling the citizen a "customer" of public administration. A summary of the literature review is given in Section 2.4.

2.1 Customer Relationship Management

In general, an enterprise aims to win, retain and increase a customer's revenue, once you strip away all other activities of a firm. This is true for nonprofits as well as for-profits, for public as well as private enterprise (Bergeron 2002; Peppers/Rogers 2004: 5). These enterprises are usually structured and managed around the products and services they provide (Homburg 2003). While the 1980s was characterized by the recognition that an external focus on customers was important, businesses in the 1990s recognized that customers are individuals with distinctive attributes (McKean 2004). Businesses had to cope with constantly changing buying behaviour (Kracklauer 2003) that resulted in shorter product life and briefer patent protection periods (Schumacher/Meyer 2004: 12). Furthermore, a rise in consumer exposure to information through various channels (Freeland 2002), and increasing competition through globalization along with developments in information technology (Payne/Frow 2004) made it increasingly difficult to gain or keep a competitive advantage (Porter 1985; Barney 1991; Dyer/Singh 1998).

Building a closer relationship with customers through CRM was seen as a possible solution to counter these challenges. In CRM customers are understood as long-term assets and thus major factors in establishing a competitive advantage (Peppers/Rogers 2004). Research has shown that a firm's profitability can be positively influenced by focusing marketing resources on increasing the firm's share of its customers' business rather than increasing the total number of customers (Peppers/Rogers 1993). Further advantages are supposed to be a reduction of marketing costs, a strengthening of customer loyalty and satisfaction, reduced price sensitivity, new opportunities for up- and cross-selling and the creation of exit barriers (Janssen/Wagenaar 2002). Corporations, therefore, started CRM projects with great hopes but the outcomes fell short of the expectations. One of the main reasons for failed CRM projects was too heavy a focus on the technology involved in CRM on the part of businesses. (Campbell 2003: 375;

Newell 2003:10-13), which is repeatedly mentioned in the literature. While the scope of CRM has remained constant, the focus has changed (Freeland 2002). The first CRM initiatives started in the early 1990s and were primarily focused on improving the call center as a service channel (Xu et al. 2002). For example, enterprises utilized technologies such as IVR to streamline the process of handling customer inquiries over the phone. The focus was first widened to include sales, and then widened even more in the late 1990s to include various service channels, especially the Internet. In addition, enterprises built data warehouses and customer analytics to better understand their customers. As complexity grew, companies focused on managing and integrating service and data gathering across channels.

CRM is based on different streams in marketing and other research areas (Bligh/Turk 2004). It has not yet reached the level of a coherent discipline; it more resembles a field of common interest to researchers and practitioners (Ehret 2004). CRM has its roots in relationship marketing (RM). RM is a term coined by Berry (1983), who defined it as "attracting, maintaining and serving clients in multiservice organizations". RM led to a paradigm shift in marketing theory and practice (Kotler/ Bliemel 2001). Research on business relationships, interactions and networks by Häkansson (1975), Gummesson (1987) and Grönroos (1990a) strongly influenced the conceptualization of RM (Ballantyne/Christopher/Payne 2003: 160). Grönroos (1990b; 1994) suggested that five aspects of managing customer service need to be understood. First, service management is a philosophy (culture) that guides and drives all decisions throughout the organisation. Second, decisions are customer- or market-driven. Third, service management is holistic. Fourth, service management is entirely linked to quality management. Finally, the value of employees for organisational effectiveness is recognized. Further influences on Relationship Marketing came from direct marketing (Lumpkin/Caballero/Chonko 1989), one-to-one marketing (Peppers/ Rogers 1993), database marketing (Nash 1993) and permission marketing (Godin 1999). In contrast to transaction marketing, which focused on a "discrete transaction with a distinct beginning, short duration, and sharp ending by performance" (Dwyer/Schurr/Oh 1987), relationship marketing looked at long-term relationships and interactions of business partners: customers, distributors and suppliers. Moreover, it covered the process of acquisition, which had been neglected by earlier concepts. However, some authors now argue for a pluralism in marketing, because he type of exchange determines the form of marketing (Brodie et al. 1997; Möller/Halinen 2000). Besides marketing science, CRM is influenced by research on knowledge management (Hedlund/Nonaka 1993; Nonaka/Takeuchi 1995; Alavi/Leidner 2001), total quality management (Deming 1986) and business process re-engineering (BPR) (Hammer 1990, Hammer/Champy 1993).

That there is a multitude of different definitions of CRM is readily apparent in the variety of definitions present in the growing body of literature. As a result, it is difficult to find a single robust definition of CRM (Hart/Hogg/Banerjee 2004). Zablah, Bellenger and Johnston (2004: 476) identified approximately 45 definitions that can be grouped around five areas: process, strategy, philosophy, technologies and resources (Table 2-1). These categories will be applied to this research to identify the dominating understanding of CRM by administrators. In general, many recent definitions underline the importance of a holistic approach and understanding, which I find most appropriate for this study. A narrow definition would have helped to focus but only a holistic definition serves the exploratory purpose of this research. Therefore, based on these definitions I use the following definition of CRM:

> *A holistic management concept and strategy, enabled by technology, which is designed to create a customer-centric organisation, to maintain and optimize customer relationships and to improve an enterprise's competitive advantage*

Thus, CRM requires that all corporate functions (marketing, sales, service and research) contribute to the overall customer-centric strategy, which may involve a change to the internal culture.

Basic principles of CRM are personalization (products, information, services), customer integration and customer proximity (planning processes, product development, collaboration), interaction (channels, long-term communication, surveys) and customer segmentation (identify the top 20% of customers who make up 80% of the profit, termination of unprofitable customers). Moreover, quality management, performance management, change management and a strategy that includes measures that promote a customer-oriented culture are vital to any CRM concept or project.

The main aspects of CRM are presented in this section. The relationships that a consumer is willing to engage in with a firm are believed to be guided by higher-order mental products such as trust, perceived service quality and customer satisfaction. What is meant by customer satisfaction is described in Section 2.1.1. A usual core task of CRM is categorizing customers (Section 2.1.2) and building the relationship between the customer and the enterprise (Section 2.1.3). This may lead to keeping the customer in close proximity to a firm. This concept is outlined in Section 2.1.4. CRM processes and the means of managing customer interactions are presented in Sections 2.1.5 and 2.1.6. After that, a description of the key functionalities and structure of a CRM system (Section 2.1.7)—a complex integration of hardware, software and applications—is presented. The final two sections focus on the evidence of CRM in practice (Section 2.1.8) and a review of the current discourse on CRM in government (Section 2.1.9).

Perspective	Description	Implications for CRM success	Representative conceptualization
Process	Buyer-seller relationships develop over time and must evolve to perdure. The macro level perspective includes all activities (processes) while the micro perspective focuses only on interaction management.	...is contingent upon a firm's ability to detect and respond to evolving customer needs and preferences.	Creation and leveraging of linkages and relationships with external marketplace entities, especially channels and end users. (Srivastava/Shervani/Fahey 1999: 169)
Strategy	A customer's lifetime value determines the amount and kinds of resources that are invested in a particular relationship.	...requires that firms continually assess and prioritize customer relationships based on their relative lifetime profitability.	Invest in customers that are valuable for the company, but also minimize their investments in non-valuable customers. (Verhoef/Donkers 2001: 189)
Philosophy	Customer retention is best achieved through a focus on relationship building and maintenance.	...requires that firms be customer centric and driven by an understanding of customers' changing needs.	a business philosophy aimed at achieving customer centricity for the company (Hasan 2003; Piccoli et al. 2003).
Capability	Long term, profitable relationships result only when firms are able to continuously adapt their behaviour towards individual customers.	...contingent upon a firm's possession of a set of tangible and intangible resources that allow for a flexible change of behaviour towards individual customers on an ongoing basis.	being willing and able to change your behaviour toward an individual customer based on what the customer tells you and what elese you know about that customer (Peppers/Rogers/Dorf 1999: 101).
Technology	Knowledge and interaction management technologies represent the key resources firms need to build long-term, profitable customer relationships.	...is primarily driven by the functionality and user acceptance of the technology firms implement in an attempt to build customer knowledge and manage interactions	CRM is the technology and Internet capabilities used to blend sales, marketing, and service information systems to build partnerships with customers. (Shoemaker 2001: 178; Xu et al. 2002)

Table 2-1: Dominant perspectives on CRM (Zablah/Bellenger/Johnston (2004): 47)

2.1.1 Customer satisfaction

According to a 2003 Gartner study of 174 companies, the primary objective of their CRM initiatives was to increase customer satisfaction (Gartner 2004). Research on customer satisfaction has focused predominantly on modelling the effects of the following factors on customers' level of satisfaction: expectations, disconfirmation of expectations, performance, affect and equity (Szymanski/Henard 2001). A good introduction to theoretical concepts of customer satisfaction is given by Homburg and Stock (2003). There are at least two different conceptualizations of customer satisfaction: transaction-specific and cumulative (Anderson/Fornell/Lehmann 1997). The transaction-specific views customer satisfaction as a post-choice evaluative judgement to a transactional experience. Transaction-specific customer satisfaction can be distinguished from cumulative satisfaction, which is a cumulative construct of the overall evaluation of the past, current, and future satisfaction with a product or service of a firm (Garbarino/Johnson 1999).

Figure 2-1 illustrates the relationship between the central factors that influence customer satisfaction. For example, improved performance does not guarantee positive disconfirmation when expectations rise proportionately or more than proportionately to performance. Likewise, an equity perception, that is, a fairness judgement that a consumer makes in reference to what others receive, can remain the same or decline as performance improves. Regarding services, Bitner (1990) points out that in the absence of concrete variables on which to evaluate quality, customers will use other tangibles to pre-evaluate or set expectations for service quality. These include environmental factors (temperature, odour), the behaviour of service providers and other customers, or physical evidence, such as design. Methods of measuring customer satisfaction are discussed by Hayes (1998).Within the context of CRM, customer satisfaction is a fundamental indicator of an enterprise's performance and customer orientation due to its links to behavioural and economic consequences (Anderson/Fornell/Rust 1997).

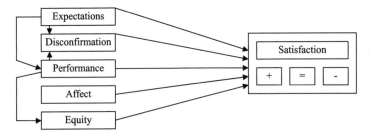

Figure 2-1: Model of antecedents of customer satisfaction (adapted from Szymanski/Henard 2001)

A variety of studies found that higher levels of customer satisfaction result in higher customer loyalty, referrals or probability of future transactions (Halstead/Page 1992; Taylor/Baker 1994; Mittal/Kamakura 2001; Olsen 2002). CRM aims to achieve these

13

goals. However, in economics the relationship between customer satisfaction and the productivity of a firm is negative. Increasing the level of customer satisfaction leads to higher costs (e.g. raw materials, production lines, employees). In addition, Figure 2-1 underlines the challenge of influencing and achieving customer satisfaction.

2.1.2 Differentiating customers

CRM concepts usually categorize customers as internal and external customers. These can be end users or intermediaries which exist both inside and outside of an organisation (Lawton 1993). End users are individuals or groups who use a service or product. Intermediaries connect end users and producers, which is a common role of retail chains for producers of consumer food products. Intermediaries may also engage in altering (e.g. repairs, enhancements) products or services. Similar analogies can be drawn for internal processes.

Most enterprises have exploited a one-to-many approach to customers. But targeting customers on a one-to-one basis is a complex task. Customer segment management, therefore, offers a more feasible customer-centric approach to managing customer relationships (Whitehouse/Spencer/Payne 2002). Customer segment management is the process of clustering groups of customers based on like attributes and value, and managing those segments in such a way (e.g. personalized newsletters or products) as to improve customer satisfaction and customer profitability.

Organisations need to identify customers before segmenting them (Peppers/Rogers 2004). Identification includes defining customer information, collecting it (e.g. loyalty cards, cookies on websites, CRM software) and linking interactions to a customer. Customer information may exist throughout the organisation in various forms (Bose 2002). It can be grouped around behaviour data (e.g. purchases, click-stream data), attitudinal data (e.g. complaints, product feature requests) and demographic information. However, customers may determine how much information they are willing to share.

Customer value and needs are the most fundamental qualities that differ from customer to customer (Peppers/Rogers 2004). Within any given customer base, there will be differences in the revenues customers generate and the resources an organisation must invest to retain them (Raaij/Verooij/Triest 2003). According to the Pareto principle, 20% of the customers are responsible for 80% of revenues. Hence, in total, customers are interpreted as capital assets, but the top-tier customers are essentially subsidising the unprofitable ones. In some cases, unprofitable customers can be terminated without negative effects on the company's overall performance (Reinartz/Krafft/Hoyer 2004; Heinrich 2005). CRM assumes that identifying profitable customers and keeping them loyal to a firm, that is, expanding the lifetime of the relationship and increasing the value of transactions, increase an organisation's overall profitability. Reichheld and Teal (1996) noted that the increase in profits from loyal customers relates to the price premium paid, the added profits from sales through referrals, profits from cost savings obtained by serving old customers and revenue growth from loyal customers due to an increase in sales to that customer. However, some research found only weak support for this assumption (Schmittlein/Morrison/Colombo 1987; Sharp/Sharp 1997; Reinartz/Kumar 2000).

To calculate the value of customers, customer lifetime value (CLV) models have become central to CRM and customer equity approaches (Malthouse/Blattberg 2005). The CLV represents the present value of expected benefits (e.g. gross margin) less the burdens (e.g. direct costs of servicing and communicating) from customers during the relationship (Bitran/Mondschein 1996; Dwyer 1997). Research on the CLV has been threefold (Singh 2003). The first set of studies focused on developing models to calculate the CLV (Berger/Nasar 1998; Jain/Singh 2002; Kumar/Ramani/Bohling 2004). The second stream of research focused on customer base analysis (Keller 1993; Schmittlein/Peterson 1994), that is, analysing existing customers and predicting future behaviour. Implications for managerial decision making (Berger/Nasar 1998; Bell et al. 2002; Raaij/Verooij/Triest 2003) were of interest to the third area of CLV research. Applying the concept of CLV in government, as a Citizen Lifetime Value (CiLV) should certainly be discussed; however, doing so is beyond the scope of this study.

Besides a value differentiation, customers may also be grouped based on a needs evaluation (Peppers/Rogers 2004). A customer need is a description of the individual benefit to be fulfilled by a product or service. Discussions with customers usually identify 200–400 customer needs per customer (Griffin/Hauser 1993). Customer needs are situational in nature and can change over time. Needs can be categorized as basic needs (assumptions about the utility of a product or service), articulated needs (personal preferences about the utility of a product or service) and exciting needs (additional utility, if fulfilled, would add additional satisfaction). Two customers might satisfy different needs with the same product or service. Therefore, firms might be able to increase the revenue from each customer by catering to those needs beyond the defined benefits of a product or service. Because this process is costly, using ICT, enterprises can create more precise customer categories over time. For example, collaborative filtering is now commonly used on the Internet (amazon.com, Web 2.0 applications) to serve a single customer's needs based on what other customers with similar needs preferred.

Customer segment management may ultimately lead to organisational changes that move towards clustering functions, budgets and operations around customer segments. Because customer behaviour changes and evolves over time, differentiating customers requires flexibility. There has to be an open dialogue between the customer and the enterprise that creates a learning relationship. Moreover, enterprises need to anticipate and respond to customer changes, which increases the need for ICT in areas of data gathering, sharing, analysis, process automation and monitoring.

2.1.3 Customer relationships

Central to CRM is managing the relationship between the customer and the enterprise. Such relationships are of special importance and are especially important in the case of services, given the unique characteristics of both relationships and services (Grönroos 1990a). While customer business relationships received attention by researchers, few studied the simultaneous relationship management of both internal and external customers as conceptualized in CRM (Beckett-Camarata/Carmarata/Barker 1998).

A relationship can be defined as "the way in which two or more people or things are connected, or the state of being connected" (Fowler/Fowler/Pearsall 2004). In order to improve a relationship, it is necessary to understand its dimensions. A relationship exists when an individual exchange is assessed not in isolation, such as a discrete transaction, but as a continuation of past exchanges and future expectations. Therefore, we have to differentiate between transactional and relational exchanges (Day 2000). Transactional exchanges include anonymous encounters with somebody at a store, as well as a series of transactions of standardized goods where participants enter a zerosum game. Relational exchanges are those that are made up of a close collaboration, with a shared interest of all involved actors, for the purpose of creating and gaining mutual long-term benefits using such means as tailoring the transactions to individual preferences in order to create long lasting relationships.

Based on a review of relationship development models, Andersen (2001) suggested four phases in relationship exchange: pre-relationship, negotiation, development and termination (Figure 2-2). First, parties identify each other as possible interaction and exchange partners. However, in this stage no interaction takes place. Second, parties explore the relationship with minimal commitment and convey preferences. In a pre-relationship phase, the social distance at the individual and organisational level is large (Ford 1980). Third, if the outcomes of the second phase prove beneficial, parties engage in further activities. Termination occurs when a party evaluates the value of a relationship as negative. This can happen at any time and can be initiated unilaterally. Planning CRM activities according to the different phases of the relationship is sometimes referred to as the customer life cycle concept in the CRM literature (Schumacher/Meyer 2004).

As noted earlier, in order for a relationship to exist, both parties have to be aware of it. Customer might not define a commercial exchange as a relationship. Relationships are highly personal concepts for individuals. Individuals are motivated to enter and maintain a relationship either because they want to, or because they have or believe themselves to have no other option (Bendapudi/Berry 1997). Peppers and Rogers (2004) listed mutuality, interaction, an iterative nature, an ongoing benefit for both parties, the willingness and ability to change behaviour, uniqueness and trust as central

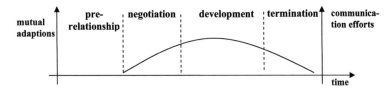

Figure 2-2: Relationship development phases adapted from (Andersen 2001)

elements of a relationship. Relationships imply mutuality, because they are based on interactions that exchange a good or service. Consequently, value is given and received (Day 2000). As the interactions are reiterated, more information and preferences are exchanged. Because of this, more benefits are offered and exit barriers are raised due to the rising costs (effort, time, costs) of creating the relationship elsewhere (Gwinner/Gremler/Bitner 1998). In addition, both parties have to adjust their behaviour as information is accumulated and individual or environmental changes occur. A relationship is not a linear process in a homogenous group. Therefore, each relationship has unique characteristics which need to be considered in order for the relationship to deliver ongoing benefits. Finally, trust is an essential part of any relationship (Singh/Siredeshmukh 2000). Trust and factors that affect trust in an exchange relationship are discussed by other authors (Moorman/Deshpande/Zaltman 1993; Hosmer 1995; Wicks/Berman/Jones 1999; Parkhe/Miller 2000).

Some authors have stressed that the customer needs to be in control of the relationship instead of the enterprise (Newell 2003). Customers should interact with a company in the way they prefer as well as with each other, fostering group learning, mutual innovation, and communities of creativity or joint intellectual capital (Gibbert/Leibold/Probst 2002).

2.1.4 Customer proximity

Interactions in a relationship may exist on various levels. The concept of customer proximity allows organisations to identify customer preferences and then design products and services accordingly. Schumacher and Meyer (2004) differentiate by organisational, contextual, process and personal customer proximity.

Organisational proximity is primarily of importance in business-to-business (B2B) relationships. In the retail sector, retail and consumer goods manufacturers sometimes closely combine their organisational structure to exchange knowledge and improve the supply chain. For example, a product that is about to go out of the retailer's stock is then automatically ordered just in time. Manufacturers may get real-time information of consumer behaviour. In contrast, contextual proximity refers to the level of knowledge about the internal structure, processes and preferences of the customer; the ability of an organisation to change internal processes based on customer demands is process proximity. Individual relationships allow the highest level of personalization and proximity. The latter can be further differentiated by the physical distance (e.g. face to face, phone, Internet), emotional distance and the type of information exchanged (Barnes 2001). However, increasing the level of customer proximity or customer integration may lead to greater complexities that result in higher costs and coordination efforts. Therefore, achieving the highest level of customer orientation might not be desirable. Indeed, Ehret (2004) noted:

> ...because customers are often not aware of their future needs, an approach based solely on explicitly expressed customer requirements, rather than potential or latent customer requirements, poses a danger to the quality of the resultant product or service. Therefore, it cannot be ignored that following a narrow approach to buyer-seller relationships can lead to a dead end [...].

2.1.5 CRM processes

CRM usually involves business process change (Galbreath/Rogers 1999). Organisational processes are highly interwoven. Most processes are done serially or sequentially, not in parallel. It is usually difficult to identify CRM and non-CRM processes. Therefore, Schumacher and Meyer (2004) suggested differentiating between primary and secondary CRM processes. Activities and direct interactions with customers are primary CRM processes. These processes include efforts by customers (e.g. filling in a form) before an interaction that may also be initiated by the customer. Secondary CRM processes are mostly internal to an organisation and non-visible to customers. As a result, they have only an indirect influence on direct customer interactions. However, primary processes can directly rely on secondary processes.

Incoming and outgoing customer contacting takes place on various channels. Managing and designing the multichannel environment is an important aspect in CRM. Face-to-face and call-center interactions are central to primary CRM processes. Interactions can involve information requests, service requests, complaints or outbound quality control. Processes may either be improved through elimination, redesign, consolidation or automation. But even within an industry, customers give different priorities to the processes that affect them (Gartner 2004). Table 2-2 lists common attributes of customer-centered products and services of importance to customers identified in the literature. Consequently, Lawton (1993) recommended starting with an analysis of expected outcomes in order to create customer-centered processes (Figure 2-3). But characteristics of services also influence service design (Lovelock 1992). For example, some services require less interaction with customers. Less interaction greatly reduces the risk of errors or a poor service experience compared to those services that involve frequent interactions. Moreover, services with long delivery process duration or scr-

Service	Product
easy to use	easy to use
timely	timely
easy to understand	durable
friendly	reliable
fast	complete
complete	style, design
relevant	inexpensive
succinct	quiet
organised	consistent
accurate	customizable
consistent	defect-free
predictable	maintainable
flexible	long-term value

Table 2-2: Common attributes of services and products expected by customers

vices with limited capacity increase the importance of informing customers. Finally, services have varying levels of complexity which may influence delivery, oversight and customer education processes.

Figure 2-3: Creating customer-centered processes

2.1.6 Customer interaction

CRM underlines the importance of interacting with customers and engaging in a learning relationship. An interaction can focus on the exchange of benefits (i.e. products and services), information exchange, social exchange or any combination of the three. Interactions occur within the context of an ongoing relationship (Peppers/Rogers/Dorf 1999; Zablah/Bellenger/Johnston 2004). Planning CRM activities according to the different phases of an interaction cycle throughout a customer relationship is sometimes referred to as the customer buying cycle concept in the CRM literature (Schumacher/Meyer 2004). According to this concept, each interaction consists of awareness, evaluation, transaction and post-transaction phases which need to be considered in business planning and management. In general, interactions should remain appropriate (e.g. frequency, timing, duration, channel, needs), relevant (degree of value generated for the customer by a transaction) and consistent with prior encounters (Greco/Ragins 2003). Many enterprises make use of a combination of channels to interact with their customers.

Table 2-3 gives an overview of these channels. The channels present a continuum from physical to virtual contact. Some channels allow synchronous interaction, and others only allow asynchronous interaction. Moreover, customers can access channels by various means (e.g. a website may be accessed with a computer or mobile phone), which influences decisions on usability and process design. Managing the multichan-

Channel	Interaction type
Sales force	synchronous
Physical location (store)	synchronous
Mail	asynchronous
Telephony (call center/ customer interaction center)	synchronous
Internet	synchronous, asynchronous

Table 2-3: Channels and interaction characteristics

nel environment and integrating it into the overall CRM strategy is central to adding value to customer interactions (Payne/Frow 2004). It involves decisions about channel design, channel mixture, the customer experience across channels and how to obtain a

360-degree view of the customer. The channel structure appropriate for any given organisation will depend upon which combination can best attract the final customers in the target segments, which in turn will depend upon the organisation's and intermediaries' ability to create value relevant to the customers needs. The channel strategy and design follow prior identification and differentiation of customers and their needs. But no matter how well channels are designed, there will likely be vertical or horizontal channel conflict (Peppers/Rogers 2004).

Furthermore, single-channel and channel-combination economics have an influence on channel-strategy decisions. Channels have differing transaction costs, infrastructural costs and relative usage (Myers/Pickersgill/van Metre 2004). In particular, electronic channels are very attractive because their self-service potential offers the chance to reduce costs (Kracklauer 2003). In order to understand channel economics, companies also have to be aware of the costs of serving similar customers across channels at any stage of the interaction process. In addition, customers may switch channels at any time during the interaction process. Companies, therefore, can offer incentives (e.g. self-service resulting in reduced waiting time) or barriers (e.g. fees) to guide customers to the right mix of channels for each product or service.

Another aspect of a channel strategy is communicating with customers and employees. For example, the migration of customers to new channels can result in redeployment of personnel and a redefinition of goals and tasks (Myers/Pickersgill/van Metre 2004). Customers' expectations and perceptions differ depending on a channel (Peppard 2000) and need to be managed. Customers might be required to learn new behaviour (e.g. self-service kiosks of airlines). Therefore, communication measures are vital in preventing channel conflicts and reducing resistance to change.

Finally, CRM systems are thought to generate a 360-degree view of the customer throughout interactions on various channels (Chen/Popovich 2003).

2.1.7 CRM systems

CRM systems represent a complex integration of hardware, software and applications. CRM systems accumulate, store, maintain, analyse and distribute customer knowledge throughout the organisation. Information systems can be differentiated from CRM systems by their content and scope (Schumacher/Meyer 2004). Communication technology like Internet applications or the telephone is not considered CRM technology. The same applies to applications or database systems. However, when integrated in one or more CRM processes, information systems are considered to be part of a CRM system. Selective CRM systems can be implemented quickly and support specific CRM processes. For example, self-service kiosks and help-desk systems are frequently used in call centers. However, they may constrain the creation of a linked system and a 360-degree view of the customer. Integrated systems, therefore, aim to bridge these shortcomings by offering additional functionality or by merging capabilities. There are generally two ways in which CRM systems may interact with customers (Bose 2002). The first way is with assistance from ICT, by means of a human intermediary between the CRM system and customer; the second way is using IT-automated interaction by means of kiosks or integrated voice response (IVR).

A widely accepted classification of CRM systems is as follows. Processes in the back and front offices are integrated through operative CRM systems (Corner/Hinton 2002). These systems may contain software for enterprise resource planning (ERP), sales automation (SA), computer-aided selling (CAS), work order management and knowledge management (KM). Analytical CRM systems manage and evaluate customer data in order to produce customer intelligence. Customer data includes individual information, transaction details about the customer and comments by those who interacted with the customer. Data warehousing and tools such as Online Analytical Processing (OLAP) and data mining solutions are typically regarded as analytical CRM systems. The data generated and subsequent CRM analytics assist managerial decision making and service interactions (operative CRM systems) in addition to providing input for product development, supply chain management and finance. Collaborative CRM systems manage and synchronize customer interaction and communication channels as well as the customer experience across channels (Kracklauer 2003; Payne/Frow 2004). They also support sharing data with external partners. Operative and analytical systems are linked to collaborative CRM systems to close the organisational loop so that all necessary information is available for those interacting with customers. For example, within a call center, call line identification (CLI) in combination with computer-telephony integration (CTI), can identify the caller and allow the call agent to access the stored customer data instantaneously.

2.1.8 CRM in private enterprises

Many companies around the world have started CRM initiatives since the strategy's emergence in the early 1990s. These organisations spend $3.5 billion yearly on CRM software, which is only a fraction of the total expense for CRM; spending on implementation, training and integration can be three or five times higher than software costs (Ebner et al. 2002). CRM project costs usually run from $60 to 130 million, and projects can take up to 36 months to complete. While CRM projects are expected to lead to improvements in many areas, academic and business research has cited failure rates between 50% and 70% (Schwetz 2001; Rigby/Reichheld/Schefter 2002; Ebner et al. 2002; Verhoef/Langerak 2003; Nairn 2002; Almquist/Bovet/Heaton 2001; Chen/ Chen 2004; Agarwal/Harding/Schumacher 2004). After analysing CRM in the American lodging industry, Piccoli et al. (2003) also concluded that only significant changes in operations and greater data-sharing collaborations would allow the studied industry sector to realize the benefits of CRM. On the contrary, Mithas, Almirall and Krishnan (2006) found that firms using CRM systems have greater levels of one-to-one marketing effectiveness.

In addition, implementation effects on accountability and data or process ownership in functional organisations are often overlooked issues. As one executive quoted an article by Kotorov (2003) summarised: "[S]o we bought a nice [CRM] toy, and now no one's using it.". Along these lines, because CRM requires organisational changes and cooperation among stakeholder groups, the real challenges lie within the limits of human resources and change management (Nairn 2002; Xu et al. 2002; Bligh/Turk 2004; Agarwal/Harding/Schumacher 2004). One of the most prevalent failures is missing executive support. Customer-centric management, therefore, requires executive sponsorship and commitment to CRM throughout and beyond the entire CRM implementation (Chen/Popovich 2003). Without it, momentum quickly diminishes. However, executives commonly fail to establish clear business goals and metrics even before launching CRM efforts because of their limited understanding of CRM (Ebner et al. 2002). Many executives still have an IT-centric comprehension of customer orientation (Brown/Gulycz 2002), while others limit CRM to a matter of tailoring special offers for customer segments.

Limiting the scope of CRM initiatives to just automating practices, without addressing redundancies or outdated processes, leaves system issues unaddressed. Moreover, organisations frequently do not evaluate their current operations and offerings from a customer perspective before they begin to focus on designing a strategy (Bligh/Turk 2004). In fact, Abbott, Stone and Buttle (2001) warned that substantial investments in CRM technology are not needed in all business sectors. For instance, in small or niche businesses, it is less difficult to maintain contact with the customer base by conventional means.

CRM implementations suffer from improperly staffed teams and technology traps (Bligh/Turk 2004). Most CRM teams are dominated by IT people and a lack of involvement of end users. With regard to CRM software solutions, Light (2003) noted that these tend to embody standardised views of relationship management processes which either require complex customizing, user training or organisational changes. Knowledge transfer from prior IT projects (e.g. ERP) is also largely absent. While there are many benefits from aligning and merging customer data, delivering too much information or functionality to organisational units can make systems slow and can burden users with too much information (Ebner et al. 2002), which can increase the existing information overflow. Furthermore, poor data quality in legacy systems or databases may lower the effectiveness of a newly implemented CRM system. Finally, many CRM initiatives ignore the issue of whether customers will be receptive to maintaining a relationship or whether they desire a different kind of relationship with an enterprise (Rigby/Reichheld/Schefter 2002). A customer's view of how a company should use its available interaction options and customer information can be significantly different from an enterprise's perspective (Newell 2003). Verhoef and Langerak (2002) noted that relationship efforts are negligible for many low-involvement products as well as for utilitarian goods and services that do not provide much value to the customer.

Gradual approaches to CRM proved more successful than doing everything at once (Gentle 2002; Ebner et al. 2002). In fact, research on enterprise-wide business process re-engineering projects (BPR) in the early 1990s identified common success factors (Al-Mashari/Zairi 1999). Thus, the greater the scope of CRM, the greater the need to re-engineer processes.

2.1.9 CRM in government

While CRM has been researched and applied in private enterprises for years, it has only recently gained attention as a concept for government. Concurrent with the emergence of eGovernment and the general tendency of transferring business concepts into the government domain, articles and studies started to address the topic. Many works on eGovernment briefly addressed CRM when referring to aspects such as one-stop government or a multichannel environment directly (Wimmer/Traunmüller/Lenk 2001; O'Looney 2002: 91-132; von Lucke 2003b; Marche/McNiven 2003; Larsen/Milakovich 2005) or indirectly (Bekkers 1999; Fountain 2001a; Brown 2005). Besides CRM, authors introduce slightly altered terms like Citizen Relationship Management (CiRM) (Daum 2002; O'Looney 2002: 96), Constituent Relationship Management (CRM) (Kavanagh 2001), Public Relationship Management (PRM) (Bleyer/Saliterer 2004) or Citizen Encounter and Relationship Management (CERM) (Trostmann/Lewy 2002) to underline a government orientation and application.

As noted in Section 2.1, the CRM literature is highly fragmented and lacks a common conceptualization (Zablah/Bellenger/Johnston 2004). It is, therefore, not surprising to find the same characteristics in the literature about its application to government. Current CiRM literature lacks a common definition, conceptualization and set of goals for CiRM. Most articles on CiRM present the general concept of private-sector CRM, technological aspects (CRM systems) and expected benefits in government (Table 2-4). CRM is supposed to build a better understanding of current and emerging citizen concerns and make government more responsive. Moreover it brings government and citizens closer together. There is general agreement that many aspects of CRM are not sector-specific. However, these aspects have not yet been translated into the context of government. Customer segmentation might help administrators to identify those customers who need help or who are about to need help. Customer retention strategies could be directed at preventing citizens from using a service again if that is the goal (Stone et al. 2003). But the termination of unprofitable customers, data mining, broadening the service range and thus choice, the issue of externalities and conceptualizing the citizen as customer (for a detailed discussion see Section 2.3.1) are believed to be harder to transfer to government.

In the literature, the term CiRM is applied in a blanket fashion to any and all citizen-focused initiatives. For instance, examples of public service provision through online portals are presented as successful CiRM projects (Pang/Norris 2002; Shine/Cornelius 2003) or the adoption of call center and CRM software for the London Borough of Haringey (Batista/Kawalek 2004). Administrators struggle with the lack of knowledge about CRM, in addition to their discomfort with CRM terminology (Accenture 2001; Janssen/Wagenaar 2002). Public administrations which claim to engage in CiRM connect it to single customer service initiatives, online portals, electronic case management, call centers, physical one-stop service centers and CRM software. However, the literature offers little to no insights into organisational, cultural or process-related changes in CiRM initiatives in terms of a holistic understanding of CRM.

King (2007) analysed the results of the British CRM Pathfinder program (2001–02) and the CRM National Programme (2003–04). The majority of the British CRM projects focused on adding CRM capabilities to call centers and one-stop shops. Municipalities that participated in the pilot project are in different stages of a proposed CRM development path which as it turned out do not have to build upon each other. Therefore, a contact center and multichannel environment were put in place without effective structural moves towards creating a customer-centric organisation (King 2007). In addition, there was little evidence for citizen analytics (segmentation, needs analysis), organisational changes (bridging departmental silos) or true multichannel access. Janssen and Wagenaar (2002) found similar results and concluded that Dutch CiRM efforts are in an "embryonic stage". Along these lines, in their survey of the current status of CRM in German public administration, Bauer, Grether and Richter (2002) reported that the CRM elements implemented were not conforming to the holistic concept of CRM presented earlier in this chapter (Section 2.1). Personalization and a closer analysis of commonly-used public services are frequent practices, while segmentation or profitability analyses remain untested domains. Among the biggest barriers to exploring CRM, German administrations mentioned their lack of human resources and the presence of time constraints. Yet they expected CRM to result in higher citizen satisfaction and trust, or an improvement in the image and acceptance of public authorities (Proeller/Zwahlen 2003). In the United States, CiRM is mostly connected to 311 non-emergency number call-center initiatives (Center for Digital Government 2005). Figure 2-4 gives an overview of the current 311 projects in the United States and Canada. Most of them are implemented on the municipal level. Kavanagh (2007) noted:

Figure 2-4: Overview of 311 initiatives in the U.S. and Canada

A government CRM initiative can encompass a number of specific activities for improving constituent relationships with government. The most common application is the constituent contact center, which provides a single point of contact for constituent inquiry. Perhaps the most well-known incarnation of a CRM contact center in government is the 311 telephone number. [Because] the telephone remains constituents' preferred means for contacting government, [...] the telephone will likely remain the focus of government CRM for at least the near future. [Yet] CRM and 311 are not synonymous. CRM refers to a discipline of constituent-focused management of government; 311 is simply one possible CRM tool, albeit an important one. Further, the presence of a 311 number does not necessarily mean that government has implemented CRM. A 311 number is just technology. If it is not built on constituent-focused processes and staff behaviors, it is not CRM.

Focus/ Perspective	Authors
Case study	Wustinger et al. 2002 (Customer Interaction Center in Vienna, Austria); Hewson Group 2002 (various US and UK cases) **; Shine/Cornelius 2003 (Florida Department of Business and Professional Regulation); Stone et al. 2003 (UK); Hanyuh/Lai 2004 (Taiwan); Myron 2004 (Baltimore, 311); GSA 2004 (1(800) FED-INFO, US and international cases); Gartner 2004: 342-344 (Baltimore) **; Richter/Cornford/McLoughlin 2005 (customer contact center, UK municipality); Center for Digital Government 2005 (US, 311); King/Burgess 2005; King 2007 (UK Pathfinder, CRM National Programme overview); Sasaki/Watanabe/Minamino 2007 (Japan);
Technology	Cohen/Moore 2000 (CRM system); Kavanagh 2001 (CRM systems); Souder 2001 (CRM system); Pang/Norris 2002 (CRM system); O'Looney 2002: 91-131 (CRM and KM); Peoplesoft 2002 (technology) **; Batista/Kawalek 2004 (CRM system); GSA 2004 (CRM system)
Survey	Accenture 2001 (PA, global) **; Bauer/Grether/Richter 2002 (PA, Germany); Janssen/Wagenaar 2002 (PA, Netherlands); Accenture 2003 (PA, global) **; Proeller/Zwahlen 2003 (PA, Switzerland); Schellong/Mans 2004 (collaborative CRM, citizens, Germany); Datamonitor 2005 (PA, US)**; Bearing Point 2006 (PA, Germany)**
Concept	Deloitte Research 2000 (CRM with focus on eGovernment)**; Bonin 2001 (CiRM); Deloitte Research 2001 (CRM with focus on eGoverment)**; Trostmann/Lewy 2002 (CERM); Daum 2002 (CiRM); Hewson Group 2002 (CRM) **; Janssen/Wagenaar 2002 (CRM); Schmitt 2003 (δCRM); von Lucke 2003a (CiRM); Jupp 2003 (CRM based on Accenture reports); Stone et al. 2003 (CRM); GSA 2004 (CRM/CiRM); Bleyer/Saliterer 2004 (PRM/CiRM); King/Burgess 2005 (CiRM); Schellong 2005 (CRM); Michel 2005 (CRM); Larsen/Milakovich 2005 (CzRM); Schellong 2006 (CiRM); Pan/Tan/Lim 2006 (CRM with focus on eGovernment); King 2007 (CiRM); da Silva/Batista 2007 (CRM, reputation); Kavanagh 2007 (CRM; 311)
Other	Tapscott 2004 (CiRM to describe eParticipation); Michel 2005 (CiRM to describe a new form of citizenship); Cooper/Bryer/Meek 2006 (citizen-centered collaborative public management); Peppers/Rogers 2004 (government CRM scenario)

Table 2-4: Overview of CiRM literature

2.2   Citizen-oriented reforms in public administration

In order to execute the functions needed to realize their goals and objectives, governments are required to supply and deliver public goods and services. Therefore, public organisations are by their very nature service organisations that must be responsive to the public. Despite being characterized by high levels of organisational–public interaction, public services exhibit substantial diversity (Laing 2003). Public services can be classified as collective, particular or merit services. Collective services are impartible, non-exclusive and inexhaustible, of monopolistic nature and collectively financed (e.g. streets). Particular services are apportionable, exclusive, exhaustible and directly financed by the beneficiary (e.g. customized license plates). Finally, merit services carry characteristics of both collective and particular services (e.g. publicly-funded theatres, subsidized food in university restaurants). Public goods and services are generally provided by public administrations and government institutions. This implies the division of functions (usually a hierarchical pyramid-shaped structure) and a given command and control structure which is commonly referred to as bureaucracy (Weber 1922).

Overregulation and increasing government complexities led to a dysfunctional model of government. Factors such as a dramatic decline in perceived bureaucratic responsiveness, a shift from production-oriented to a service-oriented economy, a continual scarcity of public resources to meet public demands and an increasingly sophisticated citizenry (information society) were factors that had an additional impetus for change. As a result, there have been various public-sector reforms in the last two decades (Pollitt/Bouckaert 2000). These reforms in general take place on four levels (Figure 2-5): internal, external, by defining a new role for government and public administration and by making citizen-orientation a central goal. In Western democracies and industrialized countries, increasing attention has been directed to the relationship between public organisations and civil society (König 2003). Government began borrowing customer service concepts from the private sector. Borins (2002) identified five building blocks of reforms: the use of a systems approach, ICT, process improve-

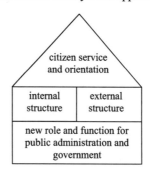

Figure 2-5: Levels and aim of administrative reforms since the 1980s (adapted from Budäus 2002)

ment, the involvement of the private or voluntary sector and empowering citizens and public servants. Governments that miss the last of these lose an important opportunity to educate citizens and to build support for reform (OECD 2000). However, reforms in the public domain face a complex set of barriers and obstacles known as the "socio-political firewall" (Vigoda et al. 2005). Among them are a lack of adaptiveness to citizens needs, and the current organisational structure, culture and values (Rogers 1983), or the political decisions and considerations, of key executive actors (Bogumil 1997a: 134).

The next section of the literature review summarises major reform movements which aimed or claimed to improve citizen-orientation in public administration. New Public Management (NPM) is introduced first, because its ideas and concepts have dominated administrative reforms and research since the 1980s. In particular, I focus on the concept of TQM. Next, I present eGovernment, which stressed external government relations with citizens via the Internet. This review allows us to identify unique aspects of CiRM in comparison with earlier concepts. In addition, we can classify the level of citizen-orientation within the spectrum of existing reforms. Finally, examining past reform projects reveals success factors and barriers which are of importance to public managers.

2.2.1 New Public Management

Public-sector reform that began in the 1980s is commonly referred to as New Public Management (NPM). Since the 1970s, reforms drawing on private-sector management concepts have become a "populist accent" (Arnold 1995) with which politicians can respond to public dissatisfaction with government performance and operations. Wilson ([1887] 1987), then a college professor and later president of the United States, had recommended, in the late 19th century, drawing insights from the field of business, since "[...] the field of public administration is a field of business". However, Hood and Peters (2004) noted that in the early days of NPM "no two authors listed the same features". The concept "loose and multifaceted and offers a kind of "shopping basket" of different elements for reform of public administration" (Christensen/Laegreid 2001). This disparity in NPM's understanding and conceptualization still exists (Brudney/Hebert/Wright 1999; Pollitt/Bouckaert 2000; Schedler 2003).

The term NPM refers to a set of normative management concepts, tools (Frederickson/Smith 2003) and goals, not policy. NPM rests largely on rational and public choice theory as well as private-sector and market models (Kelly 1998; Reinermann/Ridley/Thoenig 1998). NPM advocates oppose the traditional Weberian theory that government is best served by bureaucratic organisation and decision making (Lane 2000). According to their perspective, traditional public administration promotes an inward-looking culture serving mostly its own needs. In addition, traditional decision-making processes and structure discourage innovation. NPM aims to increase collective utility by influencing various rationalities in the decision-making process.

Reinermann (2003) identified six fundamental ideas in NPM. First, complex administrative settings should be grouped by organising (decentralization, disaggregation) agency units in modules or clusters around services. Second, process re-engineering should be conducted across hierarchical and jurisdictional boundaries as well as from the customer perspective. Third and fourth, public monopolies should be exposed to competitive market forces so that public organisations become more accountable and more client-oriented, with an increase in service quality. Fifth, human resource management should be changed so that it fosters subsidiarity, innovation and flexibility without sacrificing system integrity (e.g. wider, flatter hierarchies, output targets, limited term contracts, monetary incentives, freedom to manage). All hierarchy levels need to understand the consequences (e.g. budget cuts, other units) of their decisions and behaviour. Administrators have to steer, not row. That is, they consider recognizing a wide range of possibilities and strike a balance between resources and needs, concentrating on a single objective (Osborne/Gaebler 1992: 35). Finally, NPM is intended to empower an exemplary and visionary administrative and political leadership by their considering of the five fundamental ideas of NPM presented here. Besides an internal focus, Kißler et al. (1997: 39) identified a long-term focus of governmental reform towards "lean politics" (May 1995), similar to "lean administration". Table 2-5 summarises the differences between NPM and the former view of public administration and management.

NPM has proved difficult to define because there are no clearly identifiable variables, causal relationships or generally agreed-upon measurement methods. The meaning of NPM has also changed over time, and the term is used for all types of reforms (Ferlie/Lynn/Fitzgerald 1996; Hood 1996; Stark 2002; Bevir/Rhodes/Weller 2003). Some authors, therefore, reasoned that NPM is in a pre-theoretical stage (Klages/Löffler 1998; Christensen/Laegreid 1998, Bevir/Rhodes/Weller 2003). Hence, Reinermann, Ridley and Thoenig (1998) found that there is not enough empirical evidence on NPM implementation in large organisations. In addition, there is no common terminology that can be utilized for theory development. NPM research is mainly concentrated around three themes (Christiaens/Windels/Vanslembrouck 2004): descriptive studies of the NPM movement (Hood, 1991; Stark, 2002); critical analyses of the consequences of adopting NPM principles in different governmental organisations (Barberis, 1998; Cunningham, 2000) and studies focusing on the implementation of the new philosophy in different countries and on different levels of the public sector (Pallot, 1999; Klinger, 2000). Ridley's (1996) research showed that an institutional perspective is of importance for country comparisons and for understanding why certain elements of NPM are implemented and others are rejected. Sound evaluations of reforms, therefore, also need to review past administrative and political reforms (Klages/Löffler 1998).

	Old Public Administration	New Public Management
Primary theoretical and epistemological foundations	Political theory, social and political commentary augmented by naïve social science	Economic theory, more sophisticated dialogue based on positivist social science
Prevailing rationality and associated models of human behaviour	Synoptic rationality, "administrative man"	Technical and economic rationality, "homo oeconomicus" or the self interested decision maker
Conception of public interest	Public interest is politically defined and expressed in law	Public interest represents the aggregation of individual interest
Responsiveness	Clients and constituents	Customers
Role of government	Rowing (designing and implementing policies focusing on a single politically defined objective)	Steering (acting as a catalyst to unleash market forces)
Mechanisms for achieving policy objectives	Administering programs through existing government agencies	Creating mechanisms and incentive structures to achieve policy objectives through private and non-profit agencies
Approach to accountability	Hierarchical – Administrators are responsible to democratically elected political leaders	Market-driven – The accumulation of self-interests will result in outcomes desired by broad groups of citizens (or customers)
Administrative discretion	Limited discretion allowed administrative officials	Wide latitude to meet entrepreneurial goals
Assumed organizational structure	Bureaucratic organizations marked by top-down authority within agencies and control or regulation of clients	Decentralized public organizations with primary control remaining within the agency
Assumed motivational basis of public servants and administrators	Pay and benefits, civil-service protections	Entrepreneurial spirit, ideological desire to reduce size of government

Table 2-5: Comparing old public administration and NPM (Denhart/Denhart 2003: 28-29)

2.2.2 Critical remarks on NPM

Opposition to NPM comes from five sides. A major body of literature criticizes the economic principles of NPM. The remaining critique falls into the categories of ideology, language, generalizability and sustainability.

As noted earlier, NPM rests on the premise that private-sector management concepts and economic principles can be transferred to the public sector without any adjustment. However, market failure is a common problem for goods or services identified in neoclassical economics (Bator 1958; Krutilla 1967). The system of price–market institutions is incapable of sustaining desirable activities or preventing undesirable activities. As a result, it is generally assumed that goods or services with strong externalities (e.g. pollution, redistribution of public wealth) require a level of state regulation (Cornes/Sandler 1996). Through mergers and acquisitions, markets can also develop towards a duopoly or monopoly over time, which prevents pareto-optimality through rent seeking (Tullock 1967; Gradstein 1993). Finally, competition does not generally lead to an optimal allocation of input factors (e.g. bureaucratization in private enterprises also increases relative to their size (Meyer 2004)) or output factors such as customer satisfaction through measures like Total Quality Management (Anderson/Fornell/Lehmann 1994). This is why some thought that the NPM focus on efficiency and market-based reforms threatens to eliminate democracy as the guiding principle of public administration (Box et al. 2001) or undermines the U.S. constitution. Further critique on the economic principles of NPM comes from principal agent theory. Neo-institutional economics has shown that contractual arrangements are not necessarily superior to hierarchical relationships in government due to adverse selection, morale hazard or transaction costs (Le Grand/Bartlett 1993). Frederickson and Smith (2003: 123), therefore, argued that principal agent theory fails as a theory for public management. In fact, there is a binary principal agent situation in public administration (EO <> PA <> C) which has not yet been researched (Klages/Löffler 1998: 44). In summary, NPM's underlying market mechanisms do not automatically lead to the desired outcomes.

Another set of authors focused on more qualitative and ideological aspects of NPM. While some thought that NPM is "middle-aged", generating adverse side effects (Hood/Peters 2004), Lynn (1998) announced the "end" of NPM, and was recently supported by Dunleavy et al. (2005) who stated:

> [T]he torch of leading edge change has passed on and will not return.

But in some countries formerly resistant to NPM, such as Japan, ideas are still gaining momentum (Yamamoto 2003). Lynn (1998) wondered about NPM's generalizable applicability due the existing global variations. For example, in the UK, NPM aimed to create a minimalist state, whereas in Norway it aimed to protect the state (Bevir/Rhodes/Weller 2003). France's move to far reaching territorial decentralization in 1983 contrasts sharply with the centralizing tendencies in the UK (Hood 1996). New Zealand's structural decentralization efforts led to 300 separate agencies and 40 ministries, which proved difficult to coordinate for joint efforts and fostered a silo mentality (Gregory 2003). Consequently, there are efforts in New Zealand to reverse some of the steps in implementation.

Terms such as decentralization may also refer to changes in organisational structure or devolution to sub-national government. Furthermore, politics always needs new terms to describe administrative reforms; the term "New Public Management" quickly loses its uniqueness once newer concepts come on the scene. The latter point is quite valid if we consider that eGovernment has been on the agenda of most governments since 1999. Dunleavy et al. (2005) came to a similar conclusion. Bogumil (1997a: 135) thought that the measures of NPM and its goal of consolidating public budgets are contradictory. According to his point of view, organisational innovation and financial flexibility are difficult to realize with the current level of public debt and costs of implementing programs and ICT.

NPM aims to replace bureaucratic accountability through detailed directives, checks and balances by the public infocracy (Zuurmond 1994). Therefore, Reinermann, Ridley and Thoenig (1998) wondered who controls public executives' enactment of their available set of public information tools. Indeed, Stoker (1998) pointed to unintended behaviour by local authorities or unions and Stewart (1992; 1993) showed how NPM leads to a lack of accountability. In the "Skye Bridge" local housing projects, authorities worked both competitively and in partnership out of financial necessity but retained a traditional view of the role of public housing and service provision. Thus, the effort fell short of achieving the customer-orientation and the flexible housing provision that was envisioned by reformers. In another case of public, competitive tendering, private contractors drew the conclusion that "if a local authority does not want work to go out, it won't go out".

Empirical research by Skalen (2004) found that "NPM creates heterogeneous, conflicting and fluid organisational identities, rather than the uniform and stable business identity it is supposed to". It may have "perverse effects" (Stoker 1998) and lead to functional disruption by neglecting or threatening administrative needs (e.g. organizational operations requirements, culture) which produce "side" or "reverse effects" (Hood 1995). In addition, reforms that attempt to change government by way of focusing on results and customer satisfaction as opposed to administrative and political processes fail to account for legislative self-interest and therefore precipitate uncontrollable outcomes (Merton 1938). As Rosenbloom (1993) noted, "[E]ven if federal administration is reinvented [...] Congress may manage to reinvent its leverage over the agencies." Along these lines, Hood and Peters (2004: 270) referred to Maor's (1999) research, which found that NPM increases politicization of the administrative domain instead of the intended depoliticization. In particular, elected officials tried to gain control over the employment and disemployment of administrative executives. Of special interest to this study is Dunleavy's and Hood's (1994) observation that fragmenting bureaucracy had the unintended effect of making it harder for citizens at large to understand the bureaucratic structure and thus weakens one vital ingredient for solutions to public policy problems—informed citizen understanding of the system.

Despite their criticism, researchers generally acknowledged that NPM led to an increased focus on performance-based administration (Kickert 2000), an international dialogue on administrative reforms and an integrated approach to applying economic, social and social-psychology models in administrative science (Osborne/Gaebler 1992; Kettl/Milward 1996; Lynn 1996). In the next section, I will take a closer look at one of the tools that is central to realizing a citizen-oriented administration in NPM: Total Quality Management.

2.2.3 Total Quality Management

Total Quality Management (TQM) is based on Japanese management techniques in manufacturing. Factors and motivations bearing an impetus for organisational change through TQM are new technologies, globalization, increased competition and market saturation (Lawrence 1989; Miranda 2003). The term TQM was coined by the U.S. Department of Defence's (DOD) Naval Personnel Research Development Center (NPRDC) and Naval Air Systems Command (NAVAIR) (Secan 1996: 23; Miranda 2003: 35). The DOD *(1990)* defined TQM as follows:

> *TQM is both a philosophy and a set of guiding principles that represent the foundation of a continuously improving organization. TQM is the application of quantitative methods and human resources to improve materials and services supplied to an organization, all the processes within an organization, and the degree to which the needs of the customer are met, now and in the future. TQM integrates fundamental management techniques, existing improvement efforts, and technical tools under a disciplined approach focused on continuous improvement. (in Lin/Ogunyemi 1996)*

Irrespective of this definition, it was Deming's (1986) work that led to TQM's widespread popularity and subsequent varying definitions. Deming (1986: 23-24)

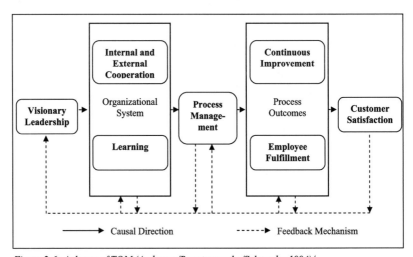

Figure 2-6: A theory of TQM (Anderson/Rungtusanatha/Schroeder 1994)/

noted 14 core points (Appendix C) based on quantitative methods that result in increased quality (Ehrenberg/Stupak 1994: 79). Quantitative methods allow to evaluate according to standards and work on continuous improvement. Anderson, Rungtusanatham and Schroeder (1994: 476) thought that there was an underlying theory (Figure 2-6), such as Taylor's (1911) scientific management or the concept of the learning organisation (Lawrence/Dyer 1983) in TQM's complex set of connected rules for intra- and inter- organisational behaviour. Ehrenberg and Stupak (1994) viewed TQM as more a part of systems theory. In systems theory, organisations are complex networks which consist of input, process, output and feedback. The role of organisational units can only be understood by analysing the external relationships (e.g. customers, suppliers) which are of a complex, dynamic and sometimes unknown nature. From a systems theory perspective, generating this kind of understanding is the aim of TQM.

Lindsay and Petrick (1997: 20) in Scharitzer and Korunka (2000: 943) defined TQM as a broad, systematic concept for all organisational customer-oriented business units, functions and employees, including external suppliers. Lin and Ogyunyemi (1996) believed that TQM is a "holistic management philosophy". Wruck and Jansen (1998: 402) noted that "TQM is a science-based, non-hierarchical and non-market–oriented

	Customer Focus	Continuous improvement	Teamwork
Principles	Paramount importance of providing products and services that fulfil customer needs; requires organization wide focus on customers	Consistent customer satisfaction can be attained only through relentless improvement of processes that create products and services	Customer focus and continuous improvement are best achieved by collaboration throughout an organization as well as with customers and suppliers
Practices	Direct customer contact. Collecting information about customer needs. Using information to design and deliver products and services	Process analysis Reengineering Problem solving Plan/do/check/act	Search for arrangements that benefit all units involved in a process. Formation of various types of teams. Group skills training
Techniques	Customer surveys and focus groups. Quality function deployment (translates customer information into product specifications)	Flowcharts Pareto analysis Statistical process control Fisbone diagrams	Organizational development methods such as the technique. Team-building methods (e.g. role clarification and group feedback)

Table 2-6: TQM – Principles, Practices and Methods (Dean/Bowen 1994: 395)

organisational technology with the potential to increase efficiency and quality". This is similar to the definition by Miranda, (2003: 36-37) who limited, however, TQM's scope to manufacturing. Because quality becomes central to an organisation's existence, so too does a customer orientation, which results in a movement from a product-only focus to a customer focus. Customer orientation, continuous improvement and teamwork (Table 2-6) are the core principles of Total Quality Management (Dean/Bowen 1994; Ehrenberg/Stupak 1994).

Process-centered TQM led to a paradigm shift in management. First, individual employees are not a key variable in explaining quality issues. Results are outcomes of teams or the system (Carr/Littman 1990: 196).

Second, the understanding of quality is reversed. In the earlier management literature, quality has a positive relation to costs, so an increase in quality can only be generated by an increase in costs (Steenkamp 1989). Deming (1986), in contrast, assumed that increasing quality results in decreasing costs.

Third, the subject of the customer did not receive much attention in organisational science. In TQM, customer interaction is important for the gathering of information that is disseminated throughout the organisation (Dean/Bowen 1994). The fundamental idea is that satisfied customers are loyal customers, which lead to satisfied employees who will assure the company's survival and competitive advantage (Anderson/Rungtusanatham/Schroeder 1994: 491). Moreover, TQM differentiates between internal (e.g. employees of different business units) and external customers (e.g. consumers, suppliers).

Customer service and customer orientation are also the guiding principles of designing a single process as well as linking organisational processes (Grant 1995: 14). Preventing variability in services or products is a key element of producing high quality. As a result of process design and teamwork ("people in research, design and sales and production must work as a team (Deming 1986)), hierarchical structures become blurred. In addition, a significant knowledge reallocation on the intra-organisational level takes place by spreading specific knowledge (e.g. strategies, complex dependencies) to all hierarchy levels with the possibility of an increase in quality on the one hand and agency conflicts (Fama 1980) on the other (Wruck/Jensen 1998). Leadership keeps its strategic role but takes up a position of facilitative coordination. But some authors thought that TQM fell short with regard to appreciating the role of strategic planning (Albrecht 1993; Godfrey 1993; Perry/Wong/Bernhardt 1995; Redman 1995; Bennington/Cummane 1997).

Fourth, continuous change in all of the above areas can only be achieved through the commitment, leadership and communication skills of executive leadership (Bennington/Cummane 1997: 366; Ehrenberg/Stupak 1994; Bennington/Cummane 1997: 82; Douglas/Fredendall 2004: 414). If management is missing these capabilities, TQM implementations will most likely fail (Reger/Gustafson 1994).

Therefore, the core elements of TQM programs can be summarised in the following 12 components (Table 2-7).

1. Committed leadership: a near-evangelical, unwavering, long-term commitment by top managers to the philosophy, usually under a name something like Total Quality Management, Continuous Improvement, or Quality Improvement

2. Adoption and communication of TQM: using tools like the mission statement, and themes or slogans

3. Closer customer relationships: determining customers' (both inside and outside the firm) requirements; then meeting those requirements no matter what it takes

4. Closer supplied relationships: working closely and cooperatively with suppliers (often sole-sourcing key components), ensuring they provide inputs that conform to customers'' end-use requirements

5. Benchmarking: researching and observing best competitive practices

6. Increased training: usually includes TQM principles, team skills, and problem-solving

7. Open organization: lean staff, empowered work teams, open horizontal communications, and a relaxation of traditional hierarchy

8. Employee empowerment: increased employee involvement in design and planning, and greater autonomy in decision-making

9. Zero-defects mentality: a system in place to spot defects as they occur , rather than through inspection and rework

10. Flexible manufacturing: (applicable only to manufacturers) can include just-in-time inventory, cellular manufacturing, design for manufacturability (DFM), statistical process control (SPC), and design of experiments (DOE)

11. Process improvement: reduced waste and cycle times in all areas through cross-departmental process analysis

12. Measurements: goal-orientation and zeal for data, with constant performance measurement, often using statistical methods.

Table 2-7: The 12 components of TQM (Powell 1995)

2.2.3.1 Critical remarks on TQM

TQM is not without some deserved criticism. Indeed, Keleman (2000: 484), Reger and Gustafson (1994) and Bennington and Cummane (1997: 366) found that up to 80% of all TQM programs fail. TQM outcomes are difficult to control by executive leadership due to the complex social relationships of teamwork and the varying perceptions of the concept (Kelemen 2000). Loss of control, feelings of inadequacy, fear of failure, change of routine habits, disruption of the social network or lack of understanding can activate strong counteracting dynamics (Galitz/Cirillo 1983). Bennington and Cummane (1997: 366-367) added the reaction of unions to the widespread changes implicit in TQM as another factor of uncertainty.

Others questioned the normative assumption that TQM is a value-free technical tool or concept (Steingard/Fitzgibbons 1993; Wilkinson/Willmott 1995; Miranda 2003). TQM derives from extensive use of metaphors. Wilkinson and Willmott (1995) urged researchers to fully understand quality and its underlying assumptions and implicit power relations. In order for the organisation to survive in a hostile environment, all interdependent components have to concentrate on the common goal set by leadership. Therefore, all individual or collective existence is to be limited to those aspects that serve the needs of the organisation (Miranda 2003), which leads to a total control of employees' subjectivity (Steingard/Fitzgibbons 1993).

2.2.3.2 TQM in government

Ehrenberk and Stupak (1994: 88) thought that "TQM was an important concept for government in the area of improving citizen satisfaction". Secan (1996: 34) saw an analogy in the common saying, "A happy customer will return and buy again." Higher levels of citizen-orientation in public administration replace scepticism with an overall positive attitude towards government.

NPM and TQM are usually used in a synonymous manner (Scharitzer/Korunka 2000; Bogumil/Holtkamp/Kißler 2001). TQM is, however, a subset within NPM-guided reforms (Reinermann/Ridley/Thoenig 1998: 43).

TQM is different from initiatives such as Zero Based Budgeting (ZBO) or Management by Objectives (MBO). In fact, Deming (1986: 54) stated that a "focus on outcomes must be abolished and replaced by leadership". The resulting steering emphasises results at the cost of processes, which facilitates short-terminism (Naschold/Watt/Arnkill 1996). Steering may lead to setting goals that are easily attainable and subjective, raising the danger of intransparency and unjustified priorities. Numerical targets are contradictory to organisational innovation and improving quality, because they create a culture of fear. Thus, from this perspective, innovations can lead to a failure in reaching goals. In addition, operational implementation and interpretation of strategic targets differ.

By contrast, TQM focuses on measuring inputs and processes throughout the organisation and hierarchies which are controlled by executives. Saueressig (1999: 27) drew the conclusion that "process-oriented approaches have a better chance of increasing the level of efficiency and external quality because they require internal reorganization". This would make it necessary to view all administrative processes as a value chain that is modelled around the respective target group (citizen, business, administration). However, Bogumil, Holtkamp and Kißler (2001: 77-78) concluded that there are "no consistent incentives", such as market competition, for TQM in government, which makes its application subject to the individual interests and efforts of administrative leadership or the regulatory environment. The latter rules ("red tape") governing public servants are usually not self-generated by bureaucracy but set by political institutions such as Congress or the Parliament (Wilson 1989). Bandemer (1998) suggested "the introduction of a process of actively managing citizens' complaint as a means to induce the necessary changes". Along these lines, Bogumil, Holtkamp and Kißler (2001: 78) expected that "TQM offered the chance to shift public administration from an inward-looking culture towards a more external (citizen)-oriented one".

Swiss (1992) found that in its "unmodified and unorthodox form" TQM does not fit the environment of government unless there are some substantial conceptual changes.

He criticised the input orientation of TQM as a retreat of the achievements realized by MBO, program budgets and performance monitoring systems. In government, "[A] move towards stressing outputs is in fact usually a move towards the desired long-range vision," and "it is stressing inputs and processes that represents short-term business as usual" (Swiss 1992). Furthermore, services are produced and consumed at the same time, making it difficult to control quality in government as it is controlled in the manufacturing of goods. He is also critical towards defining the citizen as customer, in general, which I will address in detail in Section 2.3.2. Finally, while Swiss (1992) admitted that TQM offered "innovative ideas, particularly improving processes," he concludes that the ideas of worker participation and quantitative output tracking seem like "old wine in new bottles" in government.

Despite supporting Swiss's (1992) argument for modifying TQM for government use, Rago (1994) noted that Swiss's oppositional conclusions "intimately" relate to his organisational perspective. The challenges of translating TQM into the government sphere derive from other factors than customer definition or work processes. Rago (1994) believed it is the "political culture and the unmet needs of an unlimited supply of customers that creates the real problems for the application of TQM". Along these lines, Lin und Ogunyemi (1996: 6) drew the conclusion that "TQM was applicable in government because public services are in the same category as the private services". This idea is further supported by a case study by Bennington and Cummane (1997) on a successful TQM implementation between 1989 and 1996 in the "Asset Services" of the Australian Department of Administrative Services.

- The following common errors in government TQM implementations are identified by Lin and Ogunyemi (1996: 5-9):

- One-sided focus on technology at the expense of leadership and management

- Implementation of technology before defining its specific roles and determining needs

- Training employees before support systems of TQM have been set up

- Understanding TQM as a set of measures and technical tools (e.g. benchmarking, charts and graphs, arrow diagrams) instead of a philosophy

- Understanding services as non-analysable and non-quantifiable based on their qualitative nature

- Understanding TQM as a result-oriented instead of a process-oriented method

- Lack of priority and continuous support from elected and administrative leadership

Moreover, elected and administrative leadership are neither prioritizing TQM nor offering the required long-term sponsorship. Ehrenberg and Stupak (1994: 89) noted that many are condemning TQM without a fair implementation test. "Recent changes in the public sector have had positive effects on implementing TQM successfully". For example, the Veterans Affairs Insurance Center in Philadelphia was able "to cut in half the number of veterans who had to make follow-up inquiries regarding services" (Ehrenberg/Stupak 1994: 93).

Budget constraints force public administration to optimize processes in order to increase effectiveness and efficiency at a lower level of resources (employees, budget). Privatization or contracting out is creating alternatives to government service provision monopolies. Interest groups and citizenry, taking advantage of their voice option, more often are improving the quality of existing services and choosing citizen-oriented designs when implementing policies. However, the external environment (politics, media and citizens) is more unpredictable, and is at times "[...] more influential in the public sector than the "voice" of citizens. [Therefore], it may be necessary to start with smaller organizations or sub-elements of large organizations in order to establish TQM as a useful template for organizational success" (Ehrenberg/Stupak 1994: 95).

Hirschfelder (1998) described such an approach. The German city of Saarbrücken started four partly autonomous TQM projects before attempting larger organisational changes. A more radical approach would have been rejected by citizens and public servants alike. Executive leadership intended to changed organisational culture and create a citizen-centric organisation through TQM. The initiative led to new opening hours, reduction of service delivery times (e.g. building permits) and budget savings. Moreover, the public workers union agreed to introduce a performance-based salary component. The challenges of the TQM project match findings presented earlier. Administrators were sceptical, sometimes openly opposing the rationalizing effects of TQM. Executive support and interest diminished over time. Working group results produced varying results. While some experienced regular meetings as an additional work and time burden, others feared the transparency.

Scharitzer and Korunka (2000) conducted a longitudinal case study on the effects of TQM and change management interventions from administrators' and customers' perspectives. They analysed an Austrian municipal service unit in the area of public housing. The TQM project resulted in a new hierarchical structure, customer service teams, citizen service centers and a software system. As it turned out, public servants less involved in the planning process were less satisfied and were more stressed. Internal information campaigns had an important influence on the perception of change. Twelve months after the implementation, citizen satisfaction surveys showed a significant increase in service satisfaction levels. External citizen ratings exceeded those that the public servants expected for their organisation. This dichotomy is a common observation in other studies.

Finally, administrative size is of importance. Larger cities have greater resources to invest in implementation efforts and showed higher commitment to TQM. A city's population influences public service, and information demand is significant in its association with TQM implementation (Berman/West 1995).

2.2.4 Electronic Government

From a historic perspective, public administration was among the first to utilize information and communication technologies (Reinermann et al. 1988; Lenk 1994; Adler/Borys 1996; Werner/Wind 1997; Lucke von 2003: 30). Punch-card machines were used for the census, and electronic databases were applied throughout government once the technology was available. The origin of the Internet also dates back to a government project in the 1960s. ARPANET was a DOD initiative to create an electronic packet-switching network for universities so that they could share computing power (Abbate 1994). In the early 1990s, municipalities began using e-mail, bulletin boards and other components of the Internet (Ho 2002). Advances in ICT and a rapid adoption by society in the late 1990s forced governments to draw their attention to utilizing the possibilities of the Internet and other technologies. The "Y2K problem", a flaw in software design that caused date-related processing to operate incorrectly after January 1, 2000 allowed governments to heavily invest in new technologies. At the same time, they recognized technology-related public–private interdependencies and the need for a national electronic infrastructure (Brown 2005). The role of external factors such as the evolving information society (Martin 1995; Castells 1996) in initiating this trend is believed to be far greater than in preceding government reforms (Fountain/Osiro-Urzua 2001; Schedler/Summermatter 2002; Binz-Scharf 2003).

According to Lenk and Traunmüller (2002), ICT played only an auxiliary role in NPM: to support financial management or to gather performance data (Schelin 2003). As a result, these systems were designed to support the specific needs of an agency and the general "stove-pipe" structure of public administration (Atluri et al. 2002). This rather inward-looking perspective was replaced by a greater focus on external relationships and the potential of ICT in eGovernment.

The use of ICT for internal and external government processes, obligations and activities is called electronic government (eGovernment). While there is still no commonly accepted definition of eGovernment, variations depend on the context (Allan et al. 2006) and its degree of broadness. Many researchers limited eGovernment to public information and service provision over the Internet (Dawes 2002b). Broader definitions of eGovernment underline the change of internal and external government operations through technology, electronic public services and electronic participation (Grönlund 2002). In some cases, the terms eGovernance and eGovernment are used synonymously or within the context of eDemocracy. Peri 6 (2001), for instance, described eGovernance as "digital support for policy making; decision making; group work between ministers and their juniors, senior civil servants working on policy formulation, development and management," which could instead be associated with the term eDemocracy within eGovernment. However, in this study, eGovernance refers to the role of government in regulating (e.g. adjusting property rights laws to fight illegal downloading) and facilitating (e.g. funding schools' IT equipment) growth of the information society and ICT (König/Adam 2001; Gisler/Spahni 2001). Additional terms to describe the phenomenon of eGovernment are wired government (O'Looney 2002) and digital government (McIver/Elmargarmid 2002; West 2005a). The latter is now favoured by many researchers, because there has been an excessive use of adding letters like "e" (electronic), "m" (mobile) or "u" (ubiquitous) to government-related terms. Moreover, while researchers discussed technological aspects and their potential, organisational changes and the interplay of technology in the political-administrative environment have been somewhat neglected. Along these lines, it is useful to include eGovernment, eGovernance and any future technology of ICT in our understanding of digital government in order to prevent a narrowing of our vision, which would cause us to neglect the complexity of the issue.

The following typology helps to classify research on government initiatives (Figure 2-7). The term eAdministration refers to the internal use of ICT—which might, of course, support the external use of ICT—which is subsumed under eServices. Activities and use of ICT within the field of public participation in government, whether in voting or in the policy-making process, is referred to as eDemocracy. eGovernance can focus on government, society or economy.

Following a classification theme in eCommerce (Albers et al. 2000), eGovernment relationships are differentiated into three groups (Gisler/Spahni 2001; Fountain/Osiro-Urzua 2001): Government to Citizen (G2C), Government to Business (G2B) and Government to Government (G2G) (Table 2-8). G2G involves conducting electronic exchanges between government actors on the unit, agency, local, state, federal or international level. Government to public servant relationships (Hiller/Bèlanger 2001) are a part of the G2G relationship spectrum. Transactions (data, goods, services) between

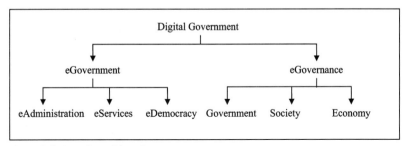

Figure 2-7: A typology of digital government

government and business are referred to as G2B. Examples are electronic public tenders or businesses achieving efficiency gains by integrating government in the value chains (e.g. tariff declaration). The third relationship is that of G2C. In this case, government establishes or maintains a direct link with citizens in order to deliver information or services. Citizens may also interact with government as part of the political process, which might result in citizen to citizen (C2C) interaction (e.g. public deliberation, eVoting).

In addition to classifying eGovernment relationships, technology-based public service delivery can reach different levels of sophistication (Symonds 2000; Gisler/Spahni 2001; Hiller/Bèlanger 2001; United Nations 2001; Layne/Lee 2001). These levels are discussed in the eBusiness literature (Heeks/Bailur 2007). The most common levels are information, one-way communication, two-way communication and full transaction. Some authors propose "transformation" as the fifth and highest

Supply side	Demand side		
	Consumer/ Citizen	Business	Government
Consumer/ Citizen	C2C Auctions, Public deliberation	C2B Job search	C2G Tax filing, Voting
Business	B2C Shops	B2B eProcurement	B2G Tax filing
Government	G2C Licenses	G2B eProcurement	G2G Immigration

Table 2-8: eGovernment and eBusiness relationships

order of eGovernment evolution (Seifert/Petersen 2001). In this case, governments initiate institutional and administrative reforms (e.g. vertical or horizontal integration, process re-engineering) (Grönlund 2002). However, I think that transformation can be part of any internal or external ICT implementation in government. Zuurmond (1994) showed that a move towards flexible, organic and horizontal structures in government are substantially facilitated by ICT's impact on data utilization, managerial control, decision making and planning.

The first stage in online sophistication is presenting information on a website. It's a passive presentation of information in various levels of detail and does not require any organisational changes. In the early days of eGovernment, websites were first developed by technology-savvy administrators on the agency level. Examples of one-way communication are downloadable forms or information about e-mail contacts. On the two-way communication level, forms can only be filled in electronically but need to be submitted to a specific agency in printed form. Data is completely processed electronically when public services reach the transaction level. Citizens and business may also be able to personalize and customize information and services. Irani, Al-Sebie and Elliman (2006) showed that online activities reaching the transaction level cease being peripheral to an agency's operations and present organisational challenges. In addition, transaction-type services require the highest levels of security and standards, because they have to ensure authenticity, integrity and confidentiality of transactions (Aichholzer/Schmutzer 1999). In practice, eGovernment project components have various levels of sophistication at the same time (Moon 2002).

Research dealing with eGovernment draws from various disciplines; in particular, it draws from political science, computer science, business and administrative science. Early studies focused mostly on outcomes and content analysis of government websites. Technical contributions covered system architecture, data mining, GIS or data security. At the moment, publications are dominated by an excess of different models and approaches, with the frameworks presented (eGovernment relationships/ sophistication levels of online provision) being the only commonly accepted models. Thus, the field can still be characterised by a lack of coherence and a lack of common bases for communication and accumulation of knowledge (Fountain 2003). This fact is further stressed by Heeks and Bailur (2006) who reviewed papers from *Government Information Quarterly, Information Polity* and *Proceedings of European Conference on eGovernment* that were published between 2001 and 2005. They pointed out that research "is dominated by over-optimistic, a-theoretical work that has done little to accumulate either knowledge or practical guidance for e-government". On the other hand, Troitzch et al. (2003) thought "that the field had left its early formation phase, characterized by definition attempts and defining of relevant research areas, and is now approaching a strong differentiation".

2.2.4.1 Central elements of ICT

eGovernment visions and concepts are largely influenced by "technological determinism" (Smith/Marx 1994), which understands ICT as a powerful agent of change and is omnipresent in government, business and the early academic literature. For instance, the President's Information Technology Advisory Committee stated that, "information technology is quite literally transforming the way we live, learn, work and play" (PITAC 1998). ICT is predicted to empower citizens and increase government efficiency (Bekkers 1999; Detlor/Finn 2002). However, ICT's transformational role in government has been poorly understood and theorized (Dunleavy et al. 2006). Following a brief review of key characteristics of ICT, I will look at its enactment and impact on government as CRM is facilitated through ICT.

Information and communication technology (ICT) allows the structuring of information processing, coordination and flows without the common boundaries of roles, organisational relationships and operating procedures of a bureaucracy (Fountain 2001a). As a consequence, the relationship between information and the physical factors of organisational size, distance, time and costs are altered. Oviatt and Dougall (1995) noted that technology supports overcoming the disadvantages of small organisational size. Digital information makes geographical dispersion irrelevant, allowing for new forms of collaboration and networks. Information technologies facilitate the speed of communication and more selectively control access and participation in a communication event or network (Huber 1990). The complexity lies in being able to operate extensively in standardized ways, such as with multiple agents distributed in time and space (Ciborra 1993). Interestingly, standardization, routinization and formalization are not only technical requirements for effective information sharing, such as in shared databases; they are also typical traits of bureaucracy (Weber 1922; Simon

1947) and to a large extent, normative categories for effective organisation (Frissen 1998: 34). Standardization indicates redundancies across agencies transparent and weakens the rationale for collecting highly redundant data by different agencies, which may result in political battles (Fountain 2001a). Organisational memory (Walsh/Ungson 1991) that was once hidden in non-digital forms (e.g. paper files) or an individual's memory can be stored, managed and analysed in digital form for knowledge acquisition or decision making. The human constraints of processing large quantities of information is reduced (e.g. search engines), and software applications allow the combining (e.g. Web-based GIS mashups like chicagocrime.org) and reconfiguring of information so as to create new information (Zmud 1983). Web-based GIS systems have improved public participation. In particular, by the availability of numerous types and sources of information on the Internet, a "new global virtual public space" is created (von Lucke 2003b). This space develops its own rules, ethics (e.g. Creative Commons, Open Source) or economics (e.g. virtual economies in "Second Life" or "World of Warcraft"). In addition, the Internet increases net effects and the distribution of power by allowing individuals to reach out and affect many other people, depending on their position within the network and their access to information resources. Information storage, provision and search costs are virtually zero once information is digitized.

Technology allows for new forms of coordination and control. Operational decisions of delivering public services are usually left to the lower-level jurisdictions (municipal level) or workers, because they are believed to have superior information and experience with regard to local needs, which results in better responsiveness. Policies such as finding balancing strategies and preventing operational biases are left to higher jurisdictions or hierarchies. As claimed by Janowitz and Delany (1957), ICT might finally connect the substantive knowledge (e.g. clients, face-to-face contacts) of lower-level employees with the functional knowledge (e.g. strategy, communication, management) of upper-level administrators or policy makers, thus avoiding their isolation from one another and providing them both with clear information. Mintzberg (1975) noted that managers require timely information, which is usually delayed as information is moving through the sequential nodes of the communication network. ICT can bring internal and external facts to the organisation's decision makers in real time. As a result, decision makers' information processing capabilities shift from depending on the system supply to the decision makers' capacity, that is, managing the information overflow (Ciborra 1996). Additionally, information systems can give clerks that are low in the hierarchy more accountability if the rules they are to follow can be embedded within the software and not emanate from the decision maker (Fountain 2001a).

On the other hand, with regard to specialization, advances in information technology can either lead to the addition or loss of job categories (e.g. as a process is replaced by the system). Therefore, ICT can mediate informal inter- and intra-group exchanges (Ciborra 1993), blur organisational boundaries (Dewan/Min 1997; Greenhill 1998), lead to simultaneous centralization and decentralization (Dewett/Jones 2001) or improve citizen-orientation (Ho 2002) through One-Stop Shops. The latter idea of creating an organisational entity that operates on top of several existing functionally different departments re-emerged as online "one-stop government" within eGovernment after being tested by agencies (e.g. social services in the United States (Calista 1986) or the "Bürgeramt" (KGSt 1974) in Germany) in the late 1970s (Hagen 2000). Online one-stop government refers to a single point of access (e.g. online portals (Reinermann/von Lucke 2002)) to electronic services and information offered by different public and semi-public authorities (Wimmer 2002).

2.2.4.2 Enacting technology in government

When governments implement ICT, outcomes vary. Online portals and online-based income tax collection have been very successful throughout the world. On the other hand, projects that aimed to introduce ICT to improve processes, data or knowledge sharing sometimes failed completely (e.g. FBI Virtual Case File (Goldstein 2005)). Out of 40 eGovernment projects in a study by Heeks (2003), 35% were reported to be total failures. Identifying and overcoming the challenges is not always easy (Gil-Garcia/Pardo 2005).

Bozeman and Bretschneider (1986) argued that there are important underlying differences between public and private management information systems (MIS). In contrast to the private sector, technology transfers and knowledge sharing are a common practice or even mandated in the public sector (Rocheleau/Wu 2002). However, risk awareness, tight budgets and the publicness of government also prevent investment into innovative ICT. ICT systems carry sunk costs and constrain subsequent choices and possibilities. Realizing a competitive advantage generally falls short of being an impetus for ICT in government. ICT is rather seen as a way to streamline governmental processes, a catalyst for organisational change or a way of cutting costs. But Kraemer and King (1986) found that job creation offset and sometimes exceeded job losses. Usually, eServices are an extra channel generating additional costs without organisational changes (Grönlund 2002). Heintze and Bretschneider (2000) also underline the direct and indirect influence of politics on IT procurement and enactment. In line with Fountain (2001a) and McIvor, McHugh and Cadden (2002), Melitski (2003) argued that organisational and cultural factors influence whether public managers will use ICT to exert central control or to empower their organisations. Decision makers in public administration many times have to resolve conflict among independent political bodies that have incompatible or competing goals (Figure 2-8).

California's state-wide automated child support system was brought to a halt due to struggles among the federal, state and county governments over the structure of the system. Federal, state and local governments usually differ in the purposes for which they want to use ICT (Rocheleau 2000). Other challenges or failures in government ICT projects derive from the purchasing process, delays in development, inflexibility, legal challenges to computing, lack of oversight, lack of risk management (The Royal Academy of Engineering 2004), organisational resistance, poor project management and training (Rocheleau 1997), indifferent senior management, lack of political will (Bannister 2001), federalism (Lucke von 2003) and dealing with or merging legacy systems and data (Peled 2000).

In particular, decisions about which data can be discarded forever are hard to make. Because data storage costs are continuously decreasing, organisations prefer to keep everything, creating data cemeteries (Lenk 1994). Sometimes interim systems bridge the incompatibilities between the old and the new system, thus keeping the legacy system alive and increasing overall system complexity (e.g. FAA-hosted computer system). When the IRS introduced Quality Information Systems (QIS) to support the Quality Teams during a TQM initiative, it never shut down the system, even though the teams do not exist anymore. The amount of work it would take to find and resolve the data-exchange routines with other systems of QIS were considered too high (Mani

Figure 2-8: Magical pentagon of organizational goals

1995). Moreover, these "electronic mounds" (Peled 2000) accumulate massive amounts of rules that conflict with changes to other systems. The possibilities of storing and searching electronic information may also justify the development of large sets of rules, so ICT does not always cut red tape. This is why Mayer-Schoenberger (2007) proposed a combination of laws and technology that reinstate a process to delete data and "revive our society's capacity to forget".

In order to understand the complexities of ICT in government, Fountain (2001a) developed the technology enactment framework (TEF). It focuses on the use and effects of ICT on organisations (government) from an institutional perspective. One key aspect of Fountain's framework (Figure 2-9) is the theoretical distinction between the ICT elements and the actors' perceptions and use of these elements. In Fountain's view, both bureaucratic structure and the behaviour of key actors will determine technology enactment and outcomes. However, this assumption was not visible in her framework. Therefore, the TEF was extended by Okumura to include the multiple roles played by career civil servants, IT decision makers and consultants in government technology enactment (Fountain 2004).

In general, the TEF presents a theory of a dynamic process than predictive outcomes. Enacted technology has four specific elements: perception, design, implementation and use. It is distinguished from "objective technology", which is hardware, software and especially the Internet, with their given set of characteristics (e.g. functionality) before people use or customize it. Take, for example, the spreadsheet software Microsoft Excel, whose broad and hidden functionality are only known and used by a limited number of people.

The most important influences on technology enactment are coming from the organizational context. Because of complex settings and organisational reforms, there is a distinction between bureaucracy and networks. Most administrators still work within one agency or department, but there is an increasing need for cross-agency collaboration, as the problems occurring in the aftermath of Hurricane Katrina revealed yet again. Network efficiency increases where there are both higher trust and richer social capital (Coleman 1988) among actors, and where information sharing is common. The actors' perceptions and the behaviours of technology are shaped by institutional arrangements. These include factors such as culture, socio-structure or legal norms. Cognitive institutions refer to mental habits and cognitive models that influence behaviour and decision making. Cultural institutions refer to shared symbols such as narratives or meanings.

The final part of the TEF is the outcome. It can take a long or a very short period of time for an impact of enacted technology to be recognized. Outcomes can affect organisational forms, institutional arrangements and enacted technology as well as objective technology, as seen in the dashed causal arrows. Causal arrows that point in both directions stress the recursive effects of variables. As such, outcomes can be direct, indirect, indeterminate, multiple and unanticipated (Fountain 2001a: 92). Even though the Fountain (2001a) framework has been criticized for a lack of originality (Norris 2003; Grafton 2003) and a lack of case study evidence to support its universal applicability (Dawes 2002a; Norris 2003), it is a useful tool to use when attempting to understand and guide the discussion of aspects of ICT within CiRM.

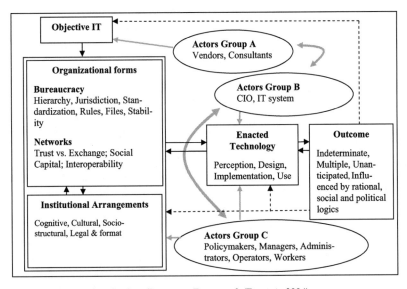

Figure 2-9: Revised Technology Enactment Framework (Fountain 2004)

2.2.4.3 Citizen-orientation and eGovernment

Concepts and discussions of eGovernment have paid particular attention to notions of citizen choice, satisfaction, orientation and building a new relationship with the citizenry (Detlor/Finn 2002). Governments design websites according to the kind of customers (Mosse/Whitley 2007) and their situation in life (Wimmer/Krenner 2001), and they offer information and services jointly on a portal (Kontzer/Chabrow 2002; Reinermann/von Lucke 2002). Citizens are supposed to go online instead of standing in line (Al-Kibsi et al. 2001).

Governments around the globe tend to stress and communicate the citizen-oriented character of their eGovernment initiatives (Cabinet Office 1999; Cabinet Office 2000; National Office for the Information Economy 2000; Northern Ireland eGovernment Unit 2000; Bundesministerium des Innern 2001; United Nations 2001; Schedler/Summermatter 2002; Ministro per L'innovazione e le Tecnologie 2002; OECD 2003; Ministerio de Administraciones Publicas 2003; OECD 2005; Bundeskanzleramt Österreich 2005). For example, Singapore, according to West (2004; 2005b), a leader in online service provision (www.ecitizen.gov.sg/ my.ecitizen.gov.sg), includes delivering integrated electronic services or being proactive and responsive by anticipating citizens' needs as two of its eGovernment programmes' five strategic goals (Siew Siew/Leng 2003). Canada also stated:

> By the year 2004, our goal is to be known around the world as the government most connected to its citizens, with Canadians able to access all Government information and services online at the time and place of their choosing. (Atlantic Canada Opportunities Agency 2004)

Furthermore, Stoltzfus (2005) noted that eGovernment plays a legitimizing role as a symbolic act towards citizens and in the international system. Therefore, states or political leadership communicate their acceptance of the effects of the ICT. Yet eGovernment supports dominant social values (Fountain 2001a). In some countries, it may be used to strengthen competitiveness and democratic values of equality and liberty, while in authoritarian states, technology can be an instrument of control and surveillance. Zhou (2004) described China's twofold strategy of digitizing all levels of the state in order to both strengthen Beijing's power in controlling its 31 administrative districts, 22 provinces and 5 autonomous territories and to improve its image in the world with regard to freedom of speech. In Switzerland, the language of citizen-orientation differs significantly in French- and Italian-speaking municipalities with an traditionally étatist culture compared to the German-speaking ones that have a more pragmatic culture (Schedler/Summermatter 2006).

Recent studies on electronic public services draw a different picture than that communicated by many governments. In the European Union, more G2B (77%) than G2C (57%) services are online, and the evolution of fully available citizen services is slowing down (Cap Gemini 2005). Similar findings are presented by the United Nations. In 2005, out of the United Nation's 191 member states, 179 were online. However, the study concludes that "[N]ot many countries utilize the full potential of eGovernment to provide information and services to their citizens" (United Nations 2004) and that "electronic systems have been large electronic reproductions of existing institutional patterns and relations" (United Nations 2003), which is still an issue. Notwithstanding the overall progress, a quarter of all countries offer transactional services, and less than 10% realized applications for online consultation. Accordingly:

> *[M]ost countries are still behind their potential in the provision of avenues for feedback and participation to the citizen even among the more mature e-ready countries. For example, whereas the United States, United Kingdom, and the Republic of Korea follow Singapore closely and are almost at full potential as measured by this survey, Australia provides 61%, New Zealand 56% and Germany 41% of stage V services (United Nations 2005).*

Therefore, eDemocracy remains a rhetorical promise (Mahrer/Krimmer 2005). American public managers (84%) were also convinced that the Internet improved addressing citizens, but only 29% of citizens shared that opinion (Lance 2002: 9). On the other hand, Bimber (1998) noted that in the historical aggregate, increases in access to information about politics have not been connected with an increased citizen engagement. Drawing on a sample of articles in key journals between 1987 and 2000 in political science and public administration, Danziger and Andersen (2002) reported that among the findings that focused on ICT in the area of "interaction between citizens and the public administration, only half conclude that there have been positive impacts, while about one-third identify negative impacts". Even though these findings are noteworthy, the analysis does not cover major eGovernment efforts and research which started in 2000 and 2001. In addition, online information provision now realized by all countries active in eGovernment has come under increased scrutiny due to censorship, costs (Eschenfelder 2004) and design.

While supplying online services and information is one aspect, demand is another. In their review of eGovernment and citizen-orientation, Schedler and Summermatter (2006) pointed out that citizen needs are higher in those public service areas which are rather complex and currently not available online. That might be a reason why the usage of many government websites has been disappointing (Dunleavy et al. 2006). Further known issues are the digital divide (OECD 2001; Kubicek 2001; Van Dijk/Hacker 2003) and lack of effective communication towards citizens. For instance, with the exception of a few highly popular services, most of Hong Kong's eGovernment services had low usage rates. Betty Fung, Deputy CIO at the Office of Hong Kong's Government Chief Information Officer, said, "The e-channel just became an additional service option, in parallel to our conventional channels, thereby increasing operating costs and reducing tangible benefits [...]; this was clearly unsustainable" (Smith 2005). Hong Kong is now trying to lead citizens and business to use lower-cost channels through various measures (e.g. changing office hours or closing down contact points). Mrs. Fung elaborated that government departments previously viewed ICT as a means of reducing costs—but not as a means to transforming their processes and reform inter-agency issues.

Similarly, Snellen (1994) found that ICT improved operations but did not affect citizen–public administration interactions. Moreover, sometimes ICT may reinforce dominant citizen administration relationships (Ingelstam/Palmlund 1991) and power structures. Nevertheless, the value of personal information could create a different kind of relationship analogous to the citizen as taxpayers (Brown 2005). Citizen information leads to a reciprocal set of obligations by the state in terms of accountability and actions. That is, the state has the obligation to protect the privacy of the citizen as well as to take action on the information provided by the citizen.

As noted earlier, there is an assumption about an underlying relationship between ranking high in eGovernment assessments, increased citizen-orientation and reputation within the international system. Rankings are based on different methods and data sets, producing diverse results. The studies analyse front-end online content, online service levels and some basic indicators related to the information society or governments' ICT budgets. However, these rankings have difficulty in capturing transformational aspects (e.g. process re-engineering, organisational changes), citizens' perceptions or participatory impacts of eGovernment efforts. In addition, studies avoid gathering information on the total number of public services and information resources for each jurisdiction within a country by creating lists of common services. But without this information, a true understanding of eGovernment progress, its transformational role and a new citizen–government relationship remains elusive.

2.3 The Citizen Public Administration Relationship

This Section reviews the theoretical discourse and empirical findings on the citizen-government relationship.

Political philosophy has long used theories of social contracts to explain the binding relationship between citizens and government (Rawls 1971; Riley 1973; Locke 1988; Rousseau 1999; Hobbes 2004). Central to the concept of the social contract is the existence of an agreement that establishes authority and obligations. Therefore, individuals accept certain obligations and limitations of their freedom in exchange for provision of certain tangible and intangible goods that would be difficult to obtain on the individual level. Public administration is often overlooked in classical references to the citizen–government relationship (Waldo 1984; Rohr 1986; Blanchard/Hinnant/Wong 1998: 488). There are also no generally agreed-upon theories of the public in public administration (Frederickson 1991). Indeed, Campbell (2005) and McSwite (2005) even claimed that the task of theorizing civic engagement and its role in public administration in a fundamentally new way is probably the most important task the field faces. This lack of theory is interesting, because public administration always played a central role in how government exerts power and citizens experience it.

The citizen–administration relationship depicts a reciprocal relation (Vigoda 2002b). An analysis of the reciprocal factors and the respective conditions allows for a deeper understanding of that relationship, which is constantly changing (Grunow 1988). Grunow (1988) thought that the concept of citizen closeness and responsiveness (e.g. the level of attention administration pays to citizen needs or participatory elements) could be applied to describe that relationship. This is considerably different from Bogumil's (1997b: 12-26) macro approach of applying common perspectives from political science, administrative science and economics/management, that is, the customer in economics/management, the participatory citizen in political science and the client in administrative science. The relationship is mostly described by the role of the citizen in the discourse on citizenship (Velditz/Dyer/Durand 1980; Flathman 1981; Thomas 1982; Levine/Fisher 1984; Marshall 1990; Stivers 1990; Cohen/Vigoda 2000; Perry/Katula 2001; Vigoda/Golembiewski 2001; Marguand/Altena 2004; Cooper 2006). The following is a very broad definition of citizenship and the citizen which underlies the discussion of the citizen administration relationship:

> *Citizenship is the status and role which defines the authority and obligations of individual members of a community. This status and role may be formally codified in terms of qualifications, rights and obligations by constitutions, charters and laws or informally determined by values, traditions and consensus. A citizen is one who qualifies for the status of citizenship formally or informally, by a particular community and is encumbered with the obligations assigned to this role by that community. (Cooper/Gulick 1984)*

Blanchard, Hinnant and Wong (1998) reviewed the evolution of the citizen–government relationship over the last 100 years. To illustrate this evolution, they developed a baseline model with four spheres: citizens, government, administration and the market (Figure 2-10). Government and citizens are connected through accountability and service linkages which make up the social contract. Citizens have further obligations through transactions with market actors. Blanchard, Hinnant and Wong (1998) identified four distinct periods: the orthodox era, the self-examination era, the diversity and implementation era, and the market-based era. The latter is marked through the dotted line in Figure 2-10.

The "orthodox era" started in the early 19th century and lasted until the early 20th century. Government and administration had a limited scope and only minor interaction with the market compared to later periods. The citizen administration relationship was mechanical and without much participation or active oversight, though there was a trend towards citizens expecting government to protect them from negative market forces (e.g. monopolies) through regulatory agencies.

In the "self-examination era" from the early 20th century to the early 1960s, the administrative state played a significant role in society. The number, size and the rate of increase of government institutions reached new levels. Between 1932 and 1939, the number of people employed in U.S. federal bureaucracy rose by 20%, from 572,000 to 920,000. Ten years later there were already 2.5 million public servants. This was influenced by factors such as economic (e.g. Great Depression (Kindleberger 1986)), political (World Wars), social and technological developments. Criticism grew as more obligations from the citizens were transferred to government and public administration in order to provide a public safety net and many other services. According to the critics, the neutrality of public administration is bound by the limited rationality of human beings, so the means of administrative procedures and formal political oversight might not prevent the potential abuse of power (Herring 1936; Simon 1947 in: Blanchard/Hinnant/Wong 1998: 495;Weber 1922).

The "implementation era" reforms changed the role of the citizen from "beneficiary" of the administrative relationship to "participant" in public administration. This era began in the early 1960s and ended in the early 1980s. The administrative apparatus and its market interactions kept on growing in size and power until the 1970s, which eventually led to a legitimacy crisis and policy implementation difficulties. The social struggles over economic and legal inequity resulted in participatory "counter measures" to bring citizens back in.

Since the early 1990s, the citizen–public administration relationship is in the "market-based reform era". Public–private and nongovernmental arrangements characterize the administrative apparatus so that the boundaries between government, administration and the market become blurred. There is also a movement to operate public administration using business methods (e.g. TQM) and creating a "customer-driven" government (Osborne/Gaebler 1992). While this movement aims to reduce the size and scope of government, it actually increases the scope of government itself. Blanchard, Hinnant and Wong (1998) argued that the market-based era has the biggest influence on the citizen–government relationship because of a shift from the traditional social contract to a social subcontract. The "social subcontract" describes a relationship condition where many administrative and government obligations are met through the market, while citizen accountability is reached through market transactions. This constellation reduces the citizen's ability (as customer) to identify and obtain political accountability and control over the (informal) administrative apparatus. One might ask what would be the next evolutionary step.

Based on some scholars' visions (Fox/Miller 1995; Smith/Huntsman 1997; Vigoda 2002b), the next period could be called the "collaborative mutual value era". According to Vigoda (2002b: 538), the citizen–government/public administration relationship "must rely on the conception of collaboration and partnership, if not citizenry ownership and control". Or, as Fox and Miller (1992: 128) put it, "[G]overnment will continue to govern [...] but the more authentic the encounters with citizens will be, the less will government be 'they' and the more it will be 'we'." This vision shares similarities with Dewey's (Dewey 1927) "colearner" or Smith's and Huntsman's (1997: 317) framing that "[P]ublic servants and citizens may be beginning to view the citi-

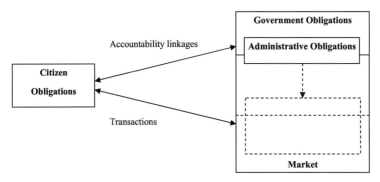

Figure 2-10: The social contract - from the orthodox era to the market-based reform era

zen–government relationship differently, not as one party overseeing the other or as one party working to satisfy the self-interested needs of the other, but as stakeholders who have common interests in increasing the worth of the community". In the new era, "the public agency setting becomes a polis, a true public space" (Stivers 1990). The visions are not new, however; they overlap with a state Aristotle (1981) called "active citizenship". The active citizen is one who, exercising practical wisdom in the public interest, joins in rendering decisive judgment about some aspect of governance. The active citizen rules and is ruled.

2.3.1 Citizen as customer/consumer

There are almost as many definitions of citizens as clients, consumers, customers or buyers as there are writers about them, with each term being applied to particular phenomena in a variety of ways (Alford 2002a). Customer and citizen-orientation are many times used in the same context in administrative reforms (Schröter/Wollmann 1998: 145). However, both terms imply a different understanding of the citizen–administration relationship and the role of each actor. Citizen and administrator roles are "intimately intertwined in advanced post-industrialist societies" (Box 1998) and "may change consecutively" (Herbert 1972). Some authors prefer to approach the discussion based on a more detailed account of the activities and social background of the citizen.

The citizen can be petitioner, complainer, performance supervisor or recipient of a document or service (Grunow 1988; Hirschmann 1999: 99). The citizen can also be politically powerful with a strong economic status or belong to the lower socio-economic spectrum, such as the homeless, without any capabilities (Daum 2002: 29). Etzinoi (1958: 252) differentiated citizens by the consumption and control function. Gilbert, Nicholls and Roslow (1998) classified public consumers into three distinct groups: first, direct buyers who are the equivalent of customers operating in an open market for a government service; second, clients who operate in a limited market with few sources for public service; and third, captives who operate in a monopoly with only one source from which to receive public service. Roberts (2004) proposed seven core roles based on competing theories (Table 2-9), which are outlined in the following paragraphs.

The citizen as subject in an authority system is the traditional point of view (Hobbes 1998; Hobbes 2004). Administrators are the link between the ruler and the ruled. Administrators are the only suitable judges of each other's performance and technical competence (Friedrich [1941] 1972). Citizens have to follow laws, regulations and decisions.

On the other hand, the citizen's role as a voter in the representative system is centered on the electoral process to vote for candidates as agents in the legislature (Riker 1982). Administrators are accountable to the elected representatives (Finer [1941] 1972). They follow laws and mandates set by legislation.

In the administrative state (Waldo 1984), decisions of public servants are rational and value-free, oriented towards generating efficient outcomes in the public interest. Politics, the public and administration are separated. Accountability to politicians is guaranteed through hierarchical structures, standardization or functional differentiation similar to Weber's (1922) description of ideal-type bureaucracy. Citizens are more of an input variable once a policy decision has been made by administrators who are in the best position to make decisions based on their neutrality and expertise. Some also refer to this limited role as the low view of citizenship (Downs 1957; Flathman 1981). The limited capacity of the citizen to make the right decision has various sources. Sometimes it's due to his relative ignorance, as in the case of patient and physician; in other instances it is a question of the need for institutionalized means of enforcing social norms, as in the case of a university or the ministry of education which determines the standards for a qualifying examination. In still other cases it is a question of long-run versus short-run interests of the citizen (Etzioni 1958); the consumer is often dominated by short-run interests, while those in control of production are often aware

System	Citizen Role	Administrator Role
Authority	Subject	Surrogate for ruler authority
Representative	Voter	Implementer of legislation
Administrative	Client	Expert, professional
Pluralist	Interest group advocate	Referee, adjudicator
Political/ market economy	Consumer, customer	Broker, contract monitor
Civil society	Volunteer, coproducer	Liaison, coproducer
Social learning	Colearner	Colearner, trustee, steward, facilitator

Table 2-9: Citizen and administrator roles in public administration models (Roberts 2004: 328)

of the necessity not to subordinate all the available resources to higher dividends or better and cheaper products but to allocate a certain proportion to reinvestment and innovation (Schumpeter 1942; Blau/Scott 2004).

In a pluralist system, democracy is best achieved through collective action. This deliberative view, supported by various researchers (Habermas 1992; Fishkin 1995a; Habermas 1996; Cohen 1996), is contrary to the former representative role. Informed citizens form groups that represent specific issues and positions. Multiple points of access and means allow these groups to participate in the political process. In this system of adversarial democracy, ambition counteracts ambition and absolute power is checked (Roberts 2004). Administrators ensure equal treatment and access, acting as brokers or referees.

In the political/market economy, the model of the citizen as consumer/customer is based on the "homo oeconomicus" (Simon 1955; Coase 1976), who aims at maximizing the individual utility as modelled in rational choice theory (Simon 1955; Downs 1957; Miller 1992). The underlying theory is primarily variations of new institutional economic theory (Aberbach/Christensen 2003). From an economist's perspective, the customer has a sovereign market position. The customer has the freedom to choose between products and services. The customer can influence content, quality and price of offerings, and producers are in competition for the customers' attention. Hirschmann (1970) explained that when consumers are dissatisfied with quality they can either choose not to purchase a good (exit) or choose to voice their dissatisfaction, depending on the degree of loyalty that they have for the brand or product. The situation is, of course, more complex than this, because the willingness to exit depends on the existence of a viable alternative (Dibben 2006). Therefore, the need for customer orientation only exists in market competition because the interests of producers are disciplined and directed by the power of consumers (voice, exit, loyalty). In public services, producer interests can range unchecked, because consumers are locked into monopoly provision and unable to exercise choice or control (Etzioni 1958; Niskanen 1968; Lake/Baum 2001; Finlayson 2003). Recipients usually have limited or no options. Government services or goods are often monopolistic because of a lack of demand for services, their meritoric character, legal barriers to entry of competitors or critical shortages in resources for the required production or provision (Lowery 1998). In the market economy model, however, agencies are in competition and stand to lose their public service provision to other arrangements, depending on the citizens' signalling. Services are provided through public, public–private or completely private constructs forming complex networks. To enable these arrangements, steering and production functions of government are separated (Roberts 2004). Administrators act as liaisons, brokers among service vendors and contract monitors. Management techniques such as TQM or MBO are assumed to be universally applicable and supportive to the administrator's multiple roles. Overall, government is deregulated and networked (Goldsmith/Eggers 2004), forming a set of small, decentralized and flexible units.

From the civil society perspective, the citizen ideal is closer to "high citizenship" (Flathman 1981; Kalu 2003b) or the "homo politicus" as an active participant in the policy-making process who may act altruistically for the common welfare (Schröter/Wollmann 1998: 146). Civic engagement includes volunteer activities for the community as well as the citizen's role as a coproducer. The latter are typically agency collaborations with neighbourhood associations or client groups to redesign or deliver public services mostly at the local level. A central aspect of this type of arrangement is that it supports building social capital (Coleman 1988) and maintaining a deliberative democratic system (Putnam 1993).

The citizen as colearner in a social learning process rests on Dewey's (1927) ideal form of governance in which democratic institutions and cultural habits of thought enable citizens and experts to act publicly to solve their collective problems and to recognize and comprehend the surprising consequences of their actions. Social learning occurs through collaborations among citizens, administrators and elected officials who are required to make value judgements on the trade-offs of competing problem definitions. As such, there are similarities to the pluralist system perspective. For instance, the Learning and Design Forum (Kathi/Cooper 2005) instituted in the City of Los Angeles sought to build trust and a shared understanding of common social concerns between city agencies and city neighborhood councils (Byrer 2006). In the social learning model, administrators serve as facilitators of the joint deliberative learning process. Government structure is less hierarchical and less complex, and supports local autonomy through a decentralized structure. Roberts (2004) concluded that only the social learning perspective is able to produce a state where citizen and administrator are equal partners. Yet the problem of "how to reconnect the broken reciprocal linkages between the spheres of society and state remains largely unanswered" (Evans 2000).

There are some other aspects to the customer role in the public sphere. There is usually a linear relationship between producer and customer in a market relationship. A customer can be a single entity such as a person or can consist of multiple entities such as subunits within one organisation. Customer producer linearity in the public sphere is somewhat blurred. While there is a relationship between the welfare recipient and an agency, there is an intangible aspect of doing a service for the whole citizenry by keeping the social system stable. Furthermore, many public transfers are one-sided, without any direct return to the agency. In fact, consumption is separated from direct financing, which is common to most public services. Administrative fees charged are only a small proportion of the actual costs of a service. Although there is considerable variation, in general, participation in consumption of public services by a given segment of the public is inversely related to its participation in financing (Etzioni 1958). Additionally, a rise in demand may not necessarily be related to an increase in customer satisfaction but rather a sign of quasi-market failures (Lowery 1998), such as free riding due to the non-excludability of the public good (Conybeare 1984). Finally, while the homo oeconomicus underlying the role of the citizen in the administrative and market economy models received wide criticism (Green/Shapiro 1994), Nyborg's (2000) attempts to include both views could overcome some of it. According to her model, every individual has two different preference orderings and utility functions: the "personal well-being function" of the individual and the "subjective social welfare function" of social state (Nyborg 2000: 305).

In conclusion, we have to differentiate between the general differences of the citizen in the public as well as the customer in the market and the more philosophical/theoretical accounts on the roles of the citizen. In practice, administrators may refer to citizens as their clients or customers while at the same time accepting or facilitating their more participatory roles. But the consumerist notion of deconstructing the citizen as customer raises concerns among researchers (Barnes/Prior 1995; Hood 1995) which are usually mixed with criticism of market-driven reforms and a certain understanding of governance.

2.3.2 Critical remarks on the citizen as customer/consumer

Criticism of the concept of the "citizen as customer/consumer" and a customer-oriented government is numerous, trenchant and sometimes aggressively phrased (Hirschmann 1999). The criticism is either arguing that the idea undermines democratic roles of the citizen or that the customer concept is not able to capture the complex relationship of citizen and government.

Haque's (1999) based his critique on the considerable transformation of the citizen–administration relationship characterized by the dominance of market ideology, demonization of the welfare state, emergence of neoliberal regimes, proliferation of promarket policies and the erosion of public service in terms of its scope, role, capacity and commitment. Osborne and Gaebler (1992) were the first to introduce the term "customer-driven" administration. They argued:

> *Today's environment demands institutions that are responsive to their customers, offering choices of non-standardized services; that lead by persuasion and incentives rather than commands; that give their employees a sense of meaning and control, even ownership. It demands institutions that empower citizens rather than simply serving them (Osborne/Gaebler 1992: 15).*

This was quickly put on the political agenda by the Clinton-Gore Administration (Gore 1993) in form of the National Performance Review, which has changed the mission of the U.S. public bureaucracy, affected the nature and composition of its services to citizens and thus transformed its relationship with them.

The core problem of interpreting citizens as customers is that the term customer implies an exchange relationship involving a monetary transaction (Bogumil 1997b; Haque 1999). It is mostly favourable to the rich but quite adverse for the poor. For example, the introduction of fees for education and health services became less affordable to the poor in some African countries. Public–private partnerships are also supporting (corporate) elites and diminishing subsidized and non-yielding social services. Along these lines, Smith and Lipsky (1999: 118-119) were concerned that the citizen–government relationship becomes "eroded when private agencies produce public services". Furthermore, the extensive role of non-government third parties and complex networks of public service delivery and policy making (Marsh/Rhodes 1992) promote the "hollowing out" of the state (Milward/Provan/Else 1993; Holliday 2000; Milward/Provan 2000; Milward/Provan 2003), thus further undermining the state's and democracy's already diminishing legitimacy (Blanchard/Hinnant/Wong 1998). In addition, the more business-oriented principle of exchange may adversely affect the public service culture that is supposed to emphasize the provision of services to all deserving citizens, including those who do not have the financial capacity to pay for such services. The administrator is more concerned with efficiency, productivity, cost-effectiveness and competition than with established public service ethics (equality, objectivity, fairness and justice). Haque (1999) concluded that "customer-oriented reforms" actually lower the service level. The decline in capacity of public administration serving citizens' basic needs is caused by the trend towards a reduction in resources through divestment and downsizing.

Bogumil (1997b) and Pegnato (1997) pointed out that the term customer is not suitable in areas where government sovereignty has to limit citizens' individual preferences and behaviour (e.g. public safety standards for food, emission regulations, prisoners). The reverse would limit government's capacity to act in the public interest as well as political accountability (Swiss 1992; Wilson/Durant 1993; Behn 1995; Carroll 1995; Frederickson 1996; Kettl 1998; Terry 1998; Hirschmann 1999; Ryan 2001). A democratic polity needs preferences that do not focus predominantly on improving the efficiency of administrative processes, because such improvements can be very harmful to the very polity that governments are supposed to help (Waldo 1984; Kirlin 1996; Kelly 1998; Kalu 2003a). Moe and Gilmour (1995) added concerns centered around constitutional issues.

Pollit (1993) as well as Barnes and Prior (1995: 58) noted that the generic model of the consumer in the private sector and the public sector misses the relationship that can develop during transactions. Pollit (1993) called it a people-developing relationship in contrast to a people-processing interaction (Thompson 1976) that occurs over the counter between producer and consumer. In fact, citizens' individual and social preferences are shaped in part by their relationship with public administration, which has the obligation to shape the relationship without guardianship (manipulation) but rather a form of trusteeship (Vigoda 2000: 173; Fountain 2001b).

Ryan (2001) identified two additional issues associated with constructing citizens as consumers (Barzelay 1992; Gore 1993; Vardon 2000). First, limiting the role of the citizen to that of a consumer would neglect the citizen's role in governance and policy generation. Second, the simplistic approach taken to the relationship between citizen and government would redefine it as a passive commercial transaction, rather than an interactive political engagement. Constructing the citizen–government relationship as one of supplier and consumer contributes to the notions of elitist government, because citizens would be withdrawn from engaging in policy implementation in favour of a being a passive consumer of public commodities existence (Schachter 1997; Smith/Huntsman 1997; Peters/Pierre 1998; Patterson 1998; Box 1999). However, Ryan (2001) thought that features (e.g. surveys, focus groups, service councils) with a customer orientation to service delivery provide new forms of participation, though the participation may only be symbolic:

> *It seems that co-optation is more often applied in communications from those in control to the clients than the other way around. Co-optation is often used in order to create a semblance of communication [...] without effective communication really existing. [...]When co-optation is manipulated or fictitious, not only does it not fulfil the function of co-opting the consumer, but it blocks the expression of his needs. Simulated co-optation [...] only conceals the need for real communication and influence. [...] The problem of the gap in communication between the consumer and those who control his consumption is sometimes partially solved by molding consumer's desires. While basic needs are difficult to mold, the manner in which they are satisfied seems to be quite open to manipulation. Furthermore, additional needs can be created simultaneously with the means of satisfying them. Thus, to the extent that the supplier of goods and services is able to create satisfaction, there is little need for communication from consumer to controller. (Etzioni 1958: 261)*

Barnes and Prior (1995) took a critical look at the aspect of consumer choice. Like "community" or "democracy", "choice" has become a term which carries moral authority, making it difficult to question whether, in fact, choosing which service to use is necessarily a high priority for citizens and is automatically a benefit to them. The introduction of markets in public services can limit the information available to the public, because that information can be regarded as a threat to organisations. For instance, the NHS Trust has been reluctant to provide public information about the percentage of their budget spent on management compared to direct patient care. Choice is frequently invoked as a tool to replace analysis of (1) the circumstances, (2) the ways in which people use services, and (3) whether choosing has any real meaning in particular circumstances (Barnes/Prior 1995: 53-54). They suggest analysing public services along five dimensions in order to identify whether prioritizing choice should be a goal of public policy:

1. **Coercion:** Is the decision to use a service made freely by the user, or is the decision one that is compelled by circumstances?

2. **Predictability:** Can the user find out about the likely effects of the service in advance of the decision to use it, or can the effects only be discovered in the process of use?

3. **Frequency:** Will use of a particular service be a frequent activity, thus enabling the user to develop expertise and experience in the outcomes the service can deliver?

4. **Significance:** Is usage of the service likely to be of considerable importance either in meeting certain of the user's major needs or in substantially affecting the user's life chances?

5. **Participation:** Do successful outcomes depend on the active involvement of the user as a coproducer of the service, or is the user's role merely that of a passive recipient of the service?

Based on these dimensions, it is possible to construct cases where choice is unlikely to be empowering. Examples of this are when there is not enough information (e.g. available options, differences, effects) available on which to base decisions, when people have no influence on the available options or they do not have the appropriate knowledge. Citizens sometimes describe their experience to find out about and gain access to public services as an "uphill struggle" or "fight" (Barnes/Wistow 1992). Even if citizens are well informed, they will probably only be able to influence the production side of public services (e.g. access channels, opening hours, form design) but not that of strategic allocation. Barnes and Prior (1995) concluded that choice may be of value in some circumstances but true user empowerment, as embodied in the notion of consumers and choice, should rather be achieved through improving mechanisms of participation in policy making, resource allocation, planning, organisation and management, as well as consumption.

Fountain (2001b: 59) noted that customer orientation is not always successful in the private sector. Products are of low quality or in a non-market–ready condition, work is being transferred back to the customer (self-service) or those serving customers are not trained well. Many times services are kept at a level that is just preventing consumers from using their voice option. The citizen as customer is significantly different from consumers in the private sector. "Consumers have no obligation, be it moral or legal, to understand, support or engage closely with their transaction partners" (Fountain

2001b). They are not loyal in any socially meaningful sense of that term. Consumers do not care much about the future of their product or service supplier and fellow clients "except to the extent that continuity and stability is concerned" (Fountain 2001b: 69). However, for the citizen, all that is the case (Stewart/Ranson 1988; Alford 2002a).

A macro perspective reveals further deficits of the term customer in government (Fountain 2001b: 62-62). Various institutions serve the customer in different or even contradictory ways (Halachmie 1995), especially in the executive and legislative branch. Besides, fragmentation and jurisdictional boundaries of public institutions make a unified service approach almost impossible. Segmenting citizens or varying service levels are also not applicable, because citizens represent no homogenous set of expectations and need to be treated uniformly. Any segmentation that occurs in the service delivery process must be viewed as a political rather than a managerial decision. While identification of preferences is already difficult, individual preferences must be aggregated in ways that support public service design and operation, sustain political legitimacy and minimize inequality. Citizens who can argue their case more effectively and have a better understanding of the complex environment and government processes are much more likely to take advantage of their voice option (Cox 1973; Fountain 2001b). Public servants are also not motivated by customer retention strategies. Moreover, customer service requires quality and performance management. But it is difficult to find appropriate measures for government program goals that are "ambiguous, vague or conflicting" for political reasons (Fountain 2001b: 63).

Even if an agency aims to serve their "customers" well, this strategy may quickly be demystified by the overwhelming demand of clients, inadequate resources or Lipsky's (1980) street-level bureaucracy mechanisms (favoritism, stereotyping, discretion). Customer service ideas "oversimplify the task environment of public servants and the role of culture in institutional behaviour" (Giddens 1984; March/Olsen 1989; DiIulio 1994 in Fountain 2001b: 66). The "customer service mantra also ignores the time dimension of preferences"—that is, short-term–oriented preferences prevail over achieving long-term–oriented collective goals (Vigoda 2000; Blanchard/Hinnant/Wong 1998). Furthermore, if politicians understand the value of customer-oriented practices in public administration and exploit citizen insights, a better understanding of preferences might improve the probability of getting re-elected. The political sphere casts doubt on the customer and market-oriented government model.

2.3.3 Citizens' preferences and expectations of public services and administration

Preference is a concept used in the social sciences, particularly economics. It assumes a real or imagined "choice" between alternatives and the possibility of a rank ordering of these alternatives, based on satisfaction, gratification, utility and so on. Decisions follow preferences but are now understood to be a highly contingent form of information processing, sensitive to task complexity, time pressure, response mode, framing, reference points and other contextual factors (Lichtenstein/Slovic 2006). The analysis of citizens' preferences can be directed at product, process or outcome level.

In general, administrative science lacks a well-grounded analysis of citizens' preferences and expectations of public services, which is also true for consumer research in the private sector (Keeton 1982; Pippke 1990; Hohn 1997: 161;Vigoda 2000: 169; Abramson/Means 2001: 6;Daum 2002: 31; Pino 2002; Reddick 2005). In fact, there is also a need for understanding and application of the public's (as opposed to institutions', authorities' and agencies') criteria of effective public participation, including their preferred methods. Testing consumer research concepts in public administration, therefore, remains a field to be explored by researchers.

Research on interactions between the citizen and the administrator (Finer 1931; Janowitz/Delany 1957; Lipsky 1980; Goodsell 1981; Hart 1984; Lewis 1990; Berman 1997; Melkers/Thomas 1998; Petts/Leach 2000; Roberts 2002; van Sylke/Roch 2004; Yang 2005) are of value, as are insights from the urban policy literature on citizen satisfaction (e.g. socio-economic and demographic factors are important), but the latter are dated (Kelly 2005). Individual satisfaction with bureaucratic encounters has also been researched at the federal level (Serra 1995), across jurisdictions (Swindell/Kelly 2002) or in the area of egovernment (Sharpe 2000; Burke 2002; Thomas/Streib 2003; Schellong/Mans 2004). However, survey-based satisfaction research in practice tends to focus on existing service rather than the complexity of customers' (future) needs (Skelcher 1992; Wisniewski 2001). Greenberg and Drew (1980) also concluded that the primary method of considering public service demand and citizen satisfaction is reacting to voluntary complaints, compliments and other informal contacts. Thus, the impact of citizen surveys depends on the extent to which administrators believe that results are valuable information. In fact, Poister and Thomas (2007) pointed out that a stream of research over the past 25 years "has shown only weak or inconsistent correlations between citizens' ratings of or satisfaction with services, on one hand, and more "objective" indicators of program performance used by agencies on the other hand. There is also no organised diffusion of respective studies initiated by public administration to other administrations or into academic research and discourse, except if they were conducted by consultants. But most of them do not present the methodology in detail. Indeed, Stipak (1979; 1980) warns that the use of a subjective measure (e.g. expressed satisfaction) to evaluate an objective measure (e.g. services delivered) without incorporating particular statistical techniques and manipulations (e.g. multivariate methods) to reduce problems of confounding variables and spurious relationships can cause overall shortcomings. Such problems had already been noted in the 1950s:

> *In each of the three agencies studied the administrators' desire to have the type of data we were collecting for clients' perspectives toward agencies with mass clienteles is indispensable. Until public agencies are able to develop support for such research, university-based work will have to be a temporary stopgap. (Janowitz/Delany 1957: 162)*

This claim is further stressed by Callahan and Gilbert, who identified three research gaps:

> *[There] is a need for empirical research with market-like surveys from outside the public agency to gain insight about public agency effectiveness - there is need for surveys that move away from perceptual measures of employees in the workplace (e.g. Brewer/Selden 2000: 696)*

away from perceptual measures of employees in the workplace (e.g. Brewer/Selden 2000: 696) or of administrators assessing their agencies' progress in meeting goals (Burke/Wright 2002: 10-11). A need for empirical research that links public satisfaction explicitly with specific design features that cut across varied levels of public agencies, moving beyond a focus at one level of government [...];[...] that examines the relationship between end-user discretion in choosing public services or products available to them, design features of public agencies, and end-user satisfaction (Thomas/Melkers 1999; Kelly/Swindell 2003). (2005: 59-60)

The following paragraphs briefly summarise citizens' preferences that are of interest for further discussion in this study. One of the major reasons for citizens' dissatisfaction is their limited knowledge of agencies, processes and programs (Lenk 1990). Their lack of knowledge does not allow them to make informed decisions about the quality of public services, so they choose other factors, such as a timely return call by a public servant, to assess the relationship (Whitley 1991: 163; Berman 1997). Interestingly, Poister and Gary (1994) even reported that there is no discernible difference between public and private services in the minds of recent users. These circumstances might have been the reason public-sector managers retained a high level of confidence in their internal performance measures and didn't change anything at all in the way they operated, despite recent initiatives to change their procedures (Levine/Fisher 1984; Watson/Juster/Johnson 1991; Kearney/Feldman/Scavo 2000; Behn 2002; Heikkila/Isett 2007).

Many citizens only have a few (every 3–5 years) interactions with public administration and perceive these interactions as a waste of time, causing them unnecessary monetary expense and sometimes even anxiety (Pippke 1990; Daum 2002: 30). The quality of consultation, in particular, is a determining factor in the citizen administration relationship (Klages 1982: 24 et seqq.; Grunow 1988: 33) because interpersonal contact appears to be an important element in service satisfaction (Hero/Durand 1985; Bogumil 1997b: 55). Creating a citizen-oriented consultation experience depends on various factors (Pippke 1998). Public servants need to have a complete overview of the citizen's issue, ensure that the information provided is correct, use comprehensible language, act proactively even when the issue spans multiple boundaries and try to avoid standardized treatment. The latter means using a flexible interpretation of existing laws and regulations (Bogumil 1997b: 47). Of course, body language (Pippke 1998) and social intelligence (Albrecht 2006) are of equal importance. Accordingly, as argued in contemporary psychological theory, when a citizen is surrounded with an emphatic and supportive environment, levels of stress, strain and anxiety dramatically decrease (Vigoda 2000).

Using regression analyses of citizen satisfaction survey data in New York City, van Ryzin et al (2004) discovered that, for example, roads and schools have a particularly strong influence on overall perceptions of urban quality, and that high overall satisfaction strongly correlates with citizens' confidence in city government.

Research conducted by Hewson Group (2004) in the UK found that public service users are willing to accept a delay in getting a service request completed if, in return, the council could guarantee a definite date and time. In addition, over 95% of all incoming telephone calls to an agency concerning mortgage applications were simply ascertaining progress. Daum (2002: 72-87) also found that in phone interactions, resolving issues at first contact with an administrator is as important as the overall process duration. Similar trends are true for e-mail. Hewson Group (2004) claimed that 70% of incoming traffic to an agency can be eliminated. Both examples illustrate that citizens prefer to be continuously informed about their service status

Forms remain another essential part of the delivery of a wide range of government services. Filling in forms is one of the most frequent ways that citizens interact with agencies. If forms are well-designed and easy to handle, then errors will be fewer, leading not only to better access to services but also considerable efficiency gains. Hence, how forms are designed can have an important effect upon how people view the responsiveness and accessibility of government. The National Audit Office (2003) analysed six forms that are filled in by up to 45 million people in focus groups in the UK. Administrative processes behind these forms were also reviewed. Central government forms used by citizens on average require between 40 and 60 pieces of information. How much time and effort citizens are willing to devote to a form depends on what the form is for. They would also prefer a quick-start guide instead of lengthy explanations. Citizens worry about supplying too many personal details and dislike re-supplying information they have already given, whether on the form or at a later stage in the service process. The biggest problem for focus group respondents concerned complexities in the sequencing of questions. Agencies often prefer to have a single form suitable for multiple types of users, rather than several forms targeted at different groups. Nonetheless, some agencies seem to have serious gaps in their knowledge of their clients and their form preferences. In only one of the agencies was it easy to find information specifically relevant for forms.

2.3.4 Administrative contacting as public participation

Citizens initiate contacts with public administration to gather information, complain or request services. Coulter (1988: 1) viewed this as a "critically important mode of citizen participation in urban political systems" and a pure form of Hirschman's (1970) voice option. This perspective is of special interest to CiRM.

Compared to the dialogue with elected officials, all citizens are in contact with administrators throughout their lifetime. Indeed, as Alexander Hamilton noted three centuries ago, "[I]t is not necessarily true that [...] the confidence of the people will easily be gained by good administration. This is the touchstone" (Morone 1990). Citizens contacting administrators, in particular, takes place at the municipal level, which is closest to citizens (Milakovich 2003). Up to three-fifths of the U.S. population is believed to contact administrators in any given year on the local level; this a rate of participation that is unsurpassed by any other form of citizen participation (Sharp 1986).

Thomas (1982) distinguished between "discretionary" and "nondiscretionary contacts". Most citizen-initiated contacts are discretionary compared to those initiated by public administration. Citizen-initiated contacts "differ most clearly from other types of political participation by their roots in citizen needs for government services"

(Thomas/Melkers 1999). But citizen-initiated contacts (hereafter referred to as contacting) are as much of a linkage between political elites and the masses as is voting in elections (Velditz/Dyer/Durand 1980), because citizen-initiated contacts are supporting four democratic elements. These are participation, representation, responsiveness and distributional equity. Public servants are forced to deal with the outcomes of policies, administrative program designs and process while they work on and represent the issue of the citizen in an increasingly complex environment (Eisinger 1972). Administrators also need external support to maintain a favourable public image and to receive internal support and prestige (Terry 1995). Contacting makes the political system more responsive because it allows for automatic citizen feedback and control of government practices. Contacting is especially important in areas where citizens need to proactively seek to receive a service. Accordingly, distributional equity of a service can be seriously affected in such cases given the discretionary role of street-level bureaucrats (Coulter 1988: 3).

Models to explain contacting vary and are conflicting. The discourse has mostly focused on the factors inducing contacting, but not the consequences (Thomas/Melkers 1999). There is considerably less agreement on which of those factors are important, as well as on when and why they are important. Some researchers believed that contacting is related to the same factors that affect other forms of political participation, such as voting (Verba/Nie 1972; Leighley 1995). Therefore, contacting would be inversely related to socio-economic status (SES), civic orientations and skills. Others proposed the needs-awareness model (Jones et al. 1977), which says that some need and some awareness must be present for a citizen to initiate a contact. Need is mostly created through negative externalities produced by citizens' or government's actions. Awareness means that first, the citizen knows that government is legally responsible; second, the government entity will act upon contacting and third, the citizen has access to a channel of influence. Coulter's (1988) study of contacting behaviour of citizens in Birmingham, Alabama, did not conform to any of the SES studies. He found a curvilinear relationship between income and contacting, with little or no contacting behaviour in census tracts dominated by middle-income cohorts. The poorest and wealthiest areas have the highest degree of contacting—because the poor have to counter various social and environmental conditions, and the wealthy have an incentive to preserve and protect their social and economic situation. Coulter found the need model theoretically more appealing and thus concludes that:

> [C]ontacting is dominated by need for government services, motivated by specific dissonance with the political system's current level of performance, and represents the role of the citizen as consumer in a service polity. Contacting is consumer politics. (1988: 94)

In fact, many public programs cannot be effective, from the perspective of citizens and administrators, unless the two sides collaborate in producing the service (Thomas 1999). Mintrom (2003) added that collaboration promotes organisational innovation and allows leaders to make more informed decisions. On the other hand, participation offers citizens intrinsic rewards that result from the feeling of increased control, greater discretion, opportunities to make choices, sociality and the presence of expressive values (Lengnick-Hall 1996; Alford 2002b). Van Ryzin (2004) also showed that personal contact with local government is a determining factor in citizen satisfaction with urban services.

Citizens have demonstrated the capability of participating more fully in the political, technical and administrative decisions that affect them -when they have been given the chance (Roberts 2004). There are, of course, more institutionalized forms of public participation in a deliberative democracy than just electoral activities and contacting (Campbell/Marshall 2000). These can be grouped along three dimensions (Figure 2-11) - scope of participation (who participates), mode of communication and decision, and extent of authority (how far discussions affect policy and administrative actions). Common methods of participation are public hearings (de Leon 1992; Baker/Addams/Davis 2005), deliberative polls (Fishkin 1995b), negotiated rule making (Rowe/Frewer 2000), neigborhood councils (Kathi/Cooper 2005), advisory boards (Day 1997), citizens' panels (Lenaghan/Mitchell 1996), co-production (Levine/Fisher 1984), referenda (Zimmermann/Just 2000) and rather indirect forms such as surveys or focus groups (Naßmacher/Naßmacher 1998). Petts and Leach (2000) identified over 25 methods of information provision, consultation and participation, and reviewed their advantages and disadvantages. Levine and Fisher (1984) offered insights into overcoming the failures of participatory programs like community-based crime prevention groups.

However, there is some evidence that many of these forms are not effectively implemented (Mintrom 2003). King, Feltey and Susel (1998) found that although many administrators view close relationships with citizens as necessary and desirable, they do not seek the public's input proactively. Indeed, they believe that greater participation increases red tape, delays and inefficiency. This impression is supported by other researchers (Hart 1972; Cleveland 1975). Participation might also be misunderstood as

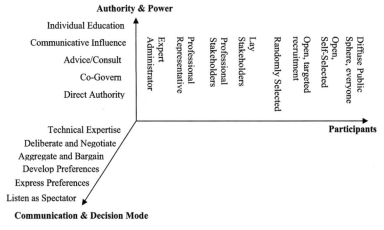

Figure 2-11: Dimensions of public participation in the democracy cube (Fung 2006: 71)

a form of co-production through citizen self-service by means of technology and automated processes (Kißler et al. 1997: 23). Moreover, Bogumil (1997b: 24-26) drew a pessimistic view of citizens' willingness to participate in activities after reviewing several studies. Even most optimistic scholars of participatory democracy estimate that the proportion of the "willing" is less than 10% of a population (Verba/Schloz-man/Brady 1995). Box (1998) calls these citizens "watchdogs". The willingness to participate depends on policy issues, expected consequences (Windhoff-Héretier 1983) and committing individual resources, and correlates negatively with the number of participants (Eisfeld 1973). Rosenbaum (1978) even thought that citizens were already too apathetic and uncommitted to participate, and Garthop and Waldo (1984) called for administrators to revitalize citizenship. However, low desire to participate depends on how a civic system for participation is set up and the ability of citizens to take advantage of it (Campbell 2005).

2.4 Summary

The first section of this chapter reviewed fundamental aspects of CRM. CRM builds on the idea that customer-centricity and relationship management allow an organization to gain advantages. CRM typically includes a variety of management practices and information technology. CRM is holistic, because it affects an organisation's vision, strategy, structure and operations. Customer interactions are managed over a variety of channels. Assessing customer needs and conducting internal process analysis are at the beginning of a CRM project. Customers are segmented and treated differently according to their segmentation. Information technology is supposed to facilitate customer analysis, building customer profiles, delivering customer service and internal knowledge sharing. These activities require or lead to organizational change, which is what presents the greatest obstacle in CRM projects. The high failure rates in CRM projects are the result of limiting CRM to its technological components and proceeding with a CRM implementation with a lack of adequate leadership. CRM has only recently gained attention as an important concept for government. Also referred to as CiRM, it is designed to allow management of the citizen–government relationship. CiRM initiatives usually start on the municipal level in contact centers.

The second section of this chapter summarised citizen-oriented reforms. In particular, NPM and eGovernment led to a paradigm shift in how public services and public participation can be organized and delivered. NPM challenged traditional public administration and aimed at introducing market-based mechanisms as well as private-sector management concepts. NPM weaknesses and critical remarks were also noted. One of NPM's management concepts of interest to this dissertation is TQM. The stream of research showed that TQM rests on a common set of assumptions and tools dealing with how to achieve quality of performance for products and services. TQM underlines the importance of customer focus and empowerment of employees, and highlights how empowerment contributes directly to customer satisfaction. Finally, a review of the literature on eGovernment revealed that ICT, especially the Internet, has the potential to improve customer service and citizen-orientation of government. However, as the reviewed cases and TEF showed, bureaucratic structure and the behaviour of key actors will determine technology enactment and outcomes.

Research on the citizen–government relationship was reviewed in the third section of this chapter. The conceptualization of citizen-orientation and citizen as customer in CRM, NPM and eGovernment have been put into perspective by a historical overview of the citizen–government relationship and the varying roles of the citizen. Scholars expected that the relationship will develop towards one of collaborative learning and production in the near future. The idea of citizen as consumer has been weakened substantially by the reviewed critique. On the citizen level, knowledge about behaviour and preferences remains fragmented due to a lack of research. Finally, a review of the literature on administrative contacting underlined its importance as an act of public participation.

The reviewed concepts have similarities. To summarise, they lack a commonly accepted definition, they are supposed to improve citizen-orientation and they stress the importance of an external customer perspective on government, its processes and services. In addition, technology is understood as an enabling factor, while success depends on leadership and communication.

3   Methodology and Data Analysis

This research used the case study method (Yin 2003). Social scientists have long used case study analysis as a method of examining public administration. The study aimed to gain deeper insights into the perception of CiRM and its implementation and impact. This chapter provides an overview of the research methodology (Section 3.1), including the three main steps taken in the study. The empirical procedure and data sources used for this study are reported in Section 3.2. Data analysis (Section 3.3) was primarily inductive, following a modified grounded theory approach (Strauss/Corbin 1998). Possible propositions from each case study were discerned, and a cross-case comparison was conducted. Special attention is given to the limitations of this research in Section 3.4. Figure 3-1 presents an overview of the research design. Further details are discussed in Chapter 0, which presents the qualitative results of the study.

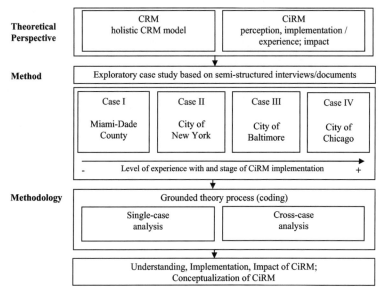

Figure 3-1: Research Design

3.1   Research method

Simon (1947) once said that "there can never be a science of public administration from the viewpoint of practice; it can only be studied scientifically through rigorous methods of social science" (Riccucci 2001). Studies of public administration as well as administrative sciences are generally criticized for their methodological deficits (Grunow 1987: 28-32). After reviewing journal articles published between 1940 and 1984, Stalling and Ferris (1988: 585) concluded that the field lacks an adequate strategy for building central research questions which are connected to appropriate methods. These deficits are a result of the large number of theoretical approaches, difficulties in methodology transfer, and the practical nature of public administration and its institutional parameters (complex and dynamic systems) (Perry/Kraemer 1986). Since individuals in public organisations directly react to "inappropriate" research strategies, which may result in a complete failure or restrictions to the research project, many dissertations and journal articles seem to skip making a thorough presentation and discussion of methods (Cleary 1992: 60). In general, qualitative methods like interviews and non-reactive methods (e.g. document analysis) are more commonly applied than quantitative methods (Perry/Kraemer 1986: 224). The case study method is thus dominant in research on public administration (Streib/Slotkin/Rivera 2001: 521).

The case study is more of a research strategy than a method (Goode/Hatt 1952; Stake 1994; Hartley 2004). As a part of this strategy, different methods like interviews, ethnography, document analysis or surveys can be applied. The broad range of data generated through a case study "allows one to gain a detailed understanding of a social organisation and its processes" (Punch 2000: 150). Variables can, therefore, "be studied in context without defining them up-front" (Neumann 1997). This is particularly helpful for generating frameworks or theories for emerging trends, processes and behaviours. CiRM is such an emerging concept in public administration. It has neither been applied widely in public administration, nor has it been studied in great detail by researchers. Accordingly, this study aims to answer questions like "how" or "why" CiRM is implemented, meeting Yin's (2003: 21-22) criteria to employ exploratory case studies for the purpose of theory construction.

A case study consists of one or more cases. A case can be an organisation, group, individual, nation, process, policy or event. Case studies can be of exploratory, explanatory or descriptive nature. According to Punch (2000: 152), case studies can be differentiated as follows:

- Intrinsic case study (Single case)
- Instrumental case study (Single case)
- Collective case study (Patchwork case study, comparative case study)

The intrinsic case study aims to generate as much knowledge as possible on a specific topic. The instrumental case study supports theory building, validation or redefinition in addition to knowledge generation. The collective case study has the same goals as the intrinsic case study except that it is based on multiple cases.

Evidence from multiple cases often makes a study more robust (Herriot/Firestone 1983). Consequently, a collective case study design of exploratory nature with multiple units of analysis was chosen for this study. Moreover, multiple-case designs provide replication of results or "contrasting results for predictable reasons" (Yin 2003:

47). CiRM initiatives were the main unit of analysis. As noted in Section 2.1.9, CiRM is currently mostly implemented in contact centers on the municipal or county level. In addition, most citizen administrative contacting also takes place on the local level, as shown in Section 2.3.4. Hence, it was justified to disregard higher jurisdictions. At the time of the study, there were roughly 30 places (cities or counties) in the United States that had started CiRM projects, which automatically limited sampling options. In order to produce contrasting results and improve external validity, selected cases differed by their stage in the CiRM implementation process, the size of the served community, the government structure and the jurisdictions. All of the research sites had progressed beyond the initial stages of implementation. The City of Chicago and the City of Baltimore had the longest history and experience in CiRM, starting in the late 1990s. Executives and elected officials from various cities and counties visited both places before starting their own initiatives. Given the size and complexity, the City of New York is currently the biggest CiRM attempt in the world on the municipal level. In addition, New York's public administration carries out tasks that are usually the domain of higher jurisdictions. Miami-Dade County offers insights from a multijurisdictional environment and unique "two-tier federation" government structure. Administrators and elected officials were the embedded units of analysis. Their understanding of CiRM and strategies of implementation was assumed to have the biggest influence on concept enactment and impact.

The most common critique is that case study results lack generalizability (Punch 2000: 153-156, Jensen/Rodgers 2001: 236). However, this depends on the type of case study. The intrinsic case study is focused on understanding the complexity and context of a specific case—not generalization. The same applies to instrumental and collective case studies, which usually include "abnormal" or special cases that one would find at the edges of a Gaussian distribution. It would not be possible to make generalizations through random sampling and choosing a high number of cases, as in quantitative methods, to meet the demands of critics. But Yin (2003: 38) pointed out how a single case study by Jacobs (1961) on New York City led to a general theory in urban planning. Case studies are more about analytical generalizability than about theoretical assumptions (Hartley 2004: 332). Single and cross-case analysis thus allowed producing generalizable findings about the understanding, implementation and impact of CiRM.

Another potential critique is that a case-oriented methodology may give inappropriate weight to cases where an expected factor is not found. The risk is to assign the cases a special or idiosyncratic theoretical status, when in fact they may simply be cases where the probability of the factor's occurrence did not hold. The absence of this factor in a particular case cannot lead to the conclusion that overall the factor does not play a significant role in other cases of that category (Vaughan 1992: 184). Because of the validity of this argument, the collective case study approach and cross-case analyses aimed at reducing this risk. Moreover, this study used interviews and document analysis to counter the constraints of a mono-method approach. Interviewees included executive-level administrators, administrative managers, public servants, elected officials and external consultants. Some interviewees had always worked in government, while others also had a working history in the private sector. Building upon multiple sources of evidence, therefore, improved the validity of the construct. Because this study did not intend to provide explanatory or causal relationships, internal validity was ignored.

Each case study involved a standardized set of steps to ensure reliability. Contacts were asked for the same documents and information using a case study protocol (Appendix A). Interviews were semi-structured (Rubin/Rubin 1995), meaning that an interview protocol was created which covered the main topics of interest based on the literature review, but the order of the topics was flexible (Weiss 1994). This allowed for new or unexpected issues to be uncovered for each case. But in general, a holistic understanding of CRM guided the design of related questions in order to answer the central question of this research. Four interview protocols were used (Appendix A) in order to take into account the interviewees' differing roles, priorities and level of involvement, and in order to ensure the validity of the data by triangulation.

3.2 Data collection and data sources

Exploratory fieldwork was conducted in order to form propositions about the understanding, implementation and impact of CiRM, an especially important step given the lack of empirical evidence in the literature. Case Studies were organised in three phases (Figure 3-2).

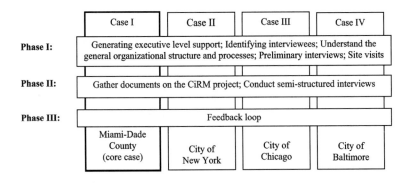

Figure 3-2: Case study design and data collection

While public managers—not necessarily from human resources—of all four cases were visiting the Kennedy School of Government for a recruiting event in the spring of 2005, I took the opportunity to make first contact before fully engaging in the detailed case study preparation.

Phase I began in September 2005 and was mainly about establishing contact with gate-keepers and developing a research prospectus. A good working relationship with a key contact, or gate-keeper, is essential for facilitating field research (Miles/Huberman 1994). After contacting executives by phone, an additional e-mail was sent to summarise the purpose, scope and value of this study. The e-mail included letters of recommendation from Jane Fountain, Director of the National Center for Digital Government (formerly at Harvard University and now at the University of Massachusetts, Amherst) and David Lazer, Director of the Program on Networked Governance at Harvard University that underlined my credibility and ensured confidentiality for the participants (Appendix A). Further, the e-mail requested help in identifying interviewees, scheduling interviews and obtaining access to documentation. After this was achieved, preliminary site visits were aimed at deepening the relationship to the executives, building a better understanding of the CiRM project and testing some of the interview questions. Except for Chicago, where detailed phone conversations with the 311 director made a preliminary site visit unnecessary, I met with all CIOs in November 2005. As a consequence of these meetings, the CIOs usually assigned an internal liaison for my research project and informed other administrative executives or elected officials.

Phase II started two to four weeks after the preliminary meetings in order to give organisations enough time to prepare for the site visits (e.g. schedule interviews) but still build on the momentum of the earlier meetings. Full-day or multiple-day site visits were conducted at the four cases from October 2005 through April 2006. Table 3-1 gives an overview of the time frame and activities for each case study. Due to the level of executive support, Miami-Dade County was studied in greater detail over a 14-day period, and thus is the core case of this study.

Site	Time Frame	Activities
Baltimore	November 2005 (2 days)	Interviews; Participation in CITISTAT meeting
Miami-Dade	December 2005 (14 days)	Interviews; Participation in meetings and daily work
	January 2006 (3 days)	Follow up interviews ; Participation in meetings (e.g. 311 State Coalition Meeting)
New York	January 2006 (1 day)	Interviews
	March 2006 (3 days)	Interviews
	April 2006 (1 day)	Interviews
Chicago	February 2006 (4 days)	Interviews

Table 3-1: Case study time frame and activity overview

Usually, some time was spent learning more about operations and project history before starting with the interviews. In each case, I was given a tour of the 311 contact center and permitted to listen in on phone calls and observe call-taker interaction. I was also invited to lunch breaks and granted access to internal meetings, which allowed collecting additional data outside of the formal interview situation. Moreover, observation of the board of county commissioners meetings provided insight into Miami-Dades political environment and the elected officials' perceptions of 311/CiRM. Field notes were taken throughout site visits and the interview process in order to record observations, interpretations and details.

Because all projects faced internal resistance, I requested to not be informed about interviewees' opinions on the overall CiRM initiative up-front. In fact, executives were specifically asked to include an unknown number of rather critical individuals. This was done to allow for unbiased data gathering and better identification of barriers. A total of 69 interviews were conducted, each lasting 60 to 90 minutes. Interviews with elected officials tended to be shorter (20–35 minutes). Including additional interviews with the same individuals, the total number of interviews was 77. Interviews were digitally recorded and mostly carried out on a one-on-one basis in the interviewee's daily working environment. To obtain individual inner perspectives, I followed a number of procedures (Rubin/Rubin 1995). These practices included following up on respondents' replies, listening more and talking less, asking open-ended questions and avoiding leading questions. Before starting an interview, the interviewees were informed about their right to refuse to answer any questions and to cease participation at any time. In addition, they were given the options of remaining anonymous and checking the interview transcript for accuracy. While all respondents declined the latter option, some explicitly requested to be quoted with their full name. When an interview was finished, interviewees received a small gift (a coffee mug from the John F. Kennedy School of Government), which they appreciated. Table 3-2 shows the number of interviews by interviewee category and case study. Interviewees were categorized according to their primary role. For instance, the category "administrators" includes all individuals who worked in public administration, regardless of their hierarchy level; this category did not include those who led a department or a broader set of organisational entities. The latter individuals were considered "executive-level administrators". Organisations used different titles to describe a function. In

	Miami-Dade County	City of New York	City of Baltimore	City of Chicago
Elected officials	8	1		
Executive-level administrators	9	6	1	5
Administrators	18	8	2	9
External consultants	1	3		
Total (69)	*36*	*18*	*3*	*14*

Table 3-2: Number of interviews per city and interviewee category

New York and Chicago, department heads are called "Commissioners", whereas the same term is used for elected officials in Miami-Dade County. Chicago elected officials are referred to as "alderman".

Besides conducting interviews, two sources of evidence, internal documents and archival data, were collected to ensure validity and reliability. First, internal documents included organisational charts, project plans, studies (produced by consultants), IT infrastructure maps, financial data, manuals, performance reports, memos or citizen surveys. These sources were either given to me or were publicly available on the Internet. They provided precise data about the organisation and project structure. Second, archival data consisted of journal and newspaper articles as well as conference presentations and promotional materials related to 311 and CiRM. This data allowed establishment of the background of each case and provided deeper insights into external communication and perceptions.

After the data was screened, feedback from interviewees on findings was solicited. Phase III of the case study process was supposed to improve construct validity.

The four cases are outlined in the sections that follow. Each case is described in terms of its location, government structure, CiRM project initiation and role in this study.

3.2.1 City of Chicago

The City of Chicago is located in the state of Illinois. Some parts of the city belong to DuPage County, while most parts belong to Cook County. The city's population is around three million, with an additional ten million living in the surrounding metropolitan area. The mayor is elected for four years and is the chief executive. He appoints commissioners that oversee departments. Richard M. Daley has been the mayor of the city since 1989. The City Council is the elected legislative branch of the city and consists of 50 "aldermen", one from each ward. In January 1999, after having analysed citizen interaction processes in 1997, Chicago implemented a technology-enabled 311 one-stop service center. Further actions to improve citizen-orientation followed. Local government officials from across the United States, as well as Canada and the UK, have visited Chicago to learn more about its CiRM activities. The city has been committed to sharing its experience and to supporting other cities in their CiRM efforts. Chicago received Harvard University's "Innovations in American Government Award" for its 311 system in 2003.

Given these facts, a case study of Chicago promised a rich data set from its own CiRM initiative and those of other cities. Furthermore, because I was in Cambridge, I was able to utilize the resources of Harvard University's Ash Institute for Democratic Government and Innovation which had given the award to the City of Chicago in 2003.

3.2.2 City of Baltimore

The City of Baltimore is located in the state of Maryland and has the status of an intergovernmental city. Baltimore, therefore, relies on federal and state funds while providing federal, state and municipal policy mandates. Its budget is around $2 billion. The city's population is around 640,000 and is declining (Henderson 2003). An additional 2.6 million live in the surrounding metropolitan area. Between 1999 and April of 2006, Martin O'Malley served as mayor of the city, which had approximately 16,000 employees. The city council consists of 14 elected representatives for Baltimore's districts and one elected president. The council's main role is oversight and approval of the budget. While Baltimore was the first place to offer a N-11 (311) number for non-emergency services in 1996, it was not until March 2001 that the CiRM strategy was implemented by the Mayor's Office of Information Technology (MOIT). Baltimore's initiative was strongly influenced by Chicago and adapted Chicago's plans to its own situation. Besides the CiRM initiative, the mayor initiated the CitiStat program, which is a unique management tool for performance management.

Although Baltimore serves as an auxiliary case for this research, it provided information how CiRM data was utilized for performance management.

3.2.3 City of New York

The City of New York is located on the East Coast in the state of New York. New York is composed of five boroughs: Manhattan, Queens, the Bronx, Brooklyn and Staten Island. The city's population is around 8.2 million, with an additional 19 million living in the surrounding metropolitan area. Like Chicago and Baltimore, New York is governed by a strong mayor–council form of government. Michael Bloomberg, who has been mayor since 2001, has almost total administrative authority. However, unlike Chicago, which has no term limits, the mayor and council members in New York are limited to two four-year terms. The City Council consists of 41 members. Many government services delivered by the city, such as education, correctional institutions or welfare services, are, in other municipalities, the responsibility of higher jurisdictions. New York's total budget for public services is around $50 billion. Implementing a 311 system was first discussed during the Giuliani Administration, but the project was stalled due to conflicts with the New York Police Department (NYPD). However, CiRM became a major initiative of Mayor Bloomberg's first term, and he announced the program in his State of the City Address in early 2002. The Department of Information Technology and Telecommunications (DoITT) was given one year for the implementation process by the mayor. The 311 contact center began operation in March 2003 and has received a lot of worldwide media coverage since then. The integration of additional services and departments is still taking place.

The complexity of New York's public administration, the number of citizens to serve and the scale of its CiRM initiative made it a study object of choice.

3.2.4 Miami-Dade County

Miami-Dade County (before 1997 named Dade County) is located in the state of Florida and encompasses more than 2,000 square miles (larger than the states of Rhode Island and Delaware). The county's population is around 2.3 million. More than 1 million people reside in the unincorporated area of the county, with the rest of the population living in its 35 municipalities (incorporated areas). The county operates under a two-tiered federation, that is, the municipalities and the county are separate jurisdictions that have their respective responsibilities. Public services such as police, zoning or code enforcing are provided by the municipalities and paid for by municipal taxes. The county delivers services such as the airport, public housing and transportation, which are paid for by county taxes. After a referendum in January 2007, Miami-Dade County began being governed by a strong-mayor and Board of County Commissioners (BCC) form of government. One commissioner is elected from each of 13 districts. Carlos Alvarez is the current mayor. The mayor appoints the county manager, with the consent of the BCC, and oversees daily government operations. The mayor cannot be in office more than two consecutive four-year terms; there are no term limitations for county commissioners. The BCC approves the budget recommended by the county manager, who is the head of the administrative branch. The county manager appoints or removes all department directors and can issue administrative orders, rules and regulations. Miami-Dade's CiRM efforts were the results of a long-term strategic plan which was developed in 1999. In 2001, the county launched its Web portal, and in 2002 it addressed the issue of having a multijurisdictional 311 customer contact center. In 2004, an interlocal agreement added the City of Miami's municipal services and 311 contact center operations to the county. In September 2005, after a 10-month pilot phase, the county's contact center went fully operational.

Due to the level of executive support and access to organisational members, Miami-Dade County was chosen to be the core case study. Moreover, CiRM requires intense cross-boundary collaboration, so it was interesting to see how the concept was interpreted and implemented in a multijurisdictional environment. Finally, Miami-Dade's analysis of the cities which are part of this study offered them the chance to either modify or follow existing models.

3.3 Data analysis

Upon completing the site visits, interviews were transcribed, producing approximately 1,500 pages. All interview transcripts included notes on expression of emotions, such as laughing or tapping one's fingers. Additional information was added from field notes.

This study is based on three levels of data analysis in order to come to an understanding and a conceptualization of a theoretical framework of CiRM (Figure 3-3). First, I compared the central elements of CRM to the citizen-oriented reforms outlined in Chapter 2.2. This allowed me to identify any unique contributions or aspects of CRM based on a comparison to currently active reform movements in government.

Second, the data analysis chosen for my interviews and documents was similar to Strauss and Corbin's (1998) grounded theory approach. This allowed structuring the data to do a case description of the implementation, impact and understanding of CiRM in addition to identifying salient concepts or themes. Third, the single and cross-case study data on how CiRM initiatives had been implemented was understood as an indirect source from which to derive the underlying understanding of CiRM in comparison with the definitions and explanations of CiRM interviewees had given.

Grounded theory can be classified as "the discovery of regularities" and further defined as "identification (and categorization) of elements, and exploration of their connections" (Tesch 1990: 78). The process involved multiple levels of data coding and classification. Glaser and Strauss argued against initiating qualitative analysis with any preconceived theory that dictates relevancies in concepts and hypotheses before the research (1967: 33). Doing so can cause the researcher to "force-fit" the data to the theory. However, researchers always begin a research project influenced by prior reading, experience or conversations that have shaped their perceptions or basic theoretical assumptions. For this study, it was even necessary to begin with an initial set of categories that was derived from holistic CRM concepts in order to support testing for differences and similarities in its application to government (Appendix B). As such, my research and theoretical framework are inductively grounded in data but are guided by CRM concepts as a frame of reference. This is seemingly the opposite of the premise of grounding theory in data.

Following Creswell's (2003) recommendations, the data was analysed in several steps. The analysis began by reading through the transcripts and documents to gain a

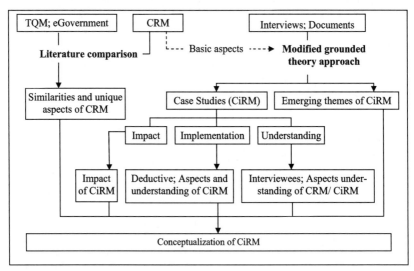

Figure 3-3: Summary of analysis process

general sense of the information and meaning. The second step was a microanalysis of each interview. Using the qualitative data analysis software ATLAS.ti 5.2, a detailed line-by-line analysis and coding was conducted. A code is a term for any category or relationship between two or more categories.

Data was coded inductive in line with the constant comparative method (Glaser/ Strauss 1967; Strauss/Corbin 1998), that is, fracturing the data into coded units (open coding) and then progressively and systematically grouping the data units that show similarities (axial coding) and relationships. Simultaneously with coding, the process of comparing all events and/or forms of social interaction identified from within the data for similarities, differences and general patterns was performed. Moreover, memos were produced throughout the coding and sorting process to support theorizing (Strauss 1987).

Results were interpreted on the individual and the aggregate case level before moving to the cross-case analysis. I looked for common patterns of an explanatory, inferential or contradictory nature. Patterns or definitions which appeared in higher frequency were considered more robust.

It emerged that various managerial incidents, events and actions were common across all cases and were sequenced at specific points in the implementation of CiRM projects. By using this method of data collection and analysis, it was possible to more readily identify the following in the cases studied:

- A series of progressive establishment stages that CiRM moved through

- An appreciation of how personal managerial relationships, both inter- and intra-organisational, can influence the management of CiRM and its outcome

3.4 Limitations to the data collection and analysis

Readers should be aware of several limitations, or caveats, to the study and its findings. These include a subjective bias, the lack of a common conceptualization of CRM, the interview data, the abundance of data, missing data and validity. A certain level of bias on behalf of myself based on cultural difference, existing knowledge or research goals cannot fully be avoided. Along these lines, the developed framework of a holistic CRM concept in itself carries a subjective bias even though it was grounded in a broad literature review. Other researchers might not accept the CRM framework, based on missing components or its broadness. Interviews are also subject to bias or distortions of the truth, which was to be countered by the process of triangulation and interview techniques. The abundance of data at the beginning, and in particular, after the analysis, acts as another limitation. Moreover, the complexity of the studied organisations and limits to my capacity of meant that all areas of interest could not be covered. Missing data might, therefore, lead to misinterpretations which can only be partly be countered by the cross-case analysis. For example, it was not possible to do a detailed analysis of the organisation and its processes before the CiRM initiatives started. Furthermore, this research did not cover the perspective of the citizen on the citizen–government relationship.

4 Results

Based on the methodology described in Chapter 3, a detailed synopsis of each of the cases included in this study is presented in this chapter, along with details about the implementation, impact and understanding of CiRM of the case. Each case analysis is divided into three sections: Implementing CiRM, Impact of CiRM and Understanding of CiRM. When describing the implementation of CiRM, I essentially give a detailed account of the 311 project as well as less detailed information on the channels and other customer service activities. The section on the impact of CiRM focuses on any kind of impact of the 311 initiatives. These may include citizen-orientation, organizational processes and roles or relationships of elected officials, administrators and citizens. The last section summarises the interviewees' opinions on various aspects of CRM and its major differences in government, as well as their definitions of CiRM. To ensure rich detail—and to prevent alterations of the meaning of interviewees' statements by my summarising their quotes in my own words—this chapter includes a large number of direct quotes. Guiding my selection of quotes was my intent to capture ideas that either represented a common, reappearing idea or were particularly unique. The case studies are presented chronologically by their date of engaging in their CiRM activities.

4.1 CiRM in Baltimore

4.1.1 Implementing CiRM

On October 2, 1996, the City of Baltimore became the first municipality in the United States to study the effects of a 311 non-emergency number. The experiment was supported by federal grants and approved by the Department of Justice. Although there was a general six-digit government information phone number available, citizens were not aware of it and dialed 911 instead. The city's introduction of 311 resulted in a reduction of police non-emergency calls to 911 by 50% within a short time. As a consequence of the successful experiment, the Federal Communications Commission (FCC) adopted the order (FCC 97-51) regarding the establishment of 311 for non-emergency access to police and municipal services on February 19, 1997. However, it also became evident that citizens did not correctly utilize 311 (Mazerolle et al. 2003). Over 60,000 calls were placed via 311 to report issues that were considered 911-type priority one calls by the police. Citizens assessed their situation differently than the police did or were confused about the most appropriate number to call due to a lack of communication. On the other hand, calls that were not considered to be a police matter were either provided with information if it was available (e.g. the time of an Orioles game) or transferred to the responsible department. Yet these type of activities were not tracked or recorded.

Shortly after Martin O'Malley came into office as mayor of the City of Baltimore in 1999, he introduced a real-time performance management accountability system called CitiStat. The idea was based on New York's CompStat model.

CompStat was developed by Police Commissioner Willam Bratton and his team at the NYPD as a crime-tracking and management tool in 1994 (Buntin 1999). In bi-weekly meetings, precinct and operational unit commanders were required to present crime trends and policing activities. They had to submit their data in advance to the CompStat Team, which compiled and analysed the data. The relevant data (e.g. different crime statistics; broken street lights) were put on computer-generated maps during those meetings. The aim of the CompStat meetings was to hold commanders accountable for responding poorly to problems and to identify effective policing measures and share that knowledge. CompStat helped the NYPD to reduce crime, motivate the police force and anticipate various internal and external problems.

While New York City's CompStat sought only to improve the performance of the police department, O'Malley believed that a similar approach would be able to improve the performance of all city departments in Baltimore. The city spent $20,000 for the purchase of necessary equipment for the operation of the CitiStat program (e.g. computers and projectors) and allocated $265,000 for operating costs (e.g. personnel) in its first fiscal year (FY01). During this time period, all of Baltimore's operating departments joined the CitiStat program. One of the key aspects of CitiStat is timely and accurate information. However, the first meetings in late 2000 and early 2001 proved difficult. Departments sometimes lacked information about their internal resources, processes or service delivery level. For example, the public works director was only able to guess the number vehicles in their fleet (6,000–6,500). In addition, some department heads claimed that they were so busy producing the statistics that they could not resolve issues identified in the meetings. One administrator remembers that "the analyst prepared a chart and put it up on the screen, and the mayor would say—aha, complaints for potholes have gone up this week, by four hundred percent. The agency head would turn around [...] and say, that data can't be right. The meeting had to stop". Because agencies were responsible for producing their own information, and because many decisions required almost real-time data, the mayor decided to create an information intake facility that was independent from any agency. The data was supposed to be generated through a centralized 24/7 phone intake for all agencies—by means of 311 (first referred to as CitiCall).

According to executive level administrators, the challenge facing them was expanding the role of the number 311. The city already had the infrastructure in place in its emergency operations center, because they started 311 in 1996, but a new customer service strategy was now needed. Until 2002, the 311 operations were handled by the police department. Therefore, the project team began by convincing the police department that "it was not important to be a police officer to answer non-emergency calls". In fact, it was necessary to de-educate the population, because—before 2002—the citizens' understanding was that when you pressed 311, "you talked to a nasty cop who didn't know much about customer service", as one administrator recalled. Furthermore, four out of ten people tended to hang up before someone could answer the phone. Departments collected various internal data (e.g. for financial accounting), but only a few tried to measure citizen satisfaction. Some departments also had phone hotlines for information and service requests. However, the project's preparation phase revealed that service levels differed significantly. Operating hours varied and usually ended by 5:00 p.m. Calls were only answered sporadically. Furthermore, callers were bounced around between departments or received different answers for the same question depending on the person they talked to. Daily call volume for city service was estimated to be around 17,000. Elliot Schlanger, Baltimore's CIO, visited the City of Chicago in order to learn from its 311 implementation experience.

Because the implementation was restricted by a tight budget and time constraints—the project was supposed to be completed within a year—the team approached its task in a very pragmatic way. It consolidated the existing call centers within the city and transferred the staff to 311. Call taker jobs within 311 were reclassified as customer service representatives (CSRs). People were provided with uniforms and a modern work environment in order to get their buy-in. However, the CSRs did not meet the newly established productivity and customer service criteria (e.g. the citizen is called customer) in the beginning. Thus, all CSRs had to go through extensive training. Some still had to be sent back to departments after a while to work on other projects because their behaviour did not change.

The project team did not create an electronic knowledge base to help answer citizens' questions. Instead, the expertise that call takers brought in from their departments served as a human knowledge base. One administrator remembered, "[If] someone had a question that was tough to answer, there was someone in the room that probably represented the agency that happened to deliver the service and would know how to answer the question. It wasn't pretty but that's what we did." Another obstacle in creating a knowledge base in a short time was that the city did not have any documented sets of procedures for the various topics or someone who was maintaining that information.

Baltimore followed Chicago's 311 setup and used Motorola Customer Service Request CSR software (referred to here as Motorola CSR) as its CRM software. Administrators named Baltimore's system CitiTrack (following the CitiStat branding). The software allows taking in service requests (SR) by a set of standardized questions. The information is then forwarded to the appropriate department. The status of the SR can be tracked at any time by the CSRs or other members of the administration. The newly-established 311 organization aimed at taking in all the information from the citizen so that agencies knew exactly what to do. However, they did not have any influence on how agencies prioritized their work. As it turned out, it was easy to answer the phone in a friendly manner but very difficult to ensure that the service delivery met citizen expectations. Now that CitiCall was the face of government to the citizens, 311 was criticized for not delivering the requested services in the promised time. These complaints revealed that many SRs reported as delivered were never taken care of. Many crews had quickly recognized that executive management only monitored the time it took to close a SR. So they just did that, believing no one would check. Another common problem was overlapping jurisdictions. The Baltimore *Sun* reported that someone called in a complaint about an abandoned vehicle that was being used by drug dealers as a base of operations (Worcester Regional Research Bureau 2003).

Since two tires of the vehicle were in an alley, and two were in a vacant lot, neither of the two partially responsible agencies, Transportation and Housing, could actually remove the vehicle. Finally, government language had to be rephrased for the interaction with citizens because it could be misleading.

The CSRs started taking calls in March 2002 and completely took over the 311 operations from the police department in August 2002. In contrast to the estimated daily call volume of 17,000 calls, the 311 call center was now receiving 3,000 to 4,000 calls per day. Call abandon rates dropped from 40% to 2% after the change in 311 call-center management. Calls lasted on average two minutes. Approximately 50% of those total calls resulted in a SR (resulting in 40,000 SRs per month), while less than 10% were follow-ups on existing SRs. The remaining calls were basic information requests. About 4% of those calls were transferred to Social Services. The 311 center started doing some outbound calls to elderly people in collaboration with the Elderly Services office during weather emergencies (e.g. a blizzard). The calls were made in order to check on an elderly person's well-being and determine whether or not they needed any assistance.

The City of Baltimore also has a Web portal that is less developed than those of other municipalities. Asked for the reason, a city official stated that "one of the things that we happen to suffer from in our city is [that] we are a rather—and this is a generalization—old, tired infrastructure [with an] underserved, high-crime [and] low-literacy population". The Web portal gives citizens access to various government information, including all CitiStat reports dating back to 2001. Citizens may also enter 67 types of service requests online using CitiTrack (Appendix D).

There are nine neighborhood one-stop service centers in Baltimore. Citizens can go there and go through the various stages of the process to get a building permit instead of walking to the various departments that are responsible for parts of that process.

Administrative executives think that technology could further automate service delivery intake and service processes in the near future. Work crews and employees could be equipped with handheld units in the future so that citizens can be connected to them in real time.

According to several administrators, the biggest key to success in the change process was having a strong leader. As one of them said, "Leadership is very important. Because you could be going around, and we have cities that talk to us all the time, that are still going around in circles, because people can't agree."

4.1.2 Impact of CiRM

The 311 contact center had an influence on how citizens interacted with Baltimore's government. In the past, when citizens had a request or complaint, they usually made four phone calls. First, they tried to call the agency responsible for the service. Then they called their council member and the mayor's office to make sure the request got priority. Finally, as extra insurance, they called an acquaintance or friend who worked in government— one who's a colleague of a colleague of the person who was responsible for the service delivery. Citizens would then call all those places repeatedly over time in order to find out what was being done in response to their request. Now, however, they are only calling 311. Elected officials are also asked to use the software or call 311 to place an SR to break the old cycle of multiple citizen calls whenever that is necessary. What's also different now is that the CSRs are required to inform callers about the status of a SR or any kind of delays.

The expectations of administrators were that people would call more frequently if they had a phone number that was easy to remember and if the service delivery actually met their expectations. However, except for some fluctuations, the daily call volume remained constant after a while. Yet the type of calls changed. In the beginning, there were repeat calls to check the status of a SR. Now the percentage of new SRs makes up 50% of the total call volume.

Almost all agencies were able to improve their performance since CitiStat and the new 311 were implemented in Baltimore. For example, in the beginning it took an agency three to six months to respond to an alley cleaning request. Now it takes under 21 days. However, now the new 311 receives more SRs and generally encounters raised expectations of the citizenry. One administrator voiced concerns that they might become victims of their own success: "Six months, it's dirt in six months. Doesn't get any dirtier, right? You only have to go there once and you have to clean it. Once you start to do it every three weeks you're going back over and over again. So the agencies were pushing back on that. [N]ot only are we trying to get it done in a short amount of time, we're creating, three times the work."

The SR intake is now automated and separated from the service delivery. During the implementation phase of the new 311, it turned out that the Recreation and Parks Department had a backlog of thousands of SRs hidden on index cards that had accumulated over 10 years. Many agencies were also forced to establish standard operating and customer service procedures at that time, because they did not previously have them.

Agencies and their executives are held accountable in new ways. As one administrator stated, "[…] if you can get past the mayor and the city council at least a couple a times a year to talk about the budget, you're safe. But when you start seeing the mayor every two weeks [in the CitiStat meeting], and things don't go away, [they] may indeed come back for resolution, then you start to become more accountable." Furthermore, 311 and agency performance data (e.g. service delivery times) were made public on the Internet. Agencies as well as politicians were afraid of the transparency but soon realized the potential once that information was systematized with tools such as a GIS. It allowed agencies to better deploy their resources and learn about the needs of the citizenry. Council members and the public were able to hold the mayor accountable for how he managed the city.

Executive administrators have been surprised by the willingness of agencies to change and accept the new approach to customer service and performance management. Usually they tend to "just hunker down and say, don't worry this [the mayor] will pass too". Administrators think that the 311/CRM approach has been institutionalized in Baltimore's government operations. As one of them concluded, "I never knew that the 311 stuff would become so integral to what we do each day. [T]hat's really the good side. [S]o the bad side is, [citizens] will still complain." By comparison, administrators expect that there will be concomitant changes in CitiStat's operation or role when there was new political leadership. Yet so far administrators do not know about the kind of positive or negative effects.

4.1.3 Understanding of CiRM

The biggest difference between CRM in the private and public sector is its aim. A senior public servant described the difference as follows:

> *So the contrast between private and public - private, make a sale, that's the goal. [In the] public, we just want to check up to make sure our people are doing the work. So from the customer's perspective, what they want, or what we want everyone to believe is we love you, and it's the customer service friendly thing to do. Check up after the interaction to make sure that you're happy. [...] In the end it's all the same, but, the motives are different*

Another aspect in CRM is building a close relationship with the customer, that is, learn all about his needs, behaviours and interactions with an enterprise. Public servants identified an additional basic ideological difference in government CRM. Agencies are more interested in the problem and the location of that problem than the caller. In fact, 20% of callers to 311 prefer to stay anonymous. The CRM software builds a history of locations rather than citizen interactions. Furthermore, the CRM software (here Motorola CSR) closes the organizational loop between work order intake, status report and delivery.

4.2 CiRM in Chicago

4.2.1 Implementing CiRM

In 1997, the City of Chicago analysed how its residents requested city services and how departments responded to those requests. Chicago residents had various ways to get in touch with their government: Aldermanic offices, community policing offices within each police district, the Internet (information, e-mail) and remote city department facilities. However, there was a proliferation of phone numbers used to market different city programs and services (e.g. 312-744-5000 for city services; 312-744-2277 for community policing; 312-744-6000 for police non-emergency services). In addition, many of the police officers who handled non-emergency calls were not trained in customer service. It was also not fully transparent whether all departments delivered services at the same service level. The mayor had to rely on the information given to him by commissioners; however, there was no hard data. Because there was considerable room for improvement, the Office of the Mayor convened discussions with the Mayor's Office of Inquiry and Information (MOII), the Office of Emergency Communications (OEC), the Chicago Police Department (CPD) and the Office of

Business Information Services (OBIS). The agenda of the meetings included the following issues:

- Y2K compliancy of the systems.

- Need to divert non-emergency calls out of the 911 dispatch system, particularly during times of crisis.

- The emergence of an additional area code within Chicago and the desire to enable residents to use one number (311) to call for information and services.

- Concern that the legacy system in use only tracked calls and did not generate work orders and data to produce management reports.

- An analysis of the associated costs of bringing the old system up-to-date versus the cost of a new system with more capability.

After a series of meetings in 1998, the Mayor's Office chose to implement 311 and expand its role beyond non-emergency police calls. In addition, the outdated mainframe was to be replaced with a modern client–server system. Furthermore, the Suncoast Scientific Inc. software SunTRACK (now Motorola CSR) was to be implemented to improve service request intake and tracking of city service processes.

Following those decisions, the OBIS and the MOII met with city departments and established the groundwork and design of the new system. The project team started mapping processes and training more than 2,000 staff members and installed the system in more than 250 remote sites by the first quarter of 2001. Because the MOII had operated a call center that forwarded calls and some service requests to city departments before 1997, it could take advantage of its existing working relationships with all city departments. However, mapping out all the business processes was a challenge in the early phase of the project. Some departments had never analysed their processes and had difficulty in identifying more efficient ways of service delivery. Moreover, departments were protective of their internal data and feared the transparency. Reluctant staff had to be convinced that the changes, while laborious, would, in fact, enable them to continue their work without interruption or major changes to their work habits. A factor that helped in overcoming the various obstacles in managing organizational change was the strong support of Mayor Richard M. Daley. Since there were no elective-office term limits in Chicago, public servants could not expect a change in leadership, because since taking office in 1989, the Mayor had enjoyed strong citizen approval. As one administrator explained:

> [T]here's that mentality of I don't have to, I can wait you out. Nobody can wait out Mayor Daley, because anybody who waited out Mayor Daley is now gone. Because he's been in [office for] sixteen years. But in order to do fundamental change, it takes time too. [...] It [takes] huge amounts of time, effort and political capital. [I]f you're in there for eight years, it's a lot harder [to wait you out].

In 1999, 311 went operational, and in the third quarter of 2000 the Mayor decided to create 311 City Services as a separate unit of local government to give it greater leverage and weight within government. For an overview of its organizational structure and embeddedness in government, see Appendix D. Because it had the same robust and scalable architecture as 911, the 311 service center also became Chicago's 911 back-up call facility. Chicago's 311 was implemented and continues to be funded with existing municipal resources. The current operating budget is around $14 million, including $9.8 million in police personnel expenses for non-emergency services. Unlike 911, however, 311 is not funded by a twenty-five-cent surcharge on wireless and landline phone lines.

In the first year of implementation, citizens placed 2.9 million calls to 311, which is available 24 hours and 7 days a week. Emergency services calls to 911 were reduced by 1 million. By 2001, the 311 call volume rose to 3.4 million, and today is around 4 million per year. The Motorola CSR application (Figure 4-1) tracked 1.6 million service requests in 2000 and is today tracking a little over 2 million service requests per year. In 2004, 311 received seven citizen comments per day. Within the Motorola CSR system, departments are sharing information on service requests so that they can coordinate activities. With regard to service requests, one senior official pointed out that around 60% of the service tickets in the system are created internally and not by the public.

At the same time as the official start of 311, the city initiated a multi-layered marketing campaign. Advertisements were placed on the public transportation system and on billboards. The local and national media were provided with information, and 311 received a lot of free media coverage. Because there was a lot of discussion about the implications for the public perception of 311, a key aspect of the campaign was to delineate the differences between 311 and 911, in addition to creating general awareness for the service number. An administrator stressed that:

> *[W]e didn't want to have a missed hit, where we have a citizen who says, "My smoke alarm's going off and the house is not on fire, I'm going to call 311," as opposed to doing the right thing and calling 911. So we had to be very cognizant that three- digit easy access has pros and cons. The pros being it's obviously very easy to remember and [...] a one-stop shop. [B]ut the down side is, if you don't methodically implement and orchestrate a media campaign, then you're going to have those folks who fall into the cracks, if you will [...].*

For quite some time, a number of local elected officials opposed the 311 initiative. The alderman believed that they might lose contact with their constituents. Taking care of service requests and citizen complaints on poor city services and having a role in helping citizens navigate through city government was an essential part of their role within government, they felt. To get their support, the members of 311 connected the alderman to the CSR system so that they could put in service requests themselves. Furthermore, the alderman's names were put on customer service letters sent to citizens in addition to the name of the commissioner of the responsible department and the mayor (Appendix D). These customer service letters serve as a feedback loop to the citizen. According to an executive level administrator:

> *[...the] tracking number is kind of your FedEx tracking number. I think it inspires confidence that we're taking their request seriously. We're professionalizing our workforce a little more,*

and if they want to call back and verify where things are at in the process, they've got a claim check, so to speak, that they can use [...]. [I]t builds trust if they see things getting done.

Initially, most departments viewed the new software system as a centralized tool for service intake and closeout of service requests, not as a management information tool. This changed in 2002 when 311 started to proactively create management reports. The "Customer Advocacy" unit was created at 311 City Services to, among other things, work closely with the Mayor's Office, the Office of Budget and Management and department managers to begin to use the information that is derived from these reports to achieve department goals and more effectively manage resources. Customer Service Advocates (CSAs) work with departmental staff to evaluate business processes and set defined lists of resolution activities and customer service goals. Together, they review and compare actual departmental performance with planned performance to determine goal achievement. They analyse the efficiency and effectiveness of programs relative to an agency's operations and assist in the establishment and revision of program policies, procedures and methods. For example, the Department of Sewers was able to reduce the average response time for service requests from 17 days in 1999 to 7 days today. The city also saved 150 gallons of water a day by identifying frequently illicitly opened fire hydrants and installing locking caps. In addition, 311 and 911 data was used by the Buildings Department to prosecute owners of properties, where appropriate, that regularly were reported as having problems. CSAs maintain regular contact with aldermanic staff and other government or outside agencies in order to evaluate usage, trends of input and special system needs. In addition, CSAs serve as conduits to

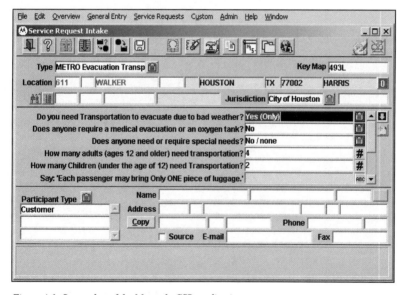

Figure 4-1: Screenshot of the Motorola CSR application

the 311 service center who provide accurate and real-time information to the operators regarding departmental policies and types of city services offered.

Chicago also operates an online Web portal that offers information and various online applications. Residents can pay their water bills and parking tickets or apply for various permits. Beginning in 2001, citizens could make a limited number of service requests online, though as one administrator noted; the city is only beginning to focus on marketing those offerings today. He also pointed out that the Internet is generally not an option for poor and elderly residents. For them, the 311 phone number would be the easiest way to reach city government. Furthermore, the phone channel is better able to cover any emergency needs for government assistance.

City departments interact with citizens to varying degrees. For example, a lot of the Department of Housing's programs, such as home ownership or foreclosure prevention, are geared directly towards citizens. The Department of Housing has different ways of interacting with constituents. There are ongoing relations between case officers and their constituents. Additionally, the department does direct mailings, leaves information postcards in aldermanic offices and organizes information events in schools or gymnasiums in Chicago's area that show patterns of high foreclosure rates. The department also collaborates with community organizations and major religious institutions to create awareness for its services. When the Department of Housing chose to be integrated into 311 City Services, the phone counsellors got together with 311 call operators to give them insights into their processes and held a session on budget counselling so that phone counsellors could better assist citizens seeking housing help. The option of an anonymous contact over the phone and the convenience of getting information anytime turned out to be a well-received option for those in need of counselling. According to one member of the Housing Department, spending the resources on outreach and prevention saves the city the substantially larger costs of handling a foreclosure.

A unit that applied the one-stop idea to the area of citywide business development was Mayor Daley's Business Express. That unit now supports anyone who wants to set up a business in the city. Instead of making the owner deal with bureaucracy, the Business Express team takes over this task.

Recognizing the potential for replication of its 311 approach, the City of Chicago is offering advice to other jurisdictions that wanted to develop their own 311 system. So far, representatives from various municipalities and counties in the United States, Canada and the United Kingdom have visited Chicago. Among them were representatives from all of the cities presented in this study. The advisory work revealed that a lot of communities thought of 311 "as a panacea". They didn't realize that once the 311 service was available, citizens expected work to get done. A member of Chicago's administration summarised the existing perception as follows:

> [P]ublic perception and the amount of times that people are going to call back 311 can either lead to [your] success or [your] failure. Cities get overly focused on answering the call and running a call center. The easiest thing about 311 is the phone center. The hardest thing is getting the city [and] the people behind the scenes to do the work. Detroit just turned it on and

had to turn it off. A whole bunch of cities turned on the phone number and then got all this work. And they're like, "Oh no," and then they turned it off.

Furthermore, managing citizens' expectations became a cornerstone of the 311 project in Chicago. Some departments were able to improve their processes; however, other departments were not able to do so because they were bound to regulations. These could negatively influence citizen satisfaction. For example, when a citizen reports an abandoned vehicle, the city has to wait two weeks before it is allowed to tow the vehicle—a fact that might not be known to many citizens.

4.2.2 Impact of CiRM

Ted O'Keefe, director of Chicago's 311 City Services, thought that the savings and efficiencies gained became much easier to recognize over time. Yet he also pointed out that it is still difficult to come up with a tangible return on investment. However, the city was to able get real-time feedback on the effects of its programs. For example, a city program to control flooding after rainstorms could be tweaked as needed after storms, and problem areas could be identified in real time because citizens were calling and reporting specific flooding issues that helped isolate the problem for the city and enabled the city to fix the problem more quickly. As a result, the city came up with a plan to tweak the vortex in those areas. Other departments were able to make better management decisions based on timely and accurate data. Historically, these decisions were based on individual assumptions about citizens' needs, internal resources or existing processes. The Department of Transportation is now trying to measure the quality of its street paving operations by tracking how long it takes until citizens start complaining about a newly paved street. Finally, all departments are using the data in their negotiations with the budget office.

All interviewees in Chicago believed that 311 and the CSR system improved internal accountability. One senior official said, "I think what we're discovering is that we can fix those finger-pointing issues. When a call is taken by 311, it's no longer the citizen that has to figure out who's responsible. [I]t becomes an internal process. If we don't feel like a department has ownership, that's when we have the ability to say, 'You're right, you don't own this, but now you own it.'" In fact, an increasing number of departments use CSR as their primary work order management system for the benefits it offers in the areas of accuracy and accountability.

Elected officials have also become more accountable. The mayor was able to give constituents exact numbers on the services the city provided for the tax dollars spent. While the aldermanic offices still process complaints and service requests, they generally have to process fewer of them because citizens can now handle the routine ones, such as requesting a new garbage cart, more easily themselves. Elected officials now spend more time on broader policy issues or in their community. In addition, they can invest their resources strategically. Each alderman has a budget available that can be invested in their ward. However, in the past, information from citizens was handled on notepads and was difficult to analyse. Now, areas of particular interest to citizens are identified by CSR and mapped in a GIS application. Performance data will soon be available to citizens, and they will have the opportunity to check how their elected official is managing their ward.

Citizens now have better access to the government of the City of Chicago than they did previously. Residents who knew someone working for local public administration usually got better and faster treatment under the old system. Now, it's a more egalitarian system, especially for citizens of lower economic status. According to one executive level administrator, "You talk to people up on the north side that are well off; they don't know [311]. They don't have to call city government. [...] They don't have graffiti [or] garbage. [...] If you go to poor neighbourhoods, they'll absolutely know it."

Creating a customer service-oriented culture is a challenge. It has not been adopted by all members of city agencies, but has become standard in some departments. Illustrating the responsiveness now apparent in some city agencies, one administrator told the story of the day he saw a city crew fixing something outside of his home. When he talked to them to point out an object that needed their attention on the other side of the road, the crew refused to take care of it because that the object was not on their schedule for that day. As a consequence, the administrator called 311 and told them about the case. One of the 311 service agents contacted the responsible department, which then contacted the crew and told it to add it to their schedule for that day.

4.2.3 Understanding of CiRM

Chicago's administrators pointed out various but very specific differences between public and private CRM. Unlike the private sector, there is less need in government for a one-to-one relationship with citizens. In fact, 311 operations showed that there was usually no link between the reported issue and the caller. Citizens may be at work, on the move or have other reasons to stay anonymous. An executive administrator noted:

> *I think, while I don't know a lot about it, New York has with their Siebel system, focused more on that customer interaction or that customer database if you will. [...] [W]e tend to focus more on what is the need, what is the issue [...] that we need to resolve. [...] If [citizens] want to give us their name, that's fine, and if they don't want to give us their name, that's fine as well. Our goal is not to necessarily discover who you are but to make sure that we can address your quality of life concerns.*

Some administrators also think that the relationship between citizens and their government is generally occurs in association with negative experiences.

> *The only contact you have with the federal government is when you pay your taxes —a negative thing. [Y]our only relationship with state government is paying your taxes. [...] Local is, they pick up your garbage; they do provide water [and] also pay taxes. [...] But by and large, public interaction with government is not a generally a positive thing. [...] You're getting a ticket. The policemen are knocking at your door. You've been robbed; now they're here to help you, but that's around a negative experience. They're crashing through your door because your house is on fire. That is a negative thing. So generally situations by which you have to interact with government, the surrounding circumstances are negative. [...] So, you don't want that customer interaction. It's kind of a one-way street. Customers come to us, they ask us for stuff, we get it done for them. [...] [If] you get that stuff done in a day, you get that stuff done quickly, [citizens are] like, "Oh, my God, government is responsive."*

In addition, they assume that citizens would prefer to avoid government interaction. One administrator put it this way:

> *[I]f the public had their wish they would never ever contact the government. If you had your druthers, you would never deal with the government on any level. [...] I mean the only thing you really need to [interact with government about might be to get] a driver's license. But if you [don't] have to get one, all the better [...].*

This is one reason why some public servants oppose closing the loop to citizens through measures like a letter once a service has been delivered. As one of them stated:

> *So, by and large you don't always want to remind people. [With] graffiti it's great that [citizens] can call in and then it's gone the next day. And then they forget about it. But you don't want to send them a notice reminding them about the graffiti that was in their neighborhood, because then now they're annoyed. Because now they're saying, "Oh, that's, it was graffiti. I do have a problem. Maybe I should move."*

While administrators thought that Chicago's CSR system is similar to a private sector CRM system, others believed that it is rather a work-relationship management system. Following this understanding, its main purpose is to control that work gets done. Citizens act as the eyes and ears for the mayor, which is preferred over responding to problems identified by the media. Moreover, a few administrators go further and stress that public CRM systems need a new classification because of the way they combine work order management, performance management and customer relationship management. However, one of the challenges of these systems is the distinct organizational disconnect between intake and delivery. An administrator explained this as follows:

> *[W]hen you call J.CREW for an item and they run a CRM [software], that operator can do your fulfilment. They [have your information], they understand the size you want and the colour you want. They take care of it. And then it's just a matter of somebody bringing it in a box. [T]hat's not filling a pothole. So typical private-sector CRM is a fulfilment and they can do it all, [but] you can't do that in the public sector.*

Furthermore, administrators voiced their concern about building citizen profiles in the future through government CRM systems. One said:

> *[I]t would have horrible impacts on those that are frequent callers. Because I have a neighbour that loves to call, but she's a concerned citizen. You know, she's not harassing [...]. But if you were to track my education versus her education. What happens when you [have] a [service agent] that sees this person has an education, this person doesn't. Do they start weighing the seriousness of what they're calling in about? [...] I think you would get into a Pandora's Box of other issues that would have to be addressed before you start modelling a person and determining what their profile is and how to interact with them. [T]here'd be a lot more issues you'd have to think through before you could create that sort of [citizen profile].*

All interviewees in Chicago pointed out that government CRM is based on a different philosophy and different goals than private-sector CRM. Government CRM is about delivering public services and not about selling goods or services. Some interviewees supported the view that managing the citizen–government relationship might not be a priority at all except in specific areas such as human services. Others stressed that CiRM would be one of the core missions defining the very existence of government. The following statement gathers together general ideas expressed by several interviewees in separate interviews:

> *I think the business-sector concern is much more on cultivating long-term customers, and identifying needs and wants, and seeing how they might be able to push certain products through the channel to market to their advantage. And so what becomes very important for them is the history of purchases and a history of relationships with that particular customer, since it's a lot cheaper for them to cultivate current customers than it is to go out and identify and mine new ones. I think with us, we're not as concerned about necessarily pushing certain products or services toward individual citizens. [T]here's a part of us that wants to do that. We want to know if people have certain needs, and we want to make sure that if there's a set of services that we need to provide, [that we do so]. [I]n the public sector, we would be more inclined to label something like that as a case management approach, so that if an individual has needs along the lines of food or shelter, housing, employment, that we make sure that we identify those needs and pull the respective departments together to provide that array of services that someone needs to get on with their life. But always managed by a lead agency [...].I think that's perhaps more analogous to customer relationship management. I know that in many ways some people call 311 or CSR public-sector CRM. And it is [CRM], I think, only in the sense that when we're looking at the customer or the citizen in a larger perspective, that we want to have a system that helps us to provide government services more effectively and more efficiently, and in that context, maintain better relationships with the citizen, but not necessarily on a one-to-one level for utilitarian purposes, or to make a better, more prolific customer out of an individual.*

However, one senior official thought differently about CRM:

> *[T]rue government CRM is used more on the regulatory side than on the delivery of city services. And let me tell you, if you don't pay your child support, you're in the system, and we know about you. Because that's where government wants to keep track of wherever you go, whoever you work for, we are going to garnish your wages, and we're going to make sure you pay child support. That's true government CRM. [I]t's going to be for people who are on the lower spectrum of the economic ladder who need help from government. [I]t's also for those people who have done bad things. [O]ddly enough, that's public-sector CRM. [P]rivate-sector CRM is all about how can we sell you more stuff [and] how can we be nice to you. Government CRM is more the bad stuff.*

In general CRM and customer service concepts are difficult to realize in government due to the public service monopoly. As one senior official noted:

> *[G]overnment is more resistant to CRM and being more customer focused because the barrier to exit is extremely high. If I am J.CREW, and you get a rude experience with me or an unfulfilling experience, you can go to L.L. Bean with the drop of a phone call. If you don't like how I deliver your garbage cart, you have to move [...].*

The same official also said:

[T]he thing that people don't understand is [...] how much work we do [that is not visible to them]. [...]We do a huge number of things really efficiently, really well, and we deliver. But, I think that's where government doesn't sell itself as well. [...]

4.3   CiRM in New York City

4.3.1 Implementing CiRM

The administration of Mayor Rudolph W. Giuliani first discussed 311 as a way to reduce the 911 non-emergency call volume. After reviewing 311 in Chicago and doing some internal analysis, exploration of using 311 was stopped because of conflicts with New York's Police Department (NYPD), which had jurisdiction over police non-emergency calls and due to the small expected effects on 911 calls (a reduction of call volume of less than 5%).

The idea reappeared when Michael Bloomberg became mayor on January 1, 2002. The mayor soon talked to Gino Menchini, the newly appointed CIO of the City of New York (Commissioner of the Department of Information, Technology and Tele-communications, [DoITT]) and announced the 311 initiative in his State of the City Address as follows, even though the city was struggling with a $6 billon budget gap:

> *[...]"Open Government" is not just a slogan; it's the only effective way to deal with compli-cated problems. As part of "Open Government," we will create a Citizen Service Center that will allow New Yorkers to reach all services by calling one phone number, 311. This will make city government accessible to every resident of this great city. Right now, New York City oper-ates more than 40 separate call centers and hotlines, which can be an obstacle course for the average citizen. There are 11 pages of listings in the phone book under NYC. No one can be knowledgeable enough to find his or her needle in a haystack that big! It will take time, but eventually New Yorkers will have only two numbers to reach government: 911 for emergencies and 311 for everything else. [...]*

Bloomberg applied his experience of building a multi-billion dollar global media and financial information business to managing the city. For him, "[G]ood companies listen to their customers, No. 1, [and] then they try to satisfy their needs, No. 2. But don't let [customers] drive the internal decisions of the company" (Lowry 2007). The mayor understood the City of New York as a corporation, its citizens as customers and its employees as talent. Therefore, he had very specific ideas about what 311 should look like:

All calls must be handled by a person and not by increasingly complex interactive voice response (IVR) systems.

- 311 must operate 24 hours a day, 7 days a week.
- 311 must be able to handle calls from all New Yorkers and visitors.
- 311 had to be able to handle all non-emergency calls.
- Implementation had to occur within one year.

The timeline was unusual for city government, because the procurement process alone for projects of that scale usually took one year. In order to meet the requested timeline, DoITT did an expedited procurement process. DoITT sent out a Request for Proposals (RFP) for a system integrator. The RFP stated that the proposal was for a "311 Customer Service Management Systems (CSMS) project which may include system integration over all aspects of the work or project components, such as: Customer Relationship Management (CRM); Procurement; Organizational Readiness; Facilities; Human Resources and Training; Telephony and voice network systems, and LAN systems and platform environment". The Mayor's Office of Operations (MOO), Office of Management and Budget (OMB), NYPD Communications (911 Division), Department of Transportation (DOT), and DoITT reviewed the vendors' proposals and selected Accenture as the Systems Integrator for 311.

Accenture had to make sure that the hardware and software were compatible with the legacy systems scattered around the city. Following the decision for the system integrator, the city hired Gartner, a technology research and consultancy firm, to do a CRM software analysis. Gartner recommended Siebel as the most suitable vendor after reviewing software solutions from Oracle, Siebel, SAP, PeopleSoft, Motorola and Computer Associates (CA). Table 4-1 gives an overview of Gartner's main selection criteria as well as its evaluation. As part of the analysis, Gartner also made some estimates on 311 call volume. A survey of city departments said that the city collectively received around six million calls per year. In contrast, Gartner expected 311 to disclose an additional hidden call demand of 15%–40% of that number and a call volume between 5–15 million in its first year of operation. In the end, DoITT decided to use

Criteria	W	Oracle	Siebel	SAP	PeopleSoft	Motorola	CA
Scale of Operation	20	E	E	BA	AA	P	P
Knowledge Management	20	AA	E	BA	A	BA	NA
Telephony Integration	8	AA	E	A	AA	P	NA
Multi-Channel Management	5	AA	AA	A	A	BA	NA
Architecture	10	A	AA	A	E	NA	NA
Vendor Market Position/ Vision	5	AA	AA	BA	A	E	NA
Vendor Support Offered	15	A	A	AA	AA	BA	BA
Product Knowledge/ Experience	7	A	E	AA	A	NA	AA
Cost	10	A	BA	BA	A	AA	NA

Key: E = Excellent / AA = Above Average / A = Average / BA = Below Average / P = Poor / NA = N/A
W = Weight

Table 4-1: Gartner's evaluation of government CRM software solution vendors

Siebel CRM software (Figure 4-2), content management from Interwoven, Inc., an Oracle database on Sun servers and a Nortel phone system. The decision for Siebel CRM, however, was not without its opponents. Administrators thought it was too slow and complex to handle and that its licensing model was too expensive.

NYPD "was by far the most critical agency in 311", said one executive administrator. So very early in the process DoITT also made a large investment in NYPD's IT infrastructure to get their buy-in. Police precincts around the city received network upgrades, computers and printers worth $5 million.

The project team and mayor decided that 311 would offer directory assistance, information provision and service request intake. The latter was supposed to allow citizens to report issues (e.g. dead animal, pothole) or to request a service. The 311 system then routes that information to the appropriate agency, and the caller is provided with a tracking number to follow up on the status. Departments in NYC had been operating using more than 45 call centers. These ranged from actual call centers to individuals or IVR to handle citizens' calls. The call centers and their services were analysed in order to determine the possibility of integrating them into 311. This process was not always received positively by agencies.

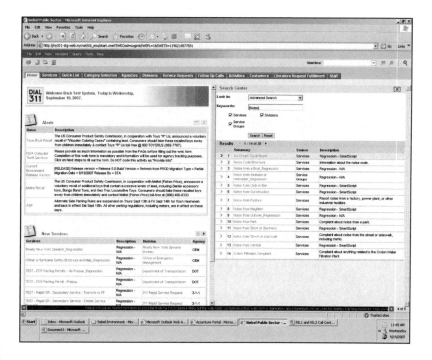

Figure 4-2: Screenshot of the Siebel application

In addition, the project generally was challenged by many elected officials and members of New York's 59 community boards. While agencies were concerned about the transparency and implications of the analysis on their budgets and operations, elected officials opposed the costs and were also afraid of losing contact with their constituency. In particular, community boards felt they would be shut out by 311 operations in their own work of helping citizens who struggled with any kind of government issue. A senior administrator said:

> The first time [the idea of 311] came out sort of like a little expense item. We were going to spend some million dollars on this project. [Elected officials] were like, "Why wouldn't we spend that on books for schools, or why wouldn't we do—there was a lot, there. [D]on't let other people tell you that they were supporters of this project early on. Nobody external of City Hall supported this project until we were this close to going live and they realized what we were going to do. There was no support. There were actually efforts to stop and complicate and make things much more difficult to happen every step of the way. [...]. [A]ny kind of budget items that [...] were put in the executive budget were questioned. [T] here were hearings [...] and, then [there] was an effort to further complicate the process by forcing us to make every single piece of data that 311 collects public before we even knew what we were collecting and how we were going to use it.[...] [C]ommissioners of other agencies in the city kind of poo-poohed the idea at first, until they realized the mayor was talking about it all the time, and he was making this a central thing, and we weren't going away. So, there was not a lot of support for this early on [...]

The transformation process benefited from the executive support of the mayor and his senior staff. Weekly steering committee meetings in City Hall served as a project accountability and escalation tool to quickly resolve obstacles that came up in the implementation process. Many 311 project members also stressed the importance of having had Emma Bloomberg, the Mayor's daughter, on the team. At that time, she was a policy analyst for the Mayor's senior advisor, Vincent LaPadula. Her role was to be the link between City Hall and the project. A consultant remembered:

> I sit down next to this young woman and I had no idea who she is [...]. So the commissioner [was] at that table, and I'm thinking,"What is the commissioner doing here? This is a call center. [T]his is like so far down." So we go around the table and introduce ourselves and she introduces herself as Emma Bloomberg and I (laughing) said [to myself],"Oh, now I understand."

DoITT began the transition to 311 on September 30, 2002. Departments[1] with the ten largest call centers and over 250 employees were gradually added to 311. The soft launch period allowed for testing the system and made the transition for operators and citizens easier. The plan included disconnecting the old agency service numbers over time. However, this phase revealed that the quality and payment of the transferred staff differed widely. Said one executive administrator, "These call centers and agencies

---

[1] The 10 departments were: Department of Sanitation (DOS); Department of Consumer Affairs (DCA); NYPD (Quality of Life); Department of Buildings (DOB); Department of Records and Information Services (DRIS); Department of Environmental Protection (DEP); Department of Transportation (DOT); Taxi and Limousine Commission (TLC); Housing Preservation and Development (HPD) and the Mayor's Action Center.

were like in the basement—both figuratively and literally, and that's where their employees were too. So we took these problem employees off their hands, attempted to train them, and bring them up to par." The 311 system had created new service titles, job requirements and payment schemes that had to be supported by all of the 14 unions that represented parts of the staff. Therefore, all unions were invited to participate in most of the stages of the planning process.

Mayor Bloomberg officially launched 311 operations on March 23, 2003. The project team of 150 members from DoITT, various city departments, Accenture and Winbourne & Costas, a consultancy, had managed to deliver the project at $21 million dollars, which was below its total budget of $25 million. A broad marketing campaign was supposed to create awareness of 311, change citizens' expectations about government interactions and to relieve 911 of non-emergency call volume. The target group of the campaign "Dial 311 – for Information and Services in NYC" was anyone from citizens to public servants. Besides the free media coverage 311 received, the city's taxis, garbage trucks, poster boards, garbage cans, and later, agency publications served as means to advertise 311. In addition, the mayor and commissioners started to mention 311 every time they interacted with the media.

Since 311 went live it has received approximately 14 million calls a year. Daily call volume can go up to 250,000 during events such as the Transit Strike of December 2006. Indeed, spikes in the call volume usually resulted in a permanently increased call volume (Figure 4-3). In peaks or emergencies, calls may also get routed to an outsourced service provider. The number 212-NEW-YORK allows callers outside of New York's telephone area code to contact 311. Calls in languages other than English are forwarded to private-sector translation services. Up to 400 customer service representatives (CSRs) now handle the calls. They are trained in service oriented behaviour and how to use the software. Before speaking to an operator, callers first hear a brief recording telling them to dial 911 in case of an emergency and providing some basic

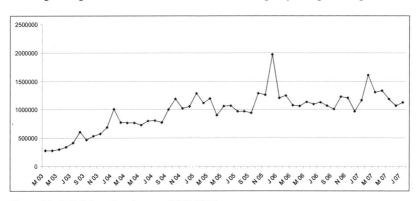

Figure 4-3: Call Volume Development (2003-2007)

service announcements. Calls are first answered by level one CSRs who determine the type of call and its solution based on information in the knowledge base, which covers a continuously growing number of topics (over 7,000).

This is supposed to happen within 30 seconds for 80% of the calls. Callers that cannot be provided with information are transferred to an agency, or if they have specific service requests, they are forwarded to level two CSRs. These CSRs are trained to handle more complex cases and how to use an agency's legacy system.This approach was chosen for several reasons. Due to the outdated IT infrastructure of many departments, it was not possible to fully integrate them into the Siebel system. Only a few agencies were able or willing to be integrated into the Siebel system. In addition, time constraints did not allow customizing the Siebel CRM system, which had originally been designed for the private sector, to government needs. "We're an incident-based model and the CRM system we use is a customer-based model," said one public servant. So a work-around using e-mail and forms was created, which led some administrators to call New York's 311 solution a "mile wide and an inch deep". The setup created many problems for 311 and city departments. First, agencies had to agree to certain service levels, that is, they had to decide on an average time needed to resolve an issue. Although many agencies opposed the idea of service levels because they did not want the information (e.g. time to close a SR) about their operation to be public, it helped reduce call volume and manage expectations. Indeed, administrators were relieved that citizens accepted and understood that many resolutions take time when they were told by the CSRs.

Second, the lack of a fully integrated system does not allow 311 CSRs to get any real-time information about the actual resolution process within an agency. Moreover, agencies do not have any method to return or forward complaints and service requests that have been mistakenly sent to them by 311 or other agencies. However, these issues are supposed to be resolved sometime in the future. Overall, the structure was still able to manage most of the service requests, which make up 10% of the monthly calls. Between 70% and 80% of the requests received are information or transfer requests (Figure 4-4).

Recently, the mayor introduced the Street Conditions Observation Unit (SCOUT), which cost the city about $1 million a year (Rivera 2007). The team of 15, whose members were drawn from five city agencies (DOS, DOT, DOB, DEP, HPD) patrols the streets to identify any kind of issue (e.g. damaged city property, homeless people in need of aid, potholes). Each member is equipped with a GPS and a Blackberry to put reports directly into the 311 system.Besides the phone channel, citizens can use physical service centers maintained by the various agencies, NYC TV and the Web portal (nyc.gov). The latter offers citizens access to information and online services such as e-payments. One-stop shop approaches can also be found on the Web portal. For instance, an application called "ACCESS NYC" serves screens relating to more than 20 city, state and federal human service benefit programs based on a set of questions. However, Gino Menchini and Lawrence Knafo mentioned that in retrospect they would now do 311 before engaging in eGovernment, because it helped them better understand citizens.

In another CiRM move, the mayor also took steps to market the city itself. In order to promote NYC to tourists, its most profitable customer base, Bloomberg hired George Fertitta, CEO of a marketing firm that had handled clients such as Disney and Coca-Cola, to head "NYC & Co". The annual marketing budget of the not-for-profit entity was tripled to $22 million so that it could better promote the city in its 14 offices around the world. In another case, the Office of Film, Theatre & Broadcasting was required to be more customer-oriented by the mayor. The agency received a new IT infrastructure and new leadership in the form of an executive who was recruited by Bloomberg from his own company. As a result, production companies were able to file for permits online or search for film locations. In addition, a 15% tax credit was offered to film and TV productions that completed at least 75% of their stage work in NYC. In collaboration with the NYPD, the agency set up a team of 33 police officers to assist productions.

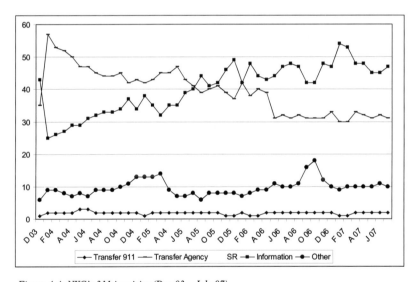

Figure 4-4: NYC's 311 inquiries (Dec 03 – July 07)

4.3.2 Impact of CiRM

In December 2004 Mayor Bloomberg stated, "New York City's 311 system not only provides everyday citizens with better access to government but also makes government more accountable and better able to respond to the changing needs of the population." In accordance with the mayor's "Open Government" idea and on the initiative of the City Council, the local law 174-A was introduced on August 17, 2005 (Hu 2006). In some cases, the concerns of community boards had become reality in late 2004. Citizen inquiries to community boards had decreased by up to a third, and the information on citizens' concerns was not forwarded to board members by 311. In addition, over half of the district managers felt that 311 reduced their access to city agencies when advocating for their district's constituents. They were told by city agencies to call 311 instead. Furthermore, 87% of the resident calls now received reported having trouble getting their complaints resolved by 311 (Shepppard/Mintz-Roth 2004; Brustein 2005).

The 174-A law required DoITT to create monthly agency reports and distribute them to the city council, the public advocate, community boards and the public through NYC's website. Since the 1970s New York held itself accountable by the annual Mayor's Management Report, which was very complex and based on a department's self-reported data. There was no formal way of tracking complaints. DoITT and the Mayor's Office of Operations worked together with the agencies to develop 311 performance metrics and reporting capabilities. The reports include data on 311's directory assistance (e.g. inquiry types). Furthermore, details on service requests such as the number of SRs received, open, closed and average time to close them. Data for 311 are also part of the Mayor's Management Report. Since DoITT started to be increasingly involved in aspects of performance management, some administrators considered taking 311 out of the organizational responsibility of DoITT and adding it to the Mayor's Office of Operations. An executive level administrator explained:

> DoITT is a technology agency, and we're a peer to many of the other agencies [s]o it's really difficult to go to another city agency and tell them that they're not doing their job the right way. [That's why] we all believe that the mayor's office is the appropriate place for this.

Operations for 311 and the ongoing process of integrating agencies into 311 uncovered many intra- and inter-agency issues. Inter-agency conflicts persistently got solved only when they were escalated to City Hall. Now, senior agency officials are hoping for multi-jurisdictional issues to be solved through meetings initiated by 311. One of these inter-agency issues was about the removal of dog excrement. An administrator explained:

> [E]very agency said, "We called the Department of Sanitation. [T]he department asked, 'Where is it? Is it on the street or is it on the sidewalk?' Well, it's on the street. 'Well, then you better call Transportation.' We called DOT and asked who deals with this. They said, 'Dog shit, we don't deal with dog shit. [I]s it a lot of it? You should call the Department of Environmental Protection. [...] [E]ventually we ended up getting in front of the right people at City Hall [...] and Sanitation was given twelve more people and now they're in charge of the problem [...]

In the case of an intra-agency issue, how the agency actually delivered its services was changed both as part of 311 and as part of a larger reform initiative. Under the existing process, architects, engineers or contractors who wanted to meet with a building inspector had to use the service of an expediter. Many of them were former Buildings Department plan examiners and as such had good relationships with people within the Department of Buildings (DOB). They made their living by facilitating the permitting and inspection process. Expediters tended to reserve many appointments with an inspector and then cancel a good number of them at the last minute if they were not hired by the architects or others who needed access. As a result, citizens who tried to get an appointment on their own had to wait several weeks. In addition, the workloads of inspectors varied widely; some had few actual meetings. Today, appointments can only be booked through 311 and the Building Information System (BIS). Inspectors are randomly assigned, and their work can be tracked online. Average wait times for an appointment were reduced from 40 days to three to five days, and expediters have been virtually eliminated.

In another agency change, the Department of Transportation started changing its strategy. It now would fill potholes based on the data provided by 311 callers. Before, DOT would set a schedule to repave the city. If for some reason potholes appeared in an area scheduled for some other time, those potholes would stay unfilled for a month or more. After the change, even though DOT receive three times the volume of potholes reports than in the past, it managed to fill them within 18 days or less by planning routes more efficiently and reorganizing their resources.

Many departments tended to control how much work they got by limiting citizens' access through the internal resources made available for their customer service unit (e.g. the number of available phone lines). In general, a small group of citizens received high levels of service because they either figured out how to use the system or knew someone within government. According to one public servant, "311 was one way of decentralizing that power and pushing out accountability." Demand was made more transparent. In fact, Dean Schloyer, 311's executive director, thought that "overall [...] there's probably some latent demand [and] it's strangely distributed across different agencies and different types of service".

An analysis of the citizen call data revealed that noise was the number one complaint; the Bloomberg administration subsequently introduced legislation to overhaul the city's 30-year-old noise code in the summer of 2004 (Lueck 2007). Moreover, as citizens started using 311 to voice their opinions to the mayor, a service called "Opinion for the Mayor" was added to 311. Ideas are summarised and then sent to City Hall.

With an operating budget of $25 million, 311 itself was never about saving money. According to executive-level administrators, it served as a tool for improving customer service and was:

> [L]ike the trojan horse. [W]e wanted to come in and say [...] we want to provide an accountability tool, but we [couldn't] sell it that way. So we're going to sell it as a one-stop shop, a 24-hour live operator service [...]

4.3.3 Understanding of CiRM

A consultant with experience in various 311 projects pointed out that most municipalities and counties in the United States that engaged in 311 never thought of them as CRM projects. All they did was start using CRM software in their 311 call centers because it was recommended by consultants. Consequently, NYC's administrators pointed out that government CRM is in many ways different from the private sector. First, government is a bigger organization than any private corporation. Second, the quantity and complexity of the services it provides far exceed those found in the private sector. Said one administrator in New York:

> [T]here's a reason the government [CRM] is very different than the private sector on [CRM]. [O]ur clients, on the government side, you think about them as our "customers" [and] their requests. [I]t would be like if you took every company in the United States, or in the world [...] and you put them into [...] one call center. [E]veryone [would be] calling for computers, telephones, shirts, [...] or food. [T]hat's the only way to compare government, even on a local level, to the commercial world on the CRM basis. So you're actually turning it around, because you're not tracking your work force, which the commercial CRM primarily will help you do. You're mostly tracking service requests. [T]here's hundreds of them [...] [and] different agencies take care of different kinds.

Officials also thought CRM's goal of generating revenue by increasing the frequency of customer interactions and doing cross-selling was irrelevant to government. Although private-sector companies can measure the effects of their CRM efforts in the growth of total or individual customer revenue, that's not possible in government due to the existence of many intangibles and the lack of a goal to generate revenue. One official said:

> But if you're calling every day to send an inspector out to a building across the street from your house that really doesn't have a problem [and] we're not smart enough to know that and we keep going there, we're wasting resources. [W]e need to control that. Whereas, a private company wants to get you to come back, you know, the more times you're in front of them, the more opportunity they have to sell to you.

Along these lines, administrators pointed out that in government increased citizen demand drives up their costs. Since agencies are constrained by their budget, there is a limit to how much of their resources they can and are willing to invest in projects that increase their workload. One said:

> [W]hy would government care about giving good customer service? Because at one level [...] the forward-thinking people in government have an answer to that, and are embracing the private-sector mentality. But there's also an undercurrent of, "Once you provide good service, then that attracts more people to use your services which pushes your costs up." [However], you're typically operating in a budget-constrained world [...]. [M]ost government organizations are very cautious about hiring additional staff, even in periods where there's a surplus. [I]f you create an increased demand for services, it's very hard to respond to that because [...] government is typically not prepared to take on additional head count.

In fact, public officials had the impression that citizens generally prefer to reduce their government interactions to a minimum. Therefore, they didn't think that CRM is irrelevant in government. In fact, CRM would help public servants in achieving the former goal. One said:

> *People don't want to deal with government. They want to limit the number of interactions with government to as few as humanly possible. [I]n some cases, [there] are customers [with] repeat business [...] but for the most part, they don't want to deal with you. So, your job is to do two things. [I]t's to become as customer-friendly and as easy to deal with as possible, so that they can spend the least amount of time with you. [O]n the back end, you need to become as efficient as possible so that you can deal with their issues as quickly as possible and make them as happy as they can be for a customer that doesn't want anything to do with you. [...] [Y]ou have to figure out what systems do I have to have in place to do that, and what systems do I have to interface, and what systems do I have to get rid of.*

In addition, citizens' expectations about government roles and services are very difficult to meet. Any efforts to improve customer service tend to quickly raise their expectations to a level that is once again hard to meet. According to the executive director of NYC's 311:

> *[N]inety percent of the time, customer frustration with city government service delivery has a lot to do with the difference between expectations and the ability to deliver. [I]f I call because it's noisy in the middle of the night in Greenwich Village at 2:00 a.m. on Friday [...] I want the noise to stop right away. [But] there's a million bars there [...]. [T]here's a huge discrepancy in some of these cases between what the city is willing to do, what the city has the resources to do, and what the customer wants. [T]hat will always exist. [...] In fact, [...] the better job we do, the more likely we're going to run into people with unmet expectations. [T]he level of service expectation has [already] increased dramatically.*

He added that in many cases the information about the individual citizen is less important than the location and type of problem.

> *[W]hat we found at least in the beginning [...] and I stress that, because I think this is something that can and should change, was [that] the important part about 311 is not customer-based, it's geography-based. In city government, the problems that we have are focused on geography. So, it doesn't matter if I call ten times, if each of those ten calls were [about] different [things], so one was a pothole, [...], they're really not related problems. So the fact that I've built this history on you, it doesn't help me. I'm not cross-selling you anything. I am not using the fact that you had a pothole to treat you better on your noise complaint. To get started, it was important for us to realize that geography really was the most important part.*

Yet a consultant in New York City thought that:

> *[T]here's much more of an anonymous relationship between the customer and government. I think [...] the next phase of CRM [in the] public sector will be to kind of test that a little and see where the value of making that a personal customer relationship [might be] [...]*

All of the interviewed administrators and consultants voiced their concern about creating a citizen profile and customer segmentation. The only area where they made an exception was for social services. Here, CRM would allow government to get a better understanding of those in need in order to support them and prevent fraud. Comments in this regard included the following:

> *[There is] a much lower acceptance of the concept of customer segmentation in the public sector than there is in the private sector. [It] would be politically challenging to figure out a way*

to segment your customers as a means to serving them differently. And I'll say there are some customers that are really on the tail end of the distribution that we do segment—they're crazy. But for the most part, we try to treat our customers the same. [...] I could imagine a process by which you would segment customers not by who they were, but by what they were calling about [...]

[We] are not trying to track individual customer behaviour. The city's very cautious about that. [I]f you call up 311, and they said, 'Hello, Mr. [Doe], we see you called about three other things in the last year, I think they're afraid that people would be concerned that this big government thing going on— Big Brother's watching you [...]

However, only one administrator thought the opposite, and said:

[U]ltimately where you want to end up is providing the optimal service for a citizen. [I]f that means it's my first time calling about a problem; we want to be able to resolve that problem quickly. And over time, as you start to call back, we want to start to look for patterns. [I]f you called a second time because there was something related to the first time, maybe we need to get you to a counsellor that can help you so that you don't have to call back a third time. Whereas if you're calling about one type of problem and we know that the city offers something that's similar, [...] sort of like Amazon, people that read this book also like this book. [...]We want to be able to provide that level of customer relationship management. And that, that's where I think we start to really unleash the power of government and you turn it around to a point where people say I didn't want to come here before, and now, wow, look at this. I come to government, I ask about one thing, and I leave with three other programs.

Finally, when asked for a definition of CiRM, administrators either limited it to providing easy access to government and making sure that services get delivered or had a very broad understanding. One said:

I don't think CRM is one thing in itself. It's not a Siebel application. It's not a call center. It's a total integration of an organization's culture—the way [an organization] is structured, its IT, its people, its everything—if it is focused on satisfying the customer. [T]ools such as Siebel and the 311 call center are just tools which help satisfy the customer. But if you get these service requests and the culture of your organization is not adapted to a customer focus you'll be a disaster. [...]I tend to think of it more holistically. [...] It's not one thing, it's many.

4.4 CiRM in Miami-Dade County

4.4.1 Implementing CiRM

Miami-Dade's CiRM efforts were the result of a long-term strategic plan, the "Blueprint for Organizational Accountability" that was designed to "deliver excellence everyday". The plan was developed by an internal task force in 1999. The task force included today's County Manager George Burgess as well as Judi Zito, today's director of the Government Information Center. Until that time, the county never had developed a strategic plan. The team concluded that to improve communications and to be more responsive to the county's residents, all of the government's organizational entities needed to adopt a customer-driven, customer-satisfaction culture similar to Disney, Florida Power & Light or Baptist Hospital.

In addition, the strategic plan underlined that the success of the proposed changes largely depended on the county's employees. Consequently, a training program was set up to improve the attitude of 7,500 county front-line employees towards citizens by July 2004. In addition, the county's "consumer outreach" was to be improved through a countywide call center and further investments in the Web portal's transaction services and information provision capabilities. Citizens were to be enabled to do self-service through various channels (e.g. kiosks). The overhaul of the technological platforms and organizational culture were expected to create an effective government operation that would diminish the current lack of consumer confidence and the frustration citizens experienced. As part of the strategy, the communications department's role was strengthened to better coordinate the advertising and public relations efforts of the county. A promotional budget of $100,000 to $150,000 was suggested to implement educational campaigns four or five times a year about government programs and services. Moreover, the radio and cable TV programs were to be better utilized to broaden the audience (e.g. webcasting of cable TV programs). Finally, the implementation of the strategic plan was to be a shared responsibility of several departments in order to foster cross-boundary collaboration and knowledge exchange.

The plan was generally adopted by the Board of County Commissioners (BCC), but until 2002, the county focused on building its Web portal and training frontline staff. Executive administrators stated that rolling customer service practices and performance metrics "through the trenches of the organization" was not easy. In fact, organizational structures and culture still pose the biggest threat for organizational change. A senior administrator described it this way:

> [...] [The] ship is going in a certain direction [...]. To turn a ship around [is] very difficult. It takes a lot of time [...]. We're going in this direction and somebody tries to turn it but it keeps going like this. [E]ventually time passes [and] players change. [...] This organization and the whole county is set in [this] way. This is the way it is. You cannot change it. I'm seeing the same thing happening now with our new director. [E]ven though he came in [and said] we're going to do this [and that] now, [...] in another three or four months he's going to be one of us (laughs). A lot of times they don't stay there long enough to really effect change.

A department director added:

> I always say, "In your organization you got a little group that thinks for everybody." [...] The rest are just like leeches. [...] [T]hey don't think. They don't participate. They don't have any ideas. And they just go with the [expletive] flow.

Nevertheless, in 2003 Judi Zito, the newly appointed CIO, presented a detailed plan to change the county's service strategy. The new concept of service was built on the following major objectives but did not make any direct references to CRM:

- Utilize technology as a key element of service delivery (Internet, phone, TV).

- Deliver services seamlessly by eliminating internal silos/stovepipes, so that the public can easily obtain services without needing to possess knowledge of county organizational structure. This may result in consolidation of services.

- Monitor service quality and utilize this information to implement a continuous service improvement program.

- Promote a continuous learning strategy in order to achieve excellent service. Establish standards and best practices for customer service.

- Establish interlocal partnerships designed to promote a vision of seamless service to all customers.

- Implement an effective communications and marketing program.

- Establish 311 as the cornerstone for government service delivery.

- Focus on both internal and external aspects of customer service.

Among other things, the idea of the "Ambassadors Club" was proposed. From Judi Zito's point of view, the employees of the county could serve as ambassadors for the county in their private life with family, friends and neighbours. The club membership was supposed to include activities such as speaking at community forums, regular meetings on a variety of customer service topics to promote continuous learning and reporting issues (e.g. graffiti) within the community. Membership was only granted to those who had a proven track record of customer service excellence. Activities were rewarded with administrative leave. Although over 500 employees had shown interest in the club, it does not yet exist.

Within the strategy was a definition of the county's customers. The plan identified five customer relationships for the county:

> In a very real sense, everyone is our customer. Every resident, business, visitor, employee, agency... every single person or organization that has a potential interaction with Miami-Dade County. These are our stakeholders. Each stakeholder has a different perspective of the organization. Each group interacts differently with County government and has different expectations, as well as opinions about what constitutes good service, as well as excellent service. Some groups feel good service is provided when they are not required to interact with government whatsoever, in essence, when government remains faceless and anonymous to them. For example, a citizen paying a parking ticket would probably prefer to conduct this transaction without ever having to interact with County staff or travel to a County facility.[...] Alternatively, a young, single mother who needs help will want to speak to someone who is compassionate and has a genuine desire to assist her. This young mother is not likely to want to deal with automated systems that provide scripted solutions to her. She needs help from a County employee that is empowered with the tools and information to assist. Service delivery is generally targeted toward specific "affinity" groups, groupings of stakeholders that are best defined by their requirement for interacting with the government.

> Government to citizen—The term citizen is used loosely to refer to stakeholders that have local, community interest in government. This includes residents (full-time and seasonal), citizens, taxpayers, local media and community organizations [...]

> Government to business—Business refers to entities wishing to do business in Miami or entities seeking to do business specifically with County government as a service provider or supplier.

Government to employee—Employees represent the largest portion of the County's budget
and it is through their efforts that the County is ultimately able to provide public service. [...]

Government to visitor—Tourism is a large part of Miami-Dade's economy. Although tourism
is not a direct responsibility of County government, County services are available to tourists
who are visiting our area, particularly in the areas of transportation and public safety. Be-
cause our community is a significant tourist destination, customer service to visitors is of ut-
most importance to our economy.

Government to government—Service delivery by the government is complicated not only by
virtue of the traditional boundaries that exist within the organization, but also because there is
often an unclear line between services provided by the County and other governmental entities
([...]municipalities, the state, [...] federal government). (Zito 2003)

Miami-Dade County analysed prior 311 initiatives in Chicago, Houston, and New
York before engaging in its implementation process. IBM Business Consultancy Services and Winbourne & Costas, a consultancy specializing in 311, were picked to do a
feasibility study and recommendation for the county. The consultancies estimated the
annual 311 call volume for the county to be between 3 and 6.5 million calls. They also
recommended:

- Using a 311 number instead of a seven- to ten-digit number

- Building a multi-channel answer center

- Organisationally, the answer center should report to the highest possible level
  of the county's executive branch in order to facilitate inter-agency cooperation and sharing of resources

- Upgrading of the telephony infrastructure

- Implementing a CRM software solution

- Extensive training for the call takers

From the consultancies point of view, the biggest risks were associated with inaccurate, insufficient, or out-of-date information from agencies, lack of proper training for
answer center staff and regulatory and cost issues.

The county operated 11 contact centers at the time of the 311 initiative. The seven
largest call centers had a combined budget of approximately $25 million dollars.
Those operated by the clerk of courts, animal control and the tax collector departments
experienced abandoned call rates of up to 40% due to limited staff resources at peak
times or poor agent utilization rates. In addition, case management systems were either
nonexistent or outmoded. Citizens were often bounced around between departments,
put on hold or forced to navigate a maze of over 1,600 agency phone numbers by
themselves. Therefore, service levels varied significantly, and many citizens were frus-
trated. According to a resident survey conducted in 2003, 69% of the respondents felt
they knew only a little about county services, and overall quality of service satisfaction

was rated at 37%. Therefore, it was the hope of county leadership that 311 would have an effect on these resident issues.

However, administrative and political leadership expressed concerns about the effects on the budget and whether the 311 project should be prioritized over other programs in the face of limited funding. Some were not supportive of 24-hour operation and felt that extended operation (9:00 a.m.–9:00 p.m.) was more feasible. Furthermore, even though the Siebel application was seen as the best product on the market, the decision was made for Motorola CSR because there were reservations about the intrusiveness of the Siebel system because of its capability to build customer profiles.

Many vendors tended to force-fit their CRM software solutions to government with the rhetoric that government should be run like a business. Yet vendors also engaged in a learning relationship with their government clients, which is what Motorola did with Miami-Dade County.

In order to establish a consolidated "311 Answer Center", the county had to get ownership of the number. The number was already in use by the City of Miami's 311 call center, which had been funded by a grant from the Department of Justice's Community-Oriented Policing Services (COPS) program in 1999. In addition, the City of Miami had signed a contract with Bell South, a telecommunication provider, in 2000 to provide the 311 services at a surcharge of $0.12 per call tariff. In 2004, Miami-Dade County obtained use of 311 after negotiating an interlocal agreement (Appendix D). By that agreement, Miami-Dade County would now be responsible for operating—along with the Miami-Dade 311 system—the City of Miami's municipal services contact center and the city's 311 contact center, both of which already existed.

The initial start-up costs for the 311 answer center were funded through a Capital Asset Acquisition Bond 2004 A/B Series, which provided $16.2 million. Using a shared services model for both the county and City of Miami, approximately 92% of the funding (approximately $8 million) was derived from general funds, and 8% was derived from the Service Level Agreements established for Web portal services. The simultaneous implementation of five major departments revealed that the challenges of each department would require a more gradual approach to growing 311. Consequently, all departments were scheduled based on the cost of implementation, the technical complexity, the relative impact on the public and their expressed level of interest. It is the county's long-term goal to collaborate with all of its 35 towns and cities in a single 311, as opposed to what happened to 911. Some have already shown their interest. Even though the county provides the primary 911 services, five cities chose to operate their own 911 emergency centers. However, at the moment, the focus of the 311 project is only on integrating all county departments and services within three to six years.

After a soft launch between November 2004 and August 2005, the county's contact center went fully operational in September 2005—two days before Hurricane Rita made landfall. One of the key lessons of the analysis and soft launch of the county's 311 program was that focusing on internal communication to gain the buy-in and support from internal stakeholders is critical to the program's success.

The contact center currently operates from 6 a.m. to 10 p.m. during the week, and from 8 a.m. to 8 p.m. over the weekend. During emergency situations, the 119 operators usually switch to 24-hour operation. Each call taker handles an average of 102 calls in English, Spanish or Haitian-Creole per day; calls usually last between 50 seconds and 02:50 minutes. A continuously updated knowledge base covering over 7,000 topics supports call takers in their responding to information requests, which make up 83% of the total annual call volume of 1.6 million (Figure 4-5). In addition, call takers are mainly working with the Motorola CSR application and also with the county's online portal, which acts as a secondary knowledge base. The scripts that guide call takers through the varied types of calls they encounter are continuously reviewed and updated by members of the 311 organization. Duplicate information intake and thus over response is prevented through the software. Information and service requests are connected to a Geographic Information System (GIS) or to other agency-specific applications. Yet service requests make up only 10% of calls, while 7% of calls need to be transferred to other entities, such as municipal, county or state agencies. According to an internal survey, the largest number of people who know about 311 and take advantage of it are welfare recipients and Hispanics aged 50 and older living on a fixed income. Projections about the effects on the 311 call volume of consolidating more

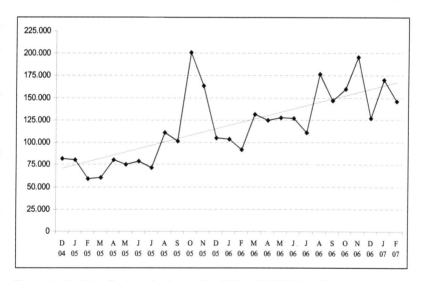

Figure 4-5: Monthly call volume development Dec 2004 to Feb 2007 (total/ linear average trend)

government entities are not viewed with great confidence. As one administrators noted, "311 seems to generate demand and phone calls."

One county outreach initiative that was taken over by the 311 contact center was the "Telephone Reassurance Program". Call takers and supervisors call participating senior citizens every other day to determine their well-being. One of the participants who lives alone and has no family said that this program "gives me peace of mind". In case of an emergency, the 311 team will call individuals listed on an emergency contact information form for the participating citizen.

In the general operation of the call center, call takers try to follow up with citizens whose requests couldn't be answered immediately. One customer service representative (CSR) noted that getting a return call from the contact center frequently astonishes citizens who are still under the impression that "call takers are just sweeping it under the rug" and that "no one's going to call me back on this". In fact, call takers may build a one-to-one relationship with citizens on certain issues. For example, one call taker mentioned the story of a young lady who lost her dog. After she spent over 15 minutes explaining the situation, he said to her, "Hey, if you need someone to talk to, give me a call." A few days later she called back to tell the call taker that she successfully found her dog. From the point of view of the call taker, this was "one of those rare instances where I prefer someone to call me directly [...] so we can solve the issue without having them have to go back into the system from the beginning".

In order to manage the cross-departmental collaboration, implement service improvements and analyse citizen data, the 311 program managers created a Customer Service Advocacy (CSA) unit. CSA unit members are responsible for the performance of a certain number of departments. CSAs provide department executive-level staff members with a monthly report based on 311 and agency data. At the moment, 311 only provides information on service requests and call volume. Although it would be of interest to CSAs and other administrators, there is no ability to analyse information topics, such as how many people asked about a certain issue. The CSA reports are given to the department director, budget analyst and the assistant county manager. CSAs also coordinate between 311 and the departments for which they are responsible in order to improve the citizen experience.

A Web-enabled reporting system ("ServiceStat"), which was part of the 2003 strategic plan, was implemented in 2006. ServiceStat combines performance data (e.g. open/closed service requests), GIS mapping and 311 call information, and is available for decision makers within departments and elected officials (Figure 4-6). In the future, this information will be made available to the public. In order to prevent short-term management interference, however, data for elected officials is delayed by two weeks.

Miami-Dade County was the founding member of the Florida 311 Coalition and also lobbied for state legislation to create a 311 grant program (www.florida311.org). However, the bill (HB 661 Governmental Service Telephone System) was vetoed by the Governor. The 311 Coalition was established in 2004 to facilitate coordination and collaboration among state, county and municipal governments in developing 311 systems. According to one administrator, the meetings indicated that:

> [...] counties and cities that had not done 311 [were] [...] afraid of opening the flood gates because [they] did not know if [they] could deal with it. If they turn it on, they can't turn it off. They can't take it away, and you are compared to others. It's a bold move, and you have to be able to meet the expectations, if not exceed them. It's a big commitment.

Before focusing on a multi-jurisdictional customer contact center in 2002, the county had launched its new Web portal in 2001. The Web portal offers over 20,000 pages and 30,000 PDF documents as well as some transaction-type services. Administrators were able to transfer many valuable lessons from Miami-Dade's portal project to the 311 implementation. Judi Zito remembered that "Internet to the phone was like the same thing over again". Departments were reluctant to adapt their intake processes to the new channel. Moreover, citizens' channel preferences depended largely on the target group and the type of service. The building industry wanted to do as much online as possible, whereas older people preferred the phone or direct contact in a service center. However, from a cost perspective the county would benefit the most if as many citizens as possible used online services. Judi Zito noted:

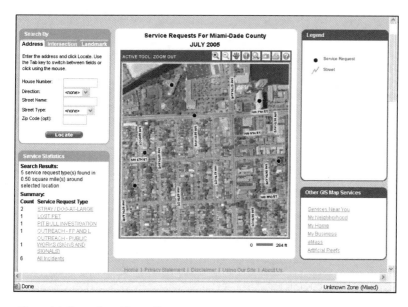

Figure 4-6: Screenshot of ServiceStat

111

> *To the extent that I can drive business away from 311 to the portal, from a cost per perspective, it is a much better scenario. But there will be certain parts of the population that will [never go there]. You can give a computer to a certain population and they will never turn them on. Some people are caught in their own "digital divide" because they have a computer but just don't want to use it.*

Hence, the county is offering over 1,200 computers and free wireless Internet access in public libraries to anyone. Team Metro, a Miami-Dade County department, also provides many services (e.g. passports, various permits, code compliance) through 15 physical over-the-counter, one-stop shops and a mobile "Government on the Go" bus unit. Its contact center was reachable through a ten-digit number for a number of years before it redirected its calls to 311 in 2005. In addition, Team Metro offers a 13-week citizens' academy program several times a year that provides citizens with information, resources and tools needed to become knowledgeable community members. The county also tried to find citizens who were willing to participate in a secret shopper program to test county services but had to outsource the task to a company after they could not find enough participants. A similar response led the county to run its Web portal usability program with county employees instead of citizens.

Further government information is provided through Miami-Dade TV. On the state level, Florida recently instituted the Open Government initiative, which provides the public, as well as state and local officials, with information on legislative processes, the state budget and details on Florida's public record laws. Citizens may also request a translation of a state government document either online or by fax.

Since May of 2006, Customer Service Advocacy (CSA) functions have been centralized in the Government Information Center (GIC). The GIC coordinates the customer service strategy and multi-channel environments such as the Web portal, 311, kiosks and physical locations, and incorporates analytical services (e.g. Customer Experience Valuation [CEV]) through its reporting unit. It is of special importance to Judi Zito, the director of the GIC, to improve the "Third Portal" in the future—that is, to improve the in-person service experience. In her view, ensuring a high and consistent level of customer service along with capturing the data of those that neither use the phone nor the computer to interact with government may provide valuable information for policy making and management.

4.4.2 Impact of CiRM

Animal Services was one of the first departments to join 311. Its operations and accessibility were influenced by the collaboration with 311. The monthly reports from the CSAs and their close collaboration with executive leadership helped the Animal Services Department to better understand citizen demand (2,500 calls a day instead of 500 calls) and the internal changes needed to meet that demand. Complaints and request intake times expanded along with the operating hours of the 311 contact center. In addition, field officers were equipped with mobile devices that allowed them to respond to service requests in close to real time. Public servants are held more accountable, because callers to 311 can always request to talk to the responsible county employee and hear about the status of their service request ticket. Other departments reported reduced calls on general issues such as operating hours. However, as 311 started providing citizens with more information instead of forwarding the calls to the responsible agency, some agency employees showed negativity towards the 311 call takers. They felt that the call takers were not qualified enough to provide the correct information.

George Burgess, the county manager, realized that the true value of 311 was the data. From his point of view, it helped them better understand what is important to different geographic areas. A senior official from the City of Miami went further and said 311 would cause significant changes in the future. Yet a department director admitted that the overall customer service initiative did not always have an effect on the time it took to react to a citizen's request. However, the evaluation of the accumulated data over time allowed them to better allocate the available resources. She said, "If [service requests are] clustered, then maybe we say look, I can get rid of four hundred of these six hundred by just doing two drainage structures." Along these lines, a number of executives were hoping that the data and internal process changes would allow them to do more with the same or even a smaller budget. In addition, the data on citizen demand made it easier for departments to go to elected officials and ask for an increase in their budget and weigh that against the county's strategic priorities. The budget office disagreed with this notion and stressed that most agencies were already properly budgeted for 95% of their service requests.

Elected officials were also astonished by the data created through 311. They identified issues that their constituents had never raised at their district office. One elected official realized that it was stray dogs and not potholes that were the biggest problem in his district. Citizens, however, still tended to follow up on 311 service requests with their commissioner to make sure they received their service. Some administrators identified elected officials as the main beneficiaries of the customer service imitative because they can take credit for a smoothly running public administration. Moreover, the performance data in ServiceStat creates a greater transparency of departments for elected officials, which has historically never been there. However, in order to prevent short-term management and make departments more comfortable, the data that is visible to elected officials is delayed by two weeks. Finally, an executive administrator thought that if commissioners have to deal less with citizens and poor service at the local level, they could strengthen their strategic and policy defining role. An elected official favoured this trend and said:

> *I don't think [...] that I'm going to lose touch with my constituents, because we're going to go to an administrative model. [In fact] we'll be kind of an audit on the system, because if something goes wrong and they're not getting their needs addressed through 311, you can be sure they're going to call their county commissioner and complain. [...] I'd love to get away from being [viewed by the citizen as being] 'the system', though, and have the administration do it. [...] I had some home chemicals that I wanted to dispose of properly, so I called the Solid Waste Department, and I didn't tell them I was a commissioner. I just called to see what the citizens [experience]. I said, where's the nearest disposal site? [T]hey said it's way on the north side somewhere, and I said, there should be one farther south. And they said, you should really contact your county commissioner about that. (Laughs) [My] thought was [that it was]*

their job to contact their boss and say look, we're getting demands from our constituents saying that they want something closer to their home. [T]hey could always contact their county commissioner, but I don't think administration ought to be telling people to contact their county commissioner. I think they ought to be trying to work it out.

What is more, the county's 311 initiative was able to provide decision makers, including FEMA representatives, with real-time situation reports based on input from citizens and county employees acting as "eyes-and-ears on the ground" during and after Hurricane Wilma in 2005 (Schellong/Langenberg 2007). Accordingly, help efforts and supply points were organized based on recognizable patterns and hotspots.

As part of their plan to improve services, an external market research firm administered a multi-language resident survey for the county in the fall of 2005. For comparison, the survey included questions from the 2003 survey. Resident satisfaction with the overall quality of county services increased from 37% in 2003 to 51% in 2005 (very satisfied and satisfied on a 5 point Likert scale). The satisfaction with the overall quality of customer service of county employees was rated at 41% while 33% remained neutral. However, compared to 2003 fewer people felt that county employees went the "extra mile" (33% in 2004 compared to 28% in 2005) or that it was easy to find someone to address their concerns (46% in 2003 compared to 44% in 2005). Residents prioritized the latter as the most important issue county government needed to improve.

Somewhat contradictory to the above data, more Miami-Dade residents stated that the county achieved its organizational goal to continuously improve its services (24% in 2003 compared to 35% in 2005. There were, however, no changes in the ratings for the organizational goal of delivering excellent public services.

Residents showed no clear opinion about whether the county's communication measures with them were effective. The county's availability of information on programs and services received a similar rating (46% neutral), although 30% were dissatisfied. Most residents (55%) that were looking for this kind of information indicated that they get it from TV (49%), the Miami *Herald* (44%) or the county's Web portal, which received a satisfaction rating of 61%. Only 7% of county residents tried to get information by calling the 311 Answer Center or another government office. Of the 54% of residents that had contact by phone or in-person contact with any Miami-Dade County Department within the last 12 months, 17% said that they contacted the 311 Answer Center. Fifty-eight percent of residents stated that they had heard of Team Metro, the department that offers many of the county's services.

4.4.3 Understanding of CiRM

Many executive-level administrators in Miami-Dade County, whether career bureaucrats or with a working history in the private sector, had embraced the customer-oriented culture. They referred to the citizen as their customer who needed to be treated with respect and in an honest way. The county manager felt the quality of how the county employees interact with citizens when they first encounter government is key to "selling government" in a way so that they feel good about government, themselves and their community. Becky-Jo Glover, the county's 311 director, also viewed the cities and departments she and her 311 team serves as customers. From her point of view, the public sector should drive how customer relationships can be managed, and good service can be provided at the lowest cost possible so that one day government can be recognized as a leader in customer service. Government will always have the obligation to serve its citizens, unlike the private sector which is only willing to invest in customer service as long as there is profit involved. However, government struggles with a negative image. A department director compared it to a "totem pole, a little better than a used car salesman".

Even though they agree that there are still a lot of things that should be done, many Miami-Dade administrators and elected officials noted that there is a limit to citizen-orientation. As service levels increase, so do citizens' expectations, which are then harder to meet. Furthermore, budget resources and citizens' willingness to provide these resources through taxes act as a barrier. As one county executive stated:

> [T]he expectation of government has gotten so low that when something positive happens they are taken aback by it. You know that won't last for long. [...] You passed our honeymoon period and essentially all these great things that you did are fueling the demand for more great things.

While one administrator thought that CRM and bureaucracy would be characterised by antagonism, most administrators approved of CRM in general. However, they identified differences in applying CRM. They felt that government services and processes are much more diverse and complex than those functions of private corporations, such as banks. Moreover, private and public entities both have mechanisms to get feedback from consumers, but government's responsibility today requires the willingness to change policies based on citizen feedback. That is, companies have no obligation to react to feedback from customers—governments, however, do. Furthermore, the location of a citizen's issue is most often more important than information about the citizen. A senior administrator explained:

> [...] we are not entirely, but we are more, event- and geography-focused than the private sector. [...] It does not matter to me who called to report the pothole but that I got the pothole fixed. And so we are more sort of incident-event-location-oriented, I think, as opposed to customer account-oriented. [...] Not that we are not concerned with the customer, because that same customer may have called 5 times and that is important, too, but the priority is to get the pothole fixed.

However, government can still add value to interactions with citizens by providing more individualized event- or geographic-specific information. Another administrator said:

> [...] There [are] two concepts [of outreach]. One is pure outreach; the second concept is added value. [W]hile there's added value in a sale in private industry, the added value's a little different in [government]. [Y]ou may call to find out if there's a teacher work day and there's no school on Friday and I might say to you as the call taker [...]: Barnes Park has camp for your kids, and if you want to take advantage and work out in the yard, we're having an Adopt a Tree function over in South Miami. Go and pick up a free tree. So you've added

value to the citizen, you've promoted county government services. [...] So you're adding value without selling something and that's an important concept [...] in government. [T]he second thing is outreach. [T]hat is when we actually use technology. [W]e use it today when there's a sexual predator living within five miles of your home. We call everybody and we [inform them about the] sexual predator. [...] Or, we're having a town meeting for one of the commissioners and we'd like the citizens in that commission district to attend. We haven't really implemented the phone technology to automatically do that, but that's something that's been discussed and it was part of the original vision. So I think in the future we'll get there, but we're not there. [...]

Only a few administrators were familiar with the term CiRM. None of the elected officials had ever heard it before. Therefore, definitions followed either a narrow or very broad understanding. Narrower definitions limited it to service intake through various channels and ensuring service delivery. Judi Zito had a very broad understanding:

Citizen Relationship Management is much bigger than 311 and much bigger than the portal. It's many things brought together that will really help us understand what the public really wants; what they need and how we can make it simple for them to access [government] in a way that is seamless. And really more than that: being able to anticipate what their needs are and having a program in place that will satisfy those needs. It's surveys, it's focus groups; it's customer service standards that we can apply across the organization not just simply in our call center but across the organization so that we really manage the relationship with the resident from beginning to end.

The county manager's definition followed a broad understanding with a special emphasis on CiRM as a philosophy for government's organizational culture:

[CiRM] is basically [...] responding to the concerns of the citizens [...]. [G]overnment is no longer out here. Government is inside [and] part of this community. [G]overnment has the task or the responsibility to respond to the concerns of the citizens. [...] It's a way of using the methods and means that we have today. [T]echnology, ethics, [...] accountability and all these things that are now available [...] in order for the citizen to be able to understand how government functions. Because [...] there is no confidence in government. [G]overnment has to show that government exists; it's here to help you. It's here to make the society better. [...] [311] is customer service; it addresses perceptions people have of government. [I]t reduces emergency call volumes and it's a great disaster management tool. [I]t's also just a strategic management tool you can use to either get information out or get information in. To me, everybody in the organization has to understand that they have a pivotal role in influencing how our customers perceive the larger organization. If I mow a lawn in Parks, I'm an ambassador for the government. If I receive tax bills over the counter downtown, I'm an ambassador for the government. If I'm one of [the] call takers, I clearly am [an ambassador]. So we talk about CRM, it's only as successful as your ability to impress upon every single one of your employees that they're a pivotal part of keeping you in business. [G]overnment will always be here, but I think we should be thinking like a business that has to succeed in keeping its customers happy for it to survive [...].[The customer is] a small piece that's critically important to the big organization's success. That [big] corporation views the experience of the customer as a hugely important thing. They provide things based on what they know their customers like and want. They want them to come back, of course, that's the business they're in. They want their customers to be happy. If they succeed; they make money. Are they in the business to make people happy? [S]ure they are. They're also in the business to make money. And they're

going to be successful making money if they're pleasing their customers. So this CRM, it's all they do. I mean, it's not something you do in an office somewhere. It's not something that's limited to 311. It's something that we have to somehow inject into the thinking of every single person who has a role in this organization.

One official felt that CiRM and eGovernment were the same:

It's all about service [and] just getting that service done. It doesn't matter who does it. [I]t's much like our portal. [...] It's all about the way that the citizens communicate with government. [...] That whole eGovernment concept, it's one and the same.

Yet there was only one critical remark regarding the implications on the civic aspect of a broader understanding of CiRM:

[...] If you want [CiRM] to be true [...] then you need to account for the whole political and civic aspect. [...] How people react to [legislation] and how they can impact change.[...] I wouldn't be very excited at the prospect of someone calling in [for] a service and discovering that there's legislation that impacts them in some kind of adverse way, that requires them to pay fees or fines. [CiRM is about] using this whole service incident as an opportunity to change this legislation. [...] CRM is the junction where you're going to decide how you're going to repurpose, you know, a regular operational interaction into some kind of policy in legislation production mechanism.

The county commissioners thought that CiRM was a core aspect of their role in government. Every time they interacted with their constituents and tried to respond to their issues they had to manage that relationship. As such, one elected official stated that CiRM is government driven by the citizen, because many complaints end up being dealt with by policies. Another commissioner focused on the philosophical values in the CiRM definition:

[CiRM] is kind of like marriage relationship management. It's courtesy, mutual respect and trying to find common ground. If there's a problem, it's negotiation. [...] I think if you apply good principles [such as] open communication, honesty and being ethical, it's telling people what your limitations are if you have them, rather than trying to bluff your way through it [...].

In contrast, the following elected official's definition of CiRM was similar to those of administrators who had a broader understanding:

[It]'s a multitude of systems whereby citizens can [...] petition their government to take care of their needs. [It's] providing government with an opportunity to create accountability to get those particular needs taken care of and resolved. [...] In addition [...] taking that feedback that we get and beginning to get a better understanding of the psyche, and the needs and the issues. And in that case, becoming proactive and resolving problems before they become a problem in the minds of the citizens [...].

5 Citizen Relationship Management

This chapter presents a discussion of the findings and contributions of the study. It begins with the search for the novel contributions of CRM to currently active reform movements. Subsequently I summarise and discuss the results of the cross-case analysis on the implementation, impact and understanding of CiRM before answering the question of whether there is a difference between private- and public-sector CRM. Consequently, I present a general model of CiRM.

5.1 Old wine in new bottles? Comparing CRM with TQM and eGovernment

Does CRM simply redefine and consolidate principles and techniques that have been studied and applied by public managers and scholars since the 1980s?

CRM and TQM are both understood as holistic management concepts and philosophies developed in the private sector as an answer to the forces such as globalization and new technologies that affect competition, consumer behaviour and other factors. Essentially, they rest on the idea that a high level of customer satisfaction and quality business information, knowledge and communication result in a competitive advantage in the market. Being market-driven means anticipating and responding to customer needs and pre-empting competitors to produce an increase in market share and/or reduce the elasticity of demand (Reed/Lemak/Montgomery 1996). Therefore, CRM and TQM do not include any particular reference to the distinctive environment found in government.

Government enactment of management concepts and technology are mediated by a number of factors, including budget scarcity, institutional arrangements, cultural norms, existing laws and regulations, policy considerations and political behaviour. However, scholars should be careful about interpreting any underlying attempt to change government into TQM and CRM. Unlike NPM, neither CRM nor TQM constitute an ideology to unilaterally impose business values, objectives and practices on government. They do not offer any normative views on governance or how to reshape the formal and informal connections between government and society. Yet both management concepts suit NPM's goals of customer satisfaction and improving government performance. In addition, generic management problems such as customer service can be addressed with due regard to their context. Of course, once enacted in government, TQM and CRM lose their neutrality because they are not without impact on governance. This effect should be analysed and discussed.

While CRM and TQM share the same goals, the means to achieve those goals rest on different premises. TQM's focus is on quality, defined as 100% customer satisfaction and zero defects. CRM's focus is on individual customer satisfaction and managing the customer relationship. The literature shows that core elements of TQM have a stronger emphasis on the internal aspects of an organisation, while the elements of CRM have a stronger emphasis on the external focus on customers. Central elements of TQM include management commitment and leadership, statistical process control and fact-based management, development of a quality culture, and removal of barriers to employee participation, continuous improvement of processes and employees capabilities. Therefore, TQM is geared towards affecting quality by working on internal processes and the interpersonal level. Central elements of CRM focus on managing customer interaction, analysing customers, creating a customer-centric organisation, developing a customer-oriented culture and utilizing technology for these management functions. Therefore, CRM is geared toward affecting customer relationships by actively managing them, working on internal processes and using technology.

Nevertheless, both management concepts share the general philosophy of the internal and external customer. CRM and TQM initiatives are always supposed to begin with a thorough analysis of customers and the organisation. A tenet of this logic is that the customer is a co-creator of value (Mele 2007). In TQM, the centrality of developing relationships with customers emerges (Norman/Ramirez 1993). Yet only CRM gives a detailed account of how these relationships can be developed and managed. In addition, in CRM customers are understood as individual entities instead of a mass that require customer-specific actions. Continuously changing customer needs oblige the organisation to engage in a learning relationship with the customer. Therefore, a firm has to have the capability to collect information, share that information and act upon the analysis of the information. In CRM this is frequently achieved through technology, but it is also accomplished through cross-boundary collaboration. Correspondingly, TQM's continuous improvement (Kaizen in Japanese) is facilitated through cross-functional teamwork, experimentation and statistical methods (Spencer 1994), because TQM advocates believe that most quality improvement opportunities lie not within the natural work group but outside it, that is, across departments.

In order to become a quality- or customer-driven organisation, the infrastructures and the cultures of organisations have to change. The act of changing roles, processes, coordination, collaboration and employee requirements results in resistance. Not surprisingly, TQM and CRM projects share the same reported failure rates of up to 70%. While both management concepts underline the importance of leadership, the CRM literature generally offers little guidance on how a firm can make the organisational transition. It mentions change management, training and communication but remains focused on the aspects of managing customer relationships. In contrast, TQM offers a detailed account of how organisational culture can be reoriented to a commitment to quality. TQM describes practices such as quality circles, self-managed teams and policies that encourage open, two-way, non-punitive communication.

Data collection and performance measurement are also fundamental building blocks of TQM and CRM. Performance measurement allows identifying and tracking progress against organisational goals, identifying opportunities for improvement and conducting benchmarking against internal and external standards. Ishikawa (1982) stressed that the ultimate purpose of data (e.g. from customer surveys, processing time, defects) in TQM is to take action based on the data. That is why employees at all levels should be trained in statistical quality-control tools and thinking concepts (Appendix C). For a CRM strategy, clear measures and standards must also be established at all levels: individual, work unit, development cycles. As such, there is no significant divergence from TQM.

Yet there are also aspects unique to CRM. These include building customer profiles, segmenting customers, calculating the customer value, and managing and offering products and services through a variety of channels in a consistent way. The evolution of ICT largely made most of these activities possible. However, building, maintaining, mining and managing comprehensive customer databases across an organisation create new issues. For example, customers are frequently uncomfortable about a perceived loss of privacy and the proactive interaction attempts of firms.

An overview (Rahman 2004) of various attempts to capture important factors of TQM lack the element of ICT. This is an additional fundamental difference from CRM and eGovernment that I will address shortly. However, it should be noted that many of TQM's elements, such as the process-oriented view of the organisation, boundary spanning teamwork or data analysis, could be facilitated by modern ICT (Au/Choi 1999).

eGovernment is in its essence about the use of ICT in government. eGovernment proponents derive their visions and concepts from the characteristics of ICT, especially the Internet. For instance, ICT allows the structuring of information processing, coordination, control and flows without the common boundaries of roles, organisational relationships and operating procedures. It also alters the relationship between information and the physical factors of organisational size, distance, time and costs.

The scope of eGovernment usually depends on the area of its application. On the one hand, filing taxes online offers citizens convenient ways of taking care of their civic duty while simultaneous automatic error checking simplifies the tax processing for government. On the other hand, ICT allows authoritarian nations to exert greater control over their citizens. Therefore, ICT is obviously part of realizing a government's mission, but only as a means to achieve the intended philosophic purpose of that government. Many eGovernment programs share the rhetoric of customer orientation and efficiency, in that way resembling the philosophy of CRM and TQM. Many authors also point to providing public services through multiple channels. The one-stop idea re-emerges in the form of Web portals and structuring digital information on the basis of major or minor life events. However, eGovernment—at least in its current form—cannot be compared with the clear boundaries and scope of management concepts found in TQM and NPM. In fact, I think eGovernment is not a management concept. It's more of a collection of practices and ideas involving ICT that are applied to government.

Governments that began implementing TQM programs already utilized ICT. Yet ICT served mostly as an important backbone of agency operations before the emergence of eGovernment. Office automation processes were extensively adapted to pre-existing organisational culture and structures. The rise of the Internet changed this and introduced new perspectives on arranging the link between government and civil society. Along these lines, Dunleavy et al. (2005) think that the digitization of government and governance (called digital-era governance) would "directly reverse changes and many others which are at a tangent to NPM priorities and orientations". Further, they identify a needs-based holism as one of the key themes of the new era, which is "a thoroughgoing attempt to prioritize away from the NPM stress on business process management and toward a genuinely citizen-based, services-based or needs-based foundation of the organization". Components of the needs-based holism activities are one-stop shops (digital and non-digital), data warehousing to develop a more holistic view of citizens' needs or self-service and co-production activities. I was surprised that Dunleavy et al. (2005) don't mention TQM or CRM and that they stress the uniqueness of the current period, because as my review of TQM has shown, their outlined trend does not reverse changes made by NPM. Instead, agencies are finally enacting ideas that were always there but never thoroughly realized. Furthermore, Dunleavy et al. (2005) outline ideas that are common to CRM, so that there seems to be a match between a variety of its concepts and government.

Based on this review, I conclude that CRM is, indeed, to a certain extent "old wine in new bottles". Nevertheless, CRM offers a well-developed set of ideas and practices on how to realize a customer-centric vision for an organisation. CRM also offers a new rhetoric of "customer relationship" to accomplish the underlying organisational change. In TQM, this is quality, and in eGovernment it is technology. Table 5-1 summarises the principles and practices of CRM, TQM and eGovernment.

	CRM	TQM	eGovernment
Principles and Components			
Goal	Customer value Customer relationship	Quality Customer satisfaction	Transformation of government
Rationale	Organisational survival Competitive advantage	Organisational survival Competitive advantage	Capabilities of technology and externalities such as the information society
Drivers	Information Knowledge	Information Knowledge	Information Knowledge
Customer	Internal External	Internal External	
Customer Relationship	Co-producer Actively managed 1-to-1	Co-producer	Multiple roles
Theoretical Background	Marketing Relationship Marketing	Systems Theory	
Organisational Structure	"Holistic" Cross-boundary Flexible, less hierarchical	Total Cross-boundary, Flexible, less hierarchical, Empowerment	Cross-boundary Networked
Technology	Facilitator		Core
Culture	Customer centric	Quality and customer orientation	
Change	Change and learning are a continuous process because customer needs are not static	Change and learning valued because they result in improving quality	
Tools	Performance measurement and management Data mining, Customer Profile, CLV	Performance measurement and management Statistics, Quality circles	ICT, Information architecture

Table 5-1: Comparing CRM with TQM and eGovernment

5.2 Implementing CiRM

Taken together, the cases reveal how 311 contact centers were implemented, but they also show that 311 or any other activity undertaken to improve citizen-orientation was not considered CRM (Table 2-1). Citizens were offered a variety of channels to interact with government before 311—agency offices, call centers and the Internet. However, the channels and service practices depended on a department director's decision and not a broader strategy. Customer service practices basically followed the jurisdictional and organisational boundaries. Service levels varied significantly.

At first, 311 was implemented as a way to reduce the 911 call burden of non-emergency calls and "freeing up officer time to engage in problem-oriented policing activities" (Mazerolle et al. 2003). Combined with organisational reform, 311 was seen as a way to facilitate community policing—at most.

While the motivation to start 311 differed, initiatives were all put on the agenda by political or administrative leadership. In Baltimore, the mayor expanded the role of 311 mainly to support his performance management program, CitiStat. In Chicago and New York, the projects were supported by the mayor to provide easy access to government information and relieve 911. Finally, in Miami-Dade County, the 311 initiative was pushed by a set of powerful commissioners and the county manager; it was the county manager who had originally envisioned the idea of the 311 Answer Center as a multi-jurisdictional, multi-channel access point for all government services in concert with other county executives during his tenure as assistant county manager.

Interestingly, many elected officials (commissioners, aldermen, and council members) were sceptical or even opposed to the projects in the beginning. Given that 311 implementations were capital-budget projects, the elected officials were concerned about the costs and about prioritising them against spending in areas such as education. There was also an underlying and deeper concern about losing contact with constituents.

In general, 311—as well as its functions—was not the result of citizen demand or voter proposition. It seems instead that 311 came from inside public administration. It is especially attractive to administrative and political leadership and allows for visible political results. This is most certainly true for the 70 U.S. implementations of 311 in the last 11 years. The adoption of 311—most have been implemented within the last three years by most of the big cities in the United States—follows the pattern (S-Shape) that Rogers (1983) described in his diffusion of innovation theory. In particular, New York's 311 received a lot of positive media coverage even though some criticized it for being "a mile wide and an inch deep". Mass media have been identified as core sources of information by diffusion research (Strang/Soule 1998) besides word-of-mouth information or best-practice stories. Furthermore, 311 must be compatible with existing routines, values and needs in municipal and county government. If it had not been (in the cases presented here), it would have slowed down the diffusion process. However, it should also be noted that the utilization of 311 differs significantly in the cases. By utilization I mean the degree of how 311 is used for non-emergency non-policing matters.

Along the lines of my preceding argument, not all of the administrators and elected officials began their initiatives with an analysis of citizen satisfaction, citizen needs and the status quo of their organisation. However, this has been identified as an important element of CRM in the literature. In addition, except for Miami-Dade County—at least to my knowledge—no holistic strategy to improve the citizen–government relationship was developed in the cases studied. It appears as though most 311 projects were very concentrated efforts to consolidate a government's call centers and centralize the phone channel for non-emergency issues of citizens. For instance, for Mayor Bloomberg, 311 was a critical political project of his first term in City Hall. Further citizen-oriented practices were being employed or tested in all of the cases studied but without an identifiable grand schema. Finally, governments around the United States were openly sharing their knowledge on the solutions and challenges of CiRM, which contrasts starkly with the proprietary nature of CRM projects in the private sector. For example, Chicago was offering advice to Miami-Dade County, Baltimore and New York, and Miami-Dade was sharing its knowledge with other counties in Florida.

Implementation of CRM also requires an organisational culture that allows change (Curry/Kkolou 2004). Successful change requires a shared vision and communication to all, but it also requires a sustainable commitment. In the three cities studied, there were very strong and charismatic mayors and some innovation-oriented department directors. Bloomberg also articulated his overall goals and specific plan for 311 at a press conference and in his State of the City Address. This exposed New York's administration and the DoITT project team in particular to the pressures of external accountability. Furthermore, regular meetings, a clear escalation path to the mayor and the involvement of Emma Bloomberg, the mayor's daughter, served as tools to secure departmental compliance.

A major undertaking of 311 was the creation of a contact center or a non-emergency call service unit. All 311 contact center implementations took approximately a year and included a soft-launch phase. However, the integration of departments remains an ongoing process that will take many years. Except in New York and Miami-Dade County, administrators did not specifically look for CRM software for their 311 operations. When Chicago began its 311 project there were simply no government-specific CRM products available on the market. By closely collaborating with the SunTrack software developer Suncoast Scientific Inc. (now Motorola) and testing the system, the city basically had a great influence stake in what Motorola CSR is today. The fact that the 311 projects studied were branded as government CRM mostly originates from the involvement and marketing activities of consultancies and software vendors. Of course, there were other ICT solutions implemented besides CRM software, which covered case management, service request management or contact management. A knowledge base, legacy applications and GIS functionality were also common features of the 311 contact centers studied. Technology (e.g. Motorola CSR, Siebel) was used to close the organisational loop between service intake, service delivery and service status tracking. Traditionally, data on citizen interaction was hidden in the departmental silos, which made transparency and identifying cross-boundary issues difficult. However, the organisational loop was only closed in terms of some service requests. Citizen data specific to an agency's operation or that was collected through other channels, especially face-to-face interactions, was not shared or collected in a data mart. Another central difference from commercial CRM systems is the type of data that was collected by government. Citizens stay anonymous most of the time; however, data on the citizen's issue and location as well as the administrator's actions are tracked and kept. In short, these steps can be classified as operational and collaborative CRM.

The tasks of 311 contact centers can be differentiated into service and non-service activities (Table 5-2). The main operations of the 311 contact centers consist of citizen-initiated interactions for directory assistance, information requests, service requests and investigation of complex citizen issues. Government-initiated interactions can be outbound information provision or customer surveys. Operating hours of the 311 contact centers are extensions of government office operating hours and are provided up to 24/7/365. While some of the 311 contact centers have the capability to process multi-channel requests, the majority of them are only managing the incoming call traffic. Interestingly, government's focus on 311 contact centers as a CiRM activity follows the path CRM once took in the private sector. In the early 1990s, private corporations began embracing CRM—first and foremost—in call centers before they introduced it elsewhere in the organisation.

Moreover, the cross-case analysis showed that public administrations were providing more personalized services in specific areas of government. In addition, customer service representatives tried to adapt to the situation and to the behaviour of each of

	Inbound Communications Citizen-initiated	Outbound Communications Government-initiated
Service Activities	Service request	Information provision (SR follow-up) Elderly reassurance
Non-Service Activities	Service status Complaint and comment handling Information provision Referrals	Citizen survey

Table 5-2: The 311 citizen contact matrix

their callers. It also is now very common to have bundled (one-stop) service offerings for target groups like the building industry (Miami-Dade) or welfare recipients (NYC) on the Web portal. Agencies such as the Housing Department in Chicago tried to personalize their foreclosure prevention outreach activities by focusing on areas with high foreclosure rates, collaborating with community leaders or offering citizens different forms of access that suited their need for anonymity.

We can also say that the more complex a service, the higher the need for personalization in government. Complexity means regulations, choice and the potential for negative consequences for the citizen or society at large. Furthermore, government is more open to adapting to the needs of their target groups if interactions result in an increase in the tax base (e.g. direct investment) or an increase in fee collection. For example, Miami-Dade's Web offerings for the building industry resulted in $1.1 million in revenue. However, New York's Office of Film, Theatre & Broadcasting may be interpreted as a counterfactual. Only after the mayor brought in an outsider from the private sector did the department become more client-oriented. The actions eventually performed should have and could have been performed much earlier. We could, therefore, ask whether departmental leadership is very important for customer service practices such as personalization or if there are other reasons that prevent departments from exerting strong leadership.

Moreover, the interviews showed that customer service and satisfaction appears to be a central metaphor for administrators and elected officials. They refer to citizens as customers. Other metaphors were brought into play to support or explain what is needed to substantiate and embody customer orientation. Phrases such as "like Disney…" dominated many interviews. A narrative difference can also be observed between interviewees. Those whose business is to directly interact with citizens describe their relationships and thoughts on what constitutes "good customer service" in greater detail. And those that were more involved on the strategic side had a more abstract understanding of the citizen–government relationship.

CRM also calls for integration of customers for product development and needs evaluations. In the cases studied there was a different kind of customer integration. Citizens, or rather their 311 SRs, complaints and comments were an important variable for everyday performance measurement, accountability and city management. Their aggregated data provided a wealth of information about service levels, employee interactions, and neighborhood conditions and trends. As such, the purpose of the integration and analysis differed. In the private sector, data mining is conducted to build individual customer profiles, segment customers, identify opportunities for up- and cross-selling and check the ROI of marketing programs. The way citizen data was integrated for performance and city management may also be interpreted as analytical CRM. However, in comparison to the private sector, the analytical process in government relied on the capabilities of the CSAs (Customer Service Advocates) or the CitiStat team (Baltimore). While the CitiStat team was using products such as MS Excel, there were no powerful data-mining solutions available. In fact, the qualitative nature of citizen comments made a manual process necessary. The analytical process also closed the loop in different ways than I have outlined earlier. That is, they facilitated knowledge sharing. The information was analysed on a monthly or daily basis, and the information on the organisational performance plus the citizens' needs was communicated throughout government.

The overall picture

Overall, the empirical evidence on the implementation of CiRM gathered from a cross-case analysis (Table 5-3) supports the premise that CRM has validity in government. In fact, I was able to identify many aspects of CRM outlined in Chapter 2.1. However, evidence was scattered, and thus the case studies do not support the notion that a holistic approach to CRM would be feasible for municipal or multi-jurisdictional CiRM initiatives. Based on interviewees' comments and further developments in the case studies of which I have become aware in recent months, I have identified the following critical success factors for CiRM activities:

- A strong leader and sustainable support.
- Budget or other funding mechanism.
- Analysing the organization and processes with the citizen in mind. Once an issue is identified, it needs to be resolved without any finger-pointing.
- Bringing in everyone with the same intensity, structure and expectations.
- Continuous communication with current and potential stakeholders on all hierarchy levels.
- A gradual approach to implementation.
- An implementation time that ensures political support (approximately one year).
- A gradual approach to external (citizen) communication (advertising).
- Starting with departments that either have a large, visible impact or have nothing to lose.
- Testing the 311 contact center in a soft launch phase for a few months.
- Performance management.
- Recognition of the fact that while technology is important, it can only facilitate customer service and organisational transformation.
- Studying best practices and open knowledge sharing.

	City of Baltimore	City of Chicago	City of New York	Miami-Dade County
Multi-channel	Yes (Web, 311, Agency)	Yes (Web, 311, Agency)	Yes (Web, 311, Agency)	Yes (Web, 311, Agency)
Citizen need analysis	Surveys, 311 data	Surveys, 311 data	Surveys, (311 data), focus groups	Surveys, 311 data, focus groups
Personalisation		Service specific	Service specific, Web	Service specific, Web
Performance Management	CitiStat	Some	CapStat	Some (ServiceStat)
Reason for 311	Data for CitiStat	Customer service	Easy access, satisfaction	Customer service, satisfaction
311 Operation since	(1996) 2002	1999	2003	2004
311 Implementation time	One year	One year	One year	One year
311 Implementation costs	0.35 Mio.	13.2 Mio.	24 Mio.	~ 16 Mio.
311 Operating costs		~ 4.3 Mio.	~ 25 Mio.	~ 6 Mio.
311 Budget sources	Grant, Budget	City budget	City budget	Bond, County budget
311 Call volume (per year)	~ 1.1 Mio.	~ 4 Mio.	~ 14 Mio.	~ 9,1 Mio.
CSA	CitiStat Team	2		4
CRM software	Motorola CSR	Motorola CSR	Siebel	Motorola CSR
Knowledgebase		Yes	Yes (~2800 topics)	Yes (~7000 topics)
GIS integration	Indirect	Indirect	Indirect	Direct
Closed loop	Yes, many agencies (SR) but not other channels	Yes, many agencies (SR) but not other channels	Yes, very few agencies (SR) but not other channels	Yes, some agencies (SR) but not other channels
Hours	24/7/365	24/7/365	24/7/365	6-10wd/8-8we/365
Multi-jurisdictional	No	No	No	Yes (City of Miami)
311 Services	Information, Referral, Service intake	Information, Referral, Service intake, Outreach	Information, Referral, Service intake, Outreach	Information, Referral, Service intake, Outreach

Table 5-3: Overview CiRM Implementation

5.3   Impact of CiRM

The CiRM initiatives had the impact on citizens, public administration and elected officials outlined in the following paragraphs. I will only present evidence that was either very unique to a particular case study or was repeatedly discovered across cases.

Looking at the past, there was already a structure in place that offered citizens the choice of different channels to interact with their government. In all of the case studies, an immense amount of information and some services were provided over the Internet, in particular, in Miami-Dade County and New York. However, today's society is increasingly mobile, with citizens spending many hours at work or on the move. Therefore, even if the criterion of computer ownership is met, individual access to an appropriate device may not be guaranteed when the need for government interaction arises. The same applies to government offices. Their operating hours, geographic distance or work contracts restrict access. Consequently, the mobile citizen uses the phone channel, whether fixed-line (landline) or mobile (cell). Mobile phones are very common today.

A 311 contact system, therefore, facilitates easy 24/7/365 access to government information, a limited amount of services and commenting/reporting to government. Groups such as seniors that tend to be excluded from the digital revolution or lower socioeconomic groups that tend to be excluded through government's complexity are now taking advantage of the 311 contact center. Call takers for 311 contact centers are well trained in customer service behaviour and act as advocates for the citizen. They help citizens identify their needs and articulate their problems, and they help citizens better understand administrative processes. Building on the argument of Moorman, Deshpandé and Zaltman (1993) on the role of trust in customer relationship, we may say that the reduced complexity through CiRM practices increases the citizen's trust in government. They thought that complexity tend to reduce trust in relationships because it reduces the chance for physical closeness. Moreover, it increases the probability of greater dissimilarities in beliefs and norms. Call takers also reduce the citizen's level of frustration at being sent to different departments by referring them to the responsible department. However, there is also some evidence that citizens still have to be aware of the administrative language required when reporting an issue. It took New York's administration over a year to correctly prioritize repair of a depression on a street because it had been mistakenly reported as a "pothole" or "sinkhole" instead of an "undermine" (Brustein 2005).

Furthermore, process changes such as those in New York's buildings department that were the result of the BPA during 311's implementation phase led to greater equality in service provision. Moreover, this was supported by the installed closed-loop SR tracking, service level agreements and performance measurement activities such as CitiStat. Responsiveness was also improved; however, there was some evidence that administrators could not ensure a uniform level of responsiveness. Overall citizen satisfaction increased. Yet it cannot be determined whether this can be derived from the CiRM activities. As I outlined in Chapter 2, customer satisfaction and citizen satisfaction are based on a complex set of factors. Further, New York's SCOUT initiative and the Internet trend of crowdsourcing (Howe 2006) inspired two citizens to start "The People's 311" (Figure 5-1). Crowdsourcing is a neologism for the Internet Web 2.0 trend to outsource a task or question to an open or more specifically defined group of people (e.g. Wikipedia, Threadless). The two New Yorker's created a Flickr[2] group where anyone can upload pictures of public nuisances (e.g. sidewalk hazards, dying trees, illegal advertising) and then "place" them on a map so that they can be located. Finally, there was, however, some evidence that citizens used the anonymity of the calls to 311 to either make false reports or wrongly denounce others. For example, even during times when no noise ordinance was actually being broken, annoyed neighbors found they could lash out at bars by anonymously calling 311 and making any kind of complaint, such as a report of a non-existent fight.

A centralized contact center, Web portal and data-driven performance initiatives are challenging to existing government structures, administrative processes and a multi-jurisdictional environment. There are several reasons for this fact. First, by making it easy for citizens to call and creating a single-call center, 311 essentially separated citizen demand from service delivery. It is a centralized, almost neutral entity that creates real-time information about citizens' needs—requests for information, service requests and comments. However, it is also noteworthy that over 60% of the SRs in Chicago are created internally. Therefore, the CiRM software happened to be quickly accepted and adopted by departments as a useful management tool.

Figure 5-1: Screenshot of the People's 311

---

[2] Flickr.com is a Web-based photo sharing and social networking platform.

Second, the separation of service intake and delivery resulted in greater transparency about citizen demand, which was formerly either not tracked because there was no process or technology in place, or because it was hidden in departmental silos. Many departments preferred the latter and tended to control their workload by limiting citizens' access. Another factor that resulted in greater internal transparency was the BPA that happened along with the process of integrating departments into 311 operations.

Third, citizen insights acquired via 311 may lead to budget or responsibility gains for some departments such as New York's sanitation department (DOS), while other departments experience losses. Yet I did not discover that the citizen insights led to organisational changes that moved toward clustering functions, budgets and operations around citizen segments.

Fourth, the performance measurement and management activities that utilized citizen and departmental data had a role in improving internal (politicians, department heads) and external (citizens) accountability. While Baltimore's CiRM activities were less sophisticated and developed than those in the other cases, its CitiStat process was the most analytical and rigorous performance management activity of all of the cases. The data acquired through the software application (Motorola CSR) provided the information on how well a department is doing. In other cases, the CSAs are trying to combine, structure and evaluate the data, but they have less leverage on changing a department's processes. The CSA process is less intrusive than CitiStat, though, and might result in incremental change.

Fifth, the data was utilized to improve public management decision making. As one administrator said, they were having the chance to do estimates instead of "guesstimates" of what is happening in the department and its area of responsibility. Issues and service requests were made visible on maps and cross-referenced with other information. However, in general, the studied governmental entities are only in the beginning stages of doing comprehensive analytics or building the capacity to do so. Furthermore, according to many administrators, the analysis helped them with allocating resources.

Sixth, customer service has historically focused on reactive problem solving and responding to complaints (Lovelock 1992). This has also been the case for public administration. The data also allows for a broader retrospective analysis aimed at continuous improvement and helps administrators to better anticipate demand. While government can certainly drive demand (e.g. public announcement about a tax rebate), there are other factors such as the weather or interlinked events that may influence demand.

Seventh, citizen demand can be overwhelming. Overall, four effects of citizen demand that are visible to all can be identified. First, it quickly identifies any inefficiency within public administration. Second, the opportunity of "voice" also raises the expectation for a response in general and usually a short response time, in particular. Accordingly, governments are under pressure to develop the capacity to analyse and react appropriately. Third, governments also need to find a balance between short-term and long-term goals and resource management. Fourth, additional and more strategic government outreach is necessary to manage citizen expectations.

Eighth, the centralized approach to 311, its data and momentum was a key source for knowledge sharing and cross-boundary collaboration. Because citizens expect 311 to provide them with all kinds of government information, departments and higher jurisdictions have to work together on a unified knowledge base. Separate departments frequently did not have access to the service activities of other departments. Difficulties of inter-agency collaboration became evident over time, and the hard data provided everyone with a good reason why issues should be approached in a holistic, coordinated and collaborative way. However, it should also be noted that overall there were no major organisational or process-related changes. Furthermore, performance management such as CitiStat consequently transcended organisational boundaries. An example of that is Baltimore's LeadStat team, which was formed with officials from different city departments and state agencies. The perception of 311 is depends heavily on all other agencies' capabilities to deliver their services in a citizen-oriented way. So the CSAs are also continuously working on reducing vertical and horizontal boundaries on the intra- and inter-agency level.

Finally, CiRM also supported emergency management. Based on the scalability of 311, government agencies were able to manage a continuous rise in information demand before, during and after a disaster. Just as in city management, the data from citizens and government employees who acted as "eyes and ears on the ground" provided emergency managers with crucial information that allowed them to monitor events and make decisions on effective emergency response measures.

Elected officials first feared losing contact with their constituency as a result of CiRM activities. Indeed, citizens' calls to their offices decreased. Many citizens contacted them for minor issues that were not related to policy but were shortcomings of administrative processes (e.g. slow delivery of a garbage can). Furthermore, citizens contacted elected officials in the hope of speeding up their service delivery, which certainly is evidence of the utility maximising behaviour described by rational choice theorists. Generally, both instances offered elected officials the opportunity to do "visible politics" that helped them justify their role. By comparison, it's much more difficult for politicians to communicate their role in policy making or provide tangible results of a policy.

CiRM offered elected officials, particularly the mayor, the chance to keep track of their policy initiatives and use hard facts when communicating with the media or citizens. It was not possible to check in the case studies if the real-time data supported short-term politics, but it certainly allowed elected officials to better react to arising issues.

Moreover, elected officials and their staff did not formerly use any sophisticated ICT solution to track and analyse citizen issues. Just like departments, they did not have information readily available about citizen issues in other areas, and they could not easily track city performance. So CiRM led to a centralized, digital intake of citizen complaints, comments and service requests. Furthermore, it somewhat mediated the cycle of elected officials interfering with departmental management by forcing them to prioritize their requests.

While Chicago initially chose to provide elected officials with 311 data and the capability to use the system, New York's councillors had to introduce law to gain access to the information. In addition, as a result of the frequency of false reports, some of New York's council members proposed legislation (Int. #509) to change the privacy policy of 311 so that callers could be traced.

Along these lines, as citizen and administrative performance data gets more meaningful and easily comprehensible, it could further politicize the domain of public administration. Maor (1999) already showed that NPM increased the politicization of the administrative domain instead of depoliticizing it. While the latter was not identified as the goal of CiRM, the reality of further politicization of the domain seems to be supported by the case evidence. Public administration has control over the data that is relevant for policy makers. By controlling the flow of and access to that information, public administration could gain greater bargaining power when negotiating with political leadership or take a more active role in policy making. On the other hand, the case of New York showed that elected officials will quickly introduce legislation to get access to information.

5.4   Understanding of CiRM

Most elected officials and administrators were not aware of the existence of CRM. Even those with a work history in the private sector who knew something about CRM had spent no time thinking about applying CRM to government. Except for CRM software, no reference to CRM could also be found in any of the reviewed documents. Moreover, none of the interviewees had used or heard of the term CiRM before the interviews were conducted. Nevertheless, a set of recurring ideas held by elected officials and administrators were identified throughout the case studies.

First, interviewees pointed out that government is more complex than the private sector in terms of its customer base and the broadness and depth of the products and services it provides. Moreover, the government monopoly in providing many public services is a constraint to the realization of customer service-oriented strategies.

Second, CiRM is based on a different philosophy than the private sector. Government is about delivering public services and delivering public value. Government is not about selling goods or services. In fact, one interviewee stressed that CiRM would be one of the core missions defining the very existence of government. Furthermore, the logic of increasing the frequency of customer interactions in order to generate more information, the chance for cross-selling and revenue does not apply to government. In most cases, it is in fact the opposite logic that applies, because fewer interactions with citizens help in reducing the cost of government operations.

Third, along these lines, administrators pointed out that there is a limit to citizen-orientation in government caused by an agency's budget and relevant policy mandates.

In addition, many believed that there is also a perceived limit to citizen-orientation based on citizens' expectations of government, which are usually complex and hard to meet. So even if government is able to meet the citizens' expectations for some time, those expectations tend to continue to rise. Then the cycle begins anew, and citizen expectations again become hard to meet due to the limited resources of government.

Fourth, with regard to public services, there is less need for generally managing relationships or in nurturing one-to-one relationships with citizens. What seems to be more important is the citizens' needs (location, particular quality-of-life issue). The only areas with a greater need for a one-to-one relationship and thus the interest of government in learning all about their clients' needs, behaviours and interactions are the areas of welfare, healthcare and law enforcement. Another recurring theme was that the citizen–government relationship usually occurs in association with negative experiences. For example, citizens have to fulfill obligations to government (e.g. get a driver's license or fishing permit, pay taxes or a speeding ticket), to request help when they are in a difficult situation (e.g. unemployment) or to request a service when government is not fulfilling its responsibilities (e.g. fill a pothole). As a result, many citizens would like to keep their interaction with government to a minimum.

Fifth, two goals of CiRM emerged throughout the interviews. On the one hand, many administrators and documents stated the goal was to increase citizen satisfaction by the measures taken (e.g. 311, multi-channel service provision, responsive service delivery). On the other hand, CiRM was understood as the pursuit of institutionalizing the underlying goal of improving accountability and government performance. Hence, 311 was understood as a central source in providing real-time citizen input for administrators and elected officials on the status quo of government's performance and citizen needs. In contrast, only one administrator thought that CiRM was more about the regulatory side (enforcement) of the citizen–government relationship.

Sixth, none of the interviewees supported the idea of creating a citizen profile based on interactions and other information. They were concerned that it would make George Orwell's "Big Brother" become reality after all. However, some noted that government has always tried to build detailed citizen profiles in welfare case management.

Finally, CiRM was either defined holistically or very narrowly. Interviewees with a holistic understanding described CiRM as a mix of channels, technologies and change of organisational culture to improve the delivery of public services. Interviewees with the narrower understanding limited CiRM to the activities and functions of 311. One elected official simply defined CiRM as the role and work of his profession.

5.5   Toward a model of CiRM

This study opened with a puzzle: Are there any differences in private and public CRM? In order to find an answer, I have looked at CRM and CiRM through four perspectives in the previous sections of this chapter: literature, implementation, impact and understanding. The experiences of three large American cities and one county suggest that CiRM is indeed a feasible concept for government. While the major focus of the case studies was on the 311 projects, it became clear that 311 is not CiRM. The case evidence and literature review also underlines that many aspects of CRM are not new to government and that some aspects of CRM need to be adapted to the government context. Therefore, I want to present a model of CiRM (Table 5-4) in this section of the chapter.

There are components of CRM that can be applied to government without further alterations; this is supported by the evidence found in the case studies. Examples include a multi-channel information and service offering, viewing everyone (internal and external) as customers, process changes based on internal and citizen analysis, or a one-to-one approach in areas like welfare. However, so far there has been no coordinated

Citizen Relationship Management (CiRM)	
Principles and Components	
Goal	Public value, transparency, accountability, equality, efficiency
Rationale	Citizen satisfaction, performance management
Drivers	Information and knowledge
Customer	Internal (PA/EO), External
Relationship	Multiple relationships, no relationship may also be desirable, blurred customer producer/provider linearity
CitizenValue	Depends on the area, producer of performance data, scout, co-producer
Theoretical Background	CRM, social contract
Organisational Structure	Horizontal and vertical cross-boundary collaboration
Technology	Facilitator
Culture	Citizen-centric
Change	Change and learning are a continuous process because citizen needs not static
Tools	Performance measurement and management, data mining, citizen profile, analysis, segmentation, surveys, channels, BPA, BPR, outreach

Table 5-4: A model of CiRM

effort with a holistic approach to CiRM on the departmental, municipal or multi-jurisdictional level. Such an implementation is mostly constrained by jurisdictions and regulations, and that is one of the reasons that departmental silos remained mostly intact. Yet it would be possible to have such implementations on a voluntary basis and with the support of a strong and visionary political and administrative leadership.

The idea of value needs to be more broadly defined in CiRM. When CiRM is applied to G2B relationships, in particular in the area of attracting foreign direct investment (FDI), governments may indeed try to collect as much information about their interactions with the business they intend to attract and to segment businesses in order to identify those that are of greatest interest to the economy (in terms of development) and government (in terms of taxes = revenue). In this case, CRM's customer value proposition could be applied to government without any changes. While the value of citizens could be measured in terms of the costs (e.g. benefits and education received) and revenues (tax paid), it would raise a set of legislative and regulatory problems. Thus, the concept of Citizen Lifetime Value should not be part of CiRM. Instead, the value of citizens can be identified in three areas. First, citizens provide their local knowledge, which can improve an administration's management. Second, citizens who frequently comment and participate allow elected officials to better understand the needs of their constituency and thus help them increase the likelihood of their getting reelected. Third, complaints and comments from citizens help everyone in holding public administration accountable.

In a firm, the boundaries of CRM are defined by the management of a company. The boundaries of the customer orientation and customer services are indirectly influenced by the customers themselves (demand) and the competition. That is, a firm will aim at providing its services or products at a level that is slightly above the expectations of its customers and the offerings of its competitors. The boundaries of CiRM in government are defined by administrators and elected officials in a bargaining process. The boundaries of citizen-orientation are indirectly set by the citizens with their complaints and votes for elected officials. That is, only if there is sufficient protest from citizens and the media will elected officials and public administration try to improve their level of citizen-orientation.

There is also a different approach to relationships in CiRM. In the private sector, firms are interested in building close and long-lasting relationships with their customers. The transfer of the concept of a one-to-one relationship has been mentioned several times in the literature on CiRM. Contrary to the literature most of the interviewees stressed their interest in a form of aggregated relationship. Again, a relationship in CiRM has two dimensions, depending on our perspective. If we think about the social contract theories outlined in Section 2.3, the citizen–government relationship can be grounded in varying streams of political philosophy. Accordingly, CiRM's components can either be altered to maintain or counter the embedded ideas on the social contract (the relationship).

However, even in the "self-examination era" (Blanchard/Hinnant/Wong 1998), that is, the timeframe from the early 20th century to the early 1960s, when an increasing number of services were expected to be provided by public administration and the citizen's role was reduced to that of the beneficiary, it was in many cases in the best interest of government to have no relationship at all with its citizens. For instance, it would be the optimal case for the police if there are no people who commit a crime that causes them to build a relationship. Employment agencies are, of course, interested in building relationships with those who are in need of a job, but it is their general goal to end the relationships (get people jobs) in the shortest time possible. Also, in many cases, the longer the relationship between citizen and a public entity exists, the higher the costs for government and ultimately society will be, so government has an incentive to keep relationships as short as possible.

Moreover, there are certain obligations (e.g. garbage collection, transportation) of government that don't really require a relationship with citizens. Citizens prefer an anonymous government, and there is no advantage for agencies in knowing more about the citizens than their address. The example of transportation points to the blurred customer provider linearity discussed in Section 2.3.1, which remains a unique to CiRM and a challenge for administrators that is difficult to overcome.

Finally, CiRM recognizes that there are varying citizen–government relationships, each of which requires different forms of management—something that actually has always been a task of government. Some relationships require the government to be in control of the relationship and be engaged in active management, while other relationships can be controlled by citizens or happen with their permission. Cultural norms and values affect citizens' privacy concerns, so unlike firms, balancing and protecting individual privacy is an important ethical goal for CiRM.

The lifecycle concept only works in CiRM on the micro level. Agencies that provide a specific service can plan their activities according to the different phases of their citizen relationships. However, from a macro perspective there is no need for the lifecycle concept in CiRM due to the monopoly of government. Unless citizens decide to migrate to another country, they have no chance to terminate their relationship with government in line with Hirschman's (1970) "exit". The same applies to government. It is not relieved of its obligation to serve the citizen until he "exits", that is, until he dies or migrates.

CiRM builds on the analysis of citizen data in order to generate citizen insights in an aggregated form. A citizen's reported issue and the location of that issue are more important and might not be linked to an individual, so there is no need to build citizen profiles. In addition, the analysis of citizen data needs to be combined with an analysis of the internal organisation and external information to produce a holistic understanding. However, one caveat should be noted. The data never speak for themselves. As Behn (Behn 2006) recently stated, "[T]he data only speak through some kind of systematic, methodological, intellectual, or ideological framework. Any bar chart or table of data establishes a framework, if only through the selection of the data and its form of presentation. The mere creation of a bar chart or table is also the creation of a framework through which the data will speak." No matter how narrowly focused a question is, it will simultaneously exclude certain kinds of answers and overemphasize other kinds (Zaltman 2003). Consequently, those who supervise (department heads, elected officials) those who do the analysis, as well as the analysts themselves, have a great responsibility. Moreover, if CiRM is understood as a general concept for government, citizen profiles need to be included in theoretical discussions, at least, because government has been collecting data to build citizen profiles in databases in law enforcement, welfare and other programs. Regardless of our perspective about the issue of customer profiles, the insights generated from the analysis need to be shared among administrative units, elected officials and ultimately citizens.

Therefore, collaborative processes on the intra- and inter-organisational level form the foundation of CiRM. This, along with open knowledge management and performance measurement processes, should result in collaborative and informed resource allocation geared towards coordinated cross-functional citizen interactions. Hence, CiRM also builds on the theory of accountability described by Kelly (2005), which states that citizens want good performance from their government and that the aspects of performance administrators can measure (in the studied cases, the key performance variable was a timely response) are the same aspects that are important to citizens.

In conclusion, I define Citizen Relationship Management as follows:

> *CiRM is a technology-enabled strategy and set of management practices aimed at maintaining and optimising relationships and encouraging citizen participation.*

5.6 CiRM and public participation

For the purpose of the following discussion, citizen participation is defined as participation in public management and administrative processes of government. I follow Coulter (1988) who identified citizen-initiated contacts with public administration as a "critically important mode of citizen participation in urban political systems". Therefore, I reason that a citizen who provides public administration with information about a broken sidewalk or a complaint adds value to government's management as well as to society. Of course, this type of participation differs from the more commonly addressed political participation studied in political science, which encompasses voting or interacting with elected officials. It also differs from the concept of civic engagement, where individuals support their community on a voluntary basis. In the context of this research, citizen participation is considered to have a direct impact on policy formulation and implementation. Among other things, CiRM provides the means for continuing participation in post-decision stages of local governance because CiRM includes mechanisms such as 311 that allow capturing citizens' needs as well as opinions in multiple ways. There is evidence in the case study analysis to suggest that the collaborative character of 311 alone is a synergistic means for achieving objectives, resolving conflict and empowering disadvantaged individuals because it provides an easy form of access. Over time these activities could influence the policy making process by providing the impetus for change through the data itself. However, the form of public participation supported by CiRM should not be understood as an alternative to other forms of participation but as complementary to those other forms.

Fung's (2006) democracy cube presented in Chapter 2.3.4 allows us to understand the governance mechanisms resulting from CiRM and compare them to other varieties of institutional design and participatory mechanisms (Figure 5-2).

CiRM allows anyone to participate—they don't have to possess a certain kind of information, and even those people who do not have citizenship (e.g. tourists, illegal immigrants) can participate. While complete openness usually fosters an overrepresentation of wealthier and educated people, this was not observed in the case studies, according to the reports from administrators. Instead, some public managers assumed that lower socioeconomic groups are overrepresented because they encounter more quality-of-life issues in their area of residence.

CiRM only leads to deliberation if the individual preferences citizens captured through CiRM systems and internal agency data are openly and widely accessible. In that case, anyone can learn about issues, engage in deliberative processes and perhaps transform their preferences. However, generally speaking, CiRM facilitates a hybrid form of the expression of preferences and technical expertise in a more conventional way, if we understand the latter as the local knowledge about community issues. It could even lead to a form of hidden agenda setting, which I will discuss later in this chapter.

The third dimension of the democracy cube addresses the impact of public participation. CiRM allows citizens to offer advice and consultation to public authorities. Administrators commit themselves to receiving an aggregated as well as individual form of input. Administrators and elected officials can base their decisions on almost real-time information. And a citizen reporting a broken sidewalk has at least some expectation of influencing administrative action, unless there are administrative processes (e.g. pothole filled in 24h rule in Baltimore) that ensure action. However, I could also imagine that freely available information would allow citizens and administrators to enter in a "cogoverning partnership" (Fung 2006) to make plans and policies.

An open and flexible form of information intake as well as sharing CiRM system and agency data with the public not only serves accountability or educational purposes but would provide the opportunity for a new form of participation—the "citizen innovator". Von Hippel (2005) described the shift of innovation to users or user communities in the business world, which is a strategy that has helped to "radically" improve business processes and products through the advances in ICT. According to Von Hippel, "[D]emocratization of the opportunity to create is important beyond giving more users the ability to make exactly right products for themselves. [...] The joy and the learning associated with creativity and membership in creative communities are also important." If we transfer the idea of "user innovation" to participation in administrative processes, the citizen as an innovator could come up with new ways of analysing, explaining or using the data in beneficial ways for society or public administration. Instead of storing information about citizens' issues and the performance of administrative processes, public administration links the information back to citizens so that they—among other things—are able to provide missing data that is important for decision making. Sharing government information with the public is not without difficulty (Rosegrant 1992). Yet if information sharing is embedded into a thoughtful process, the public can get a better understanding of public resources and the limits to customer service. This has already proven successful in some initiatives around the world (Pröhl/Plamper 2000).

Some might still question the value of the kind of participatory activity supported through CiRM in comparison to other forms of participation. In the case studies, citizens make government aware of many administrative management and low-priority policy issues; they provide a reflection of the status quo but do not participate in deliberations on the grand policy themes. Yet over time, administrative processes become hardened and are not examined for effectiveness or efficiency until there is an incident that exposes the existence of a problem such as in New York's DOB. In CiRM, this is a continuous process. Along these lines, over time the reported issues might evolve either into an incident or a priority. If streets start getting bumpy, people will at some point realize that the task they delegated to government is not being done correctly. Consequently, citizens will use their voice option. Accordingly, if the citizen receives good customer services in areas defined or accepted by the citizen as an obligation of government, and if the citizen can help government to more efficiently take care of its everyday responsibilities and then feels the impact, then this will have an incremental impact on the overall perception of government. In short, when participation is rewarded with the power to improve the quality of life, individuals contribute to problem solving and governance processes despite the obstacles of time constraints, social conflict and the like (Fung 2006). This rarely happens to voters of political parties. It also follows that satisfied citizens will do "business" with government without the usual fear or anxiety. I speculate that under a CiRM-type administration, it may be possible for people to look forward to dealing with public administration. Extending that logic, I would expect fewer citizens to engage in avoiding laws and regulations and more to engage in participation if they can see the fruits of their efforts reflected in good services and good policies.

Further, compared to other forms of participation such as town meetings, CiRM establishes a process of continuous low-intensity participation. Other forms of participation are usually a single or episodic incident rather than a process. Moreover, results of other forms of participation are highly unpredictable, delayed or hard to measure. CiRM also provides the means and mechanism to capture and analyse large quantities of ideas and comments on grand or small policy schemes, such as education or foreign policy. CiRM would lead to a diminishment of the separation between government and the public. I hereby follow Bohmann (1996: 180-200) who argued that citizens should be considered "not as passive clients but as sources of information and judgements, especially concerning the contextual features of applying laws and agreements to specific local situations". Moreover, CiRM would meet Barnes' and Prior's (1995) demand for a mechanism to allow citizens' participation in resource allocation, planning or management. As van Ryzin (2004) has shown, the confidence (trust) of citizen in government increases as the citizen's quality are solved quickly.

At first glance, CiRM supports the notion of rational actor models. Citizens try to optimize their genuine utility by reporting issues. According to rational actor theories of collective action, it makes little sense to take part in politics. Briefly, the logic is as follows. Since governmental policies are collective goods the rational, self-interested individual has no incentive to invest scarce resources in political participation. Because the efforts of any single individual are unlikely to have a significant effect on whether the desired policy outcome is achieved, the rational individual will hitch a free ride on the activity of others and thus will reap the benefits of the preferred policy without expending resources on its attainment. However, CiRM allows for a form of collective action that has yet to be explored by citizens and administrators. It supports Aristotle's (1981) "active citizenship", where citizens exercise practical wisdom in the public interest, because on the macro level the aggregate of individual preferences could shape public management decisions—not necessarily policy decisions—that increase the collective utility. The wisdom of the crowd serves the greater good. This adds to the puzzle of participation in rational choice theory (Verba/Schlozman/Brady 1995).

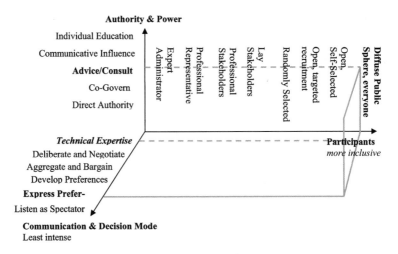

Figure 5-2: Dimensions of public participation in CiRM

5.7   Potential issues of CiRM

Taking the argument presented in the preceding paragraph further, CiRM may provide citizens with a new way to bring a matter to the attention of policy makers without the policy makers being aware of it. That is, citizens who begin to understand the analytics or processes of CiRM and the role of the data for administrative and political decision making—even when their opinions are only one factor that decision makers take into consideration—and have the capability to activate a critical mass of other citizens to report on an issue of their interest may, by their concerted participation in government, effect real change. Such a strategy would lead to a kind of hidden agenda setting on the part of the activated citizens, because 311 on its own functions like a real-time market for citizens. The greater the demand, the greater the probability of government responding. However, the opportunity or even the mandate to participate also does not ensure that quality participation will occur (Rosener 1978), as it was seen in the case of the phony noise reports in Greenwich Village. CiRM is more than 311, but the present anonymity of 311 calls and citizens' awareness of the underlying processes was abused by some citizens to denounce others.

Furthermore, if data becomes more prominent in decision making, public managers will have to adopt more rigorous mechanisms and strategies as they attempt to balance opinions and interpret results. Public managers, therefore, need training to effectively collect, analyse and translate data into meaningful statements. Those who decide what kind of data is collected, who collect the information, who analyse the data and who draw conclusions from the data have great responsibility, which demands continuous scrutiny. Because it is public administration that collects and analyzes the data, it is almost inevitable that the domain of public administration—once home to neutrality and expertise—is politicized by CiRM. Data ownership, control and validity or trust-fulness of results could be a central battleground in the future.

Heikkila and Isett (2007) also pointed out another issue of importance to CiRM. Administrators may question the validity of the citizen's subjective evaluation, contingent on its congruence with objective performance data: "There is precious little evidence, however, to suggest that agencies are choosing performance measures based on citizen priorities or revising performance criteria based on citizen preferences, especially if the agency is meeting or exceeding its performance target." Not many governments publish their service standards and resolution processes. And even fewer public entities haven taken the steps to redress citizens if government fails to meet its own standards or promises. Along these lines, King and Cotterill (2007) noted that CRM "enablement of contact centers and other channels continues to deny citizens an active role in service design or delivery" because they have no direct input as to how service is delivered or what processes are used.

CiRM is also essentially about change, and the active resistance to change experienced in public and private organisations will be a key barrier to an effective realization. Because government is not affected by market pressures, and because CiRM takes longer to implement than most political terms in office last, it will be difficult to ensure sustainable support, which is a key CiRM success factor.

CiRM facilitates cross-boundary collaboration, which has many benefits but may as well result in making government more complex than less complex. The only difference is that complexity is better obscured by more efficient channels, more effective interaction processes and higher citizen-orientation. Therefore, a very cynical counter-argument could be that CiRM will mostly be enacted to hide government's lack of capability to change.

Finally, it is of course possible to apply the argument brought forward by Bogumil, Holtkamp and Kißler (2001) against NPM/TQM that the application of CiRM is subject to individual interests and efforts of administrative and political leadership or the regulatory environment. In addition, in line with Schedler's and Summermatter's (2006) findings on citizen-orientation in eGovernment, CiRM will likely be altered by social values and culture.

6 Conclusion

The purpose of this research was to explore CRM in government. The research was developed around five key questions. How is CRM understood and implemented in government? What has been the impact of CRM initiatives? What is the contribution of CRM to currently active reform movements that aim at improving citizen-orientation? The answers to these questions were intended to support two additional objectives of this study: first, answering the fundamental question of whether there is a difference between private and public CRM, and second, conceptualizing Citizen Relationship Management, (what I refer to as CiRM) to clearly delineate CRM's application in government.

In order to find an answer to these questions, I began this study with an assessment of CRM in the business world. A literature review showed that CRM was influenced by different streams in management research—in particular, marketing science—and by developments in technology. At the core of CRM lies the goal of increasing customer revenue over the lifetime of the customer relationship to ensure the competitive advantage of a firm. While CRM definitions vary, most authors refer to the same set of components—customer analysis, segmenting customers, synchronizing customer interaction throughout channels and a customer-oriented culture. CRM is typically facilitated through ICT, but only as an enabling factor. Accordingly, CRM is now understood as a holistic management concept used in creating a customer-centric organisation. A myriad of companies struggled with their CRM projects and realized that improving customer relationships is not just a matter of installing a CRM system in their call center. These companies eventually learned that the greater the scope of a CRM project, the greater the need to re-engineer processes—and thus the greater the resistance to implementation of CRM. Use of CRM in government was not discussed until 2000. There, Citizen Relationship Management (CiRM) is intended to improve citizen satisfaction and citizen-orientation. However, CiRM lacks a commonly accepted definition or understanding of when and how government is doing CiRM. According to the scarce empirical evidence, only a few governments are engaging in CiRM. Most initiatives usually start on the municipal level and in government contact centers.

Many authors claimed that CiRM would bring about a significant increase in citizen satisfaction and improve citizen-orientation in government. In order to verify these claims I compared CRM to currently active government reform movements, in particular TQM and eGovernment. TQM underlines the importance of customer focus and empowerment of employees, and highlights how empowerment contributes directly to customer satisfaction. A review of the literature on eGovernment revealed that the characteristics of ICT have the potential to improve citizen-orientation of government. In eGovernment, ICT is understood as an enabling factor for organisational change. However, eGovernment falls more within models of limited rather than transformational change (West 2005: 2). Empirical evidence suggested that the organizational structure, culture and the behaviour of key actors will determine the enactment and outcomes of TQM or ICT. My comparative analysis showed that CRM shares many aspects with TQM and eGovernment. Whether CRM, TQM or eGovernment—all of them rest on the underlying logic that information sharing and customer focus result in positive outcomes for both customers and the organisation. Yet CRM also introduces both more detailed or new procedures and ideas about customer orientation that revolve around managing the customer relationship. Moreover, the customer is understood as an individual. Furthermore, unlike NPM, neither CRM nor TQM constitute an ideology that unilaterally imposes business values, objectives or practices on government. They do not offer any normative views on governance or any methodology for reshaping the formal and informal connections between government and society.

In addition, the focus of CRM on the customer and on managing customer relationships made it necessary to review the literature on the citizen–government relationship. The citizen–government relationship is much more complex than a customer business relationship. First, the citizen has multiple roles, such as voter, client, coproducer or customer. Defining the citizen as a customer or consumer of government was subject to a lot of criticism, which was usually mixed with criticism of market-driven reform movements such as NPM. While the discussion of the citizen as customer is generally important, this research clearly showed that administrators refer to citizens as customers but have a broader understanding of the role they actually play. That is, they call the citizen their client or customer in order to stress a customer service culture with attributes such as friendliness, but they also understand that the citizen has additional roles, such as a voter. Second, I outlined the movement of the citizen–government relationship throughout the last 100 years towards being one of collaborative learning and production. Because the analysis of customer needs is an important aspect of CRM, I briefly reviewed the literature on citizens' needs and preferences. Systematic research of citizens' preferences is sparse or dated, but the myth of citizens considering bureaucrats highly incompetent is exaggerated. Many citizens are satisfied with the performance when interacting with public administration (Goodsell 2004). However, measuring citizen satisfaction remains difficult. Finally, I outlined the importance of administrative contacting as a means of public participation in a democracy. In fact, many government programs cannot be effective unless citizens and administrators work together. Given the combination of these findings, it can be concluded that some aspects of CRM need to be adapted to the government context.

The empirical study combined a qualitative exploratory case study design and a modified grounded theory approach. The sample for this study consisted of three U.S. cities' and one county's customer services initiatives with 311 projects. The data was analysed in three steps with the aim to conceptualize CiRM. The three steps were comprised of a literature review, a single- and cross-case analysis of the implementation, understanding and impact of CiRM, and a comparative analysis of cross-case data and literature.

One major finding of this research is that 311 or any other activity undertaken to improve citizen-orientation was not considered CRM. In fact, little evidence could be found that administrators were aware of CRM at all. Even those with a work history in the private sector and knowledge about CRM did not try to apply it to government. The only reference made to CRM was during the planning process of the 311 projects when administrators were looking for an appropriate CRM software package for their contact centers. Yet administrators and elected officials pointed out various differences between CRM and CiRM. Government is more complex than a private firm in terms of the types of relationships it has with its customer base and the broadness and depth of its services. Furthermore, CiRM's philosophy is more about serving the citizen efficiently and reducing citizen interactions. The goal of CiRM is to increase citizen satisfaction while at the same time improving accountability and government performance. Except for areas such as welfare, administrators were more interested in the location and particular quality of life issue rather than building citizen profiles. Somewhat surprising was the fact that they stressed that the citizen–government relationship usually occurs in association with negative situations. That is, citizens are forced to obey a government regulation that they might not like, or they ask government for support when they have a problem caused either by government or external factors (e.g. weather, disease).

The empirical evidence on the implementation of CiRM supported the premise that CRM has validity in government. Similar to the early days of CRM in the private sector, CiRM initiatives primarily focused on call centers. However, it was possible to identify many other aspects of CRM—a multi-channel environment, the practice of personalization in specific government programs or the analysis of citizen data collected through 311. It should be noted that the latter was done on an aggregated and not on an individual basis. It also became evident that there was neither a concerted approach to CiRM nor an attempt to apply CiRM holistically. Furthermore, the fact that 311 projects were branded as CiRM mostly originated from the marketing activities of consultants and software vendors. CiRM activities were communicated as customer service initiatives but followed the hidden agenda of improving accountability by establishing a new form of performance management.

CiRM initiatives had an impact on citizens, public administration and elected officials. CiRM made government more accessible to citizens and led to greater equality in some areas. Users of 311 became an additional source of information for public administration. They became the eyes and ears on the ground and provided real-time information on their genuine needs. Furthermore, the government's commitment to solving a citizen's reported issue raises citizens' expectations for government to take action in the future. The ongoing expansion of the centralized 311 contact center and Web portal challenged existing government structures and processes. There was greater transparency about citizen demand as well as greater transparency about administrative performance. CiRM tends to expedite a more data-driven public management function. CiRM also facilitates horizontal and vertical knowledge sharing and cross-boundary collaboration. However, in general, CiRM did not lead to a significant transformation of government or governance. It did, however, allow elected officials to hold public administration accountable. CiRM also provided elected officials with the tools to better understand the aggregated needs of their constituents and to build a more visible link between their actions and citizens' issues. Overall, these findings support the conclusion that CiRM could further politicize the domain of public administration. I argue in line with Fountain (2001a) that the transparencies through CiRM and ICT will cause political battles over such issues as ownership of data.

Based on the preceding analysis, the study's main contribution is a basic conceptualization of CiRM. I argued that there are many components that can be applied to government without further alterations. The cross-case analysis supported this conclusion. Many aspects specific to CiRM depend on one's perspective. First, the idea of value needs to be more broadly defined. A citizen's value could be translated into a monetary figure, thus translating the CLV to "citizen lifetime value" (CiLV). This idea should be discussed further in future research. However, I identified the value of citizens in other areas such as accountability and public value creation. Second, the boundaries of CiRM in government are defined by administrators and elected officials in a bargaining process. The boundaries of citizen-orientation are indirectly set by the citizens with their complaints and votes for elected officials. Third, there is also a different approach to relationship in CiRM: Firms are interested in a long-lasting business relationship with their profitable customers that mainly is associated with product or service transactions. The role CiRM depends first and foremost on the theoretical point of view of the citizen–government relationship, which has been discussed by social scientists and philosophers for centuries. In addition, I concluded that it was in many cases in the best interest of government to have no relationship at all with its citizens. Furthermore, the citizen–provider linearity is blurred. Fourth, collaborative processes on the intra- and inter-organisational level form the foundation of CiRM. Finally, CiRM leads to a shift towards a greater focus on the consolidation and analysis of citizen and government data as well as data from other sources. In conclusion, CiRM is a set of management practices and strategy with a broad citizen focus that maintains and optimizes citizen interactions and encourages citizenship.

My premise of CiRM being involved with encouraging citizenship is based on my judgment that CiRM allows for more pragmatic forms of continuous low-intensity public participation. CiRM makes it easy for anyone to participate in government (e.g. through 311). CiRM facilitates a hybrid form of the expression of individual preferences and technical expertise on community issues that formerly took place in a more conventional way. I propose that sharing the data generated through CiRM with the public could facilitate the role of the citizen as an innovator in line with von Hippel's (2005) user innovation. Instead of taking all the responsibility for solving its issues, public administration can encourage thousands of individuals to work on collective problems. I argue that if the citizen can help government to more efficiently take care of its responsibilities and then feels the impact without a significant delay, then this will have an incremental impact on the overall perception of government. Therefore, in line with an argument of Fung (2006), CiRM would allow citizens to be the "shock troops of democracy": "Properly deployed, their local knowledge, wisdom, commitment, authority, can address wicked failures of legitimacy, justice, and effectiveness in representative and bureaucratic institutions." The forms, purposes and rationales of classical participatory democracy, however, fail to capture what is most attractive about CiRM. Its appeal does not lie primarily in shifting sovereignty from politicians and administrators to citizens. Instead, CiRM mobilizes citizens to address pressing deficits in existing conventional, less participatory governance arrangements and provides government with the means and mechanisms to capture and analyse large quantities of ideas and comments. Therefore, through CiRM, the active involvement of civil society and a strong administrative apparatus are neither mutually exclusive nor contradictory.

6.1   Limitations of this research

While the findings of this research are plausible, there are weaknesses and limitations to this research that militate for certain caveats. Qualitative results such as those presented here haven been criticized for their lack of generalizability. Following the logic of replication (Yin 2003), the reappearing opinions of interviewees as well as the practices identified as CRM across cases provided compelling support for my conceptualization of CiRM. Because this study took into account multiple organizations, going beyond the idiosyncratic views of one organisation or a certain set of individuals, it increased the applicability of the results to other government organisations. Therefore, other municipalities and counties would likely have comparable perspectives and activities. This assumption rests on the tenet of qualitative design that findings are applicable based on shared meanings within a culture. However, the results are valid for the studied U.S. context but do not represent the whole reality. For example, I did not study CiRM in other countries and political systems. For instance, opinions on privacy and citizen segmentation might vary. Further, the cases chosen for this research represented larger U.S. administrations on the municipal and county level. Therefore, I was not able to draw conclusions about the perspectives and applicability of CiRM in smaller administrative settings. In addition, I did not research CiRM on the state or federal level. Yet these levels of government generally have fewer relationships with citizens. Moreover, I realized that the focus on 311 projects did not allow me to fully explore CiRM as it may be used throughout entire organisations and in programs of the administrations studied in each of the cases.

An alternate research design would have been to assess the state of CiRM in a manner similar to that used in the studies undertaken by Accenture (2001; 2003), which tried to determine the penetration and perception of CRM in four specific areas of government and in eleven countries by means of a survey with senior-level executives. This alternative was rejected for several reasons. First, there were important practical considerations. It would have been a daunting, probably impossible, task to gain the necessary access to many different government organisations and executive sponsors in the planned timeframe of this research. Second, because of the emerging nature and nascent stage of CiRM in government, a survey-based approach would only have been able to reinforce existing beliefs (Deshpande 2001) and would not have been suitable to developing a new understanding. Third, a survey-based approach would also not have been able to shed light on the reasons behind the opinions held about certain aspects of CiRM.

As noted earlier, most individuals in government were not even aware of CRM. Because administrators and elected officials were the embedded but predominant unit of analysis, their opinions are slightly overrepresented in the interpretation. They may have also been influenced by their colleagues and the 311 projects. This was, in fact, true for some of the interviews where respondents' definitions of CiRM matched the basic functionality and aims of the 311 projects. Building upon multiple sources of evidence did not allow most of this difficulty to be bypassed or resolved.

It was also beyond the scope of this study to investigate the citizen–government relationship and CiRM from the perspective of the citizen. The omission could create some discrepancies to these results. It was not possible to test citizens' perceptions of whether CiRM can dramatically improve the citizen–government relationship and public services.

Although I concluded that CiRM allows for a different kind of public participation, this study could further benefit from a more detailed discussion of the results with respect to the literature on public participation and the social subcontract. It was also out of the scope of this study to further explore the role and importance citizen data played in the decision-making processes of administrators and elected officials. Moreover, this study was not able to cover the process of data analysis.

Conclusions about the impact of CiRM are essentially conclusions about 311 initiatives and not CiRM. However, I showed that many aspects of 311 initiatives matched CRM. In fact, in the private sector CRM first started in contact centers.

Finally, while I tried to ground the approach to CiRM in an extended review of the CRM literature, the decision on the essential parts of CRM that guided parts of this research were subjective in nature. Thus, other scholars might criticize my understanding of CRM as incomplete. Further, starting with a specific understanding of CRM certainly served the purpose of this study: answering the question of whether there is a difference between private and public CRM. However, this frame of reference might have also limited the possibility of conceptualizing CiRM in ways beyond our current understanding.

6.2 Implications for Theory and Research

This interdisciplinary approach has tried to advance the understanding of CiRM and conceptualize CiRM for future studies within administrative science. First, this study helped identify the similarities and dissimilarities between the private-sector and public-sector experience with behavioral, organizational, and technical variables in the CiRM process. Second, it translated CRM into the context of government by incorporating the existing literature, multiple case study evidence and views of administrators and elected officials. Prior studies on CiRM did not pursue this methodology. Their model of CiRM rests on the private-sector model of CRM and personal opinions about what aspects might be difficult to transfer to government. Their model of CiRM is mostly derived from CRM and the subjective view of the author.

This research is also the first study that linked CiRM to other government move-ments such as TQM or eGovernment. Because I was able to identify many compo-nents of CRM in TQM and eGovernment, this research somewhat demystified the claims about CiRM's uniqueness and potential impact.

Furthermore, this study linked CiRM to the discourse on citizenship and public par-ticipation. Along these lines, this research made a contribution to the ongoing debate about direct versus indirect participation. The case studies showed that direct citizen participation in administrative practice is no longer hypothetical. The discourse about public participation among social scientists has yet to recognize the new form of pub-lic participation that results from CiRM, which has been described in this research. The role and impact of aggregated forms of citizen participation is feasible and desir-able. Yet how this fits within other forms of public participation should be discussed in greater detail. Moreover, there is also a need for understanding and application of the public's (as opposed to institutions', authorities' and agencies') criteria of effective public participation, including their preferred methods for specific issues.

Administrators within this study stressed that many citizens would like to reduce their contact with government. That might actually be true. However, we should probably assume that expectations differ widely—not just on the individual level (a variance between people), but with regard to a single individual's preference of inter-action with a specific type of government function. It is important to determine what citizens value most in their relationships with government. Many customers are al-ready willing to make their detailed buying behaviour transparent to private corpora-tions over which they have no control in return for customized offers or special sav-ings. This research does not provide an answer to the pressing question of whether citizens want a "supersized" public service that is based on individual citizen profiles and aggregated citizen data analysis. The preceding paragraph and the findings of this research point to another issue of importance. Data is becoming more and more impor-tant in administrative decision making. Public decision makers must balance priorities in an environment that offers more tangible information than in the past. It is, there-fore, necessary for the academic discourse to focus on developing an appropriate gov-ernance structure as well as a better understanding of which type of data is useful and how that data can be interpreted and utilized in a mutually beneficial way. Moreover, a knowledge-centric system and organisation requires a public servant who has a broad understanding of goals, strategies, stakeholders and how their own work fits in this context. A term that has been used recently is system-level bureaucrat (Reddick 2005). How people capable of executing such a new role can be attracted to public admini-stration and how upper-level administrators will react to sharing the power of "know-ing" has yet to be determined.

With regard to a different issue, researchers in the field of public administration should never stop questioning the effects of management practices on the roles of the citizen. However, this study clearly underlines the fact that we can stop criticizing the idea of calling the citizen a customer. First, this aspect has been discussed exhaustively in the past. There is nothing left to be said. We simply need to be aware that the concept of "customer", borrowed from the private sector, will always have flaws when applied in government as Moore (1995) and others have noted. Second, most administrators are well aware that the citizens have multiple roles. Calling the citizen a customer does not necessarily result in passivity of the citizen. It also does not achieve some kind of hidden agenda of government to make the citizen a passive consumer, harkening back to the citizen–government relationship of the 19th century. If the term "customer" helps public servants to generally behave in a more courteous and friendly way—between each other or toward the citizen—that should not be criticized.

Finally, an important contribution of this study is that it highlights the need for additional research on the strategies, implementation, understanding and impact of CiRM. This study helped identify CiRM from the perspective of municipal and county government, and could be the focus of future efforts to determine if there is a similar pattern across the CiRM implementation experiences of multiple government organizations, whether municipal, county, state or federal. It would be useful to conduct a detailed study of CiRM-type activities over a longer time period, with both studies of citizens and government. It would also be very interesting to do a longitudinal study of a single case from multiple perspectives that begins before a holistic CiRM implementation is started in order to test for the real changes that occur in the citizen–government relationship. Finally, because CiRM facilitates cross-boundary collaboration, researchers are encouraged to study arrangements such as those in Miami-Dade County in greater detail.

6.3 Implications for Policy and Public Management

The results of the research suggest that CiRM offers guidance to public managers in creating a customer-centric organisation. CiRM allows the structuring and designing of the citizen experience of interacting with government. It introduces a new form of low-intensity citizen participation. And it supports the shift to a real-time, data-driven decision and performance management style. Yet it is not a panacea for the problems of government. CiRM can only be one of the strategic steps taken to cope with the challenges of shrinking budgets, a declining public workforce, issues in resource allocation and demands for citizen-orientation. In order to realize a customer-centric organisation and move beyond 311, it would be necessary to establish a centralized unit that coordinates the CiRM efforts throughout government. Miami-Dade's GIC is a step in the right direction.

Many governments focus on the automation of internal processes in their CiRM efforts in order to achieve internal efficiencies. However, establishing processes of analysing and acting upon the information from citizens and internal knowledge is predicted to lead to greater rewards. The key to effective analysis is the existence of high-quality data. My recommendation is to develop a strategy to acquire, assimilate, transform and exploit new knowledge from internal and external sources, including citizens. It is very important for public managers to abstract from the data provided by resources such as 311. With regard to 311, I doubt that all U.S. citizens will ever be able to benefit from it. The way 311 had been introduced was very pragmatic and avoided conflicts with the sovereignty of jurisdictions. Germany's attempt to introduce a countrywide networked multi-jurisdictional N-1-1 solution (115 Bürgertelefon) or Korea's N-1-1 solution (110) might offer alternatives.

Thus, 311 is a phenomenon that can mostly be found on the municipal level. However, this resulted in isolated solutions similar to those of the many the Web offerings that follow the existing demarcations of government. For instance, in the state of Massachusetts, the City of Somerville has implemented 311. The City of Boston and the City of Cambridge have not done so as of this writing. Yet for many outsiders as well as citizens it is hard to understand why there could not be a single 311 solution to serve the population living in the Greater Boston area. Further, many 311 projects simply capture non-emergency policing issues of citizens. Finally, smaller communities struggle to copy the actions taken in cities such as New York or Chicago. They need to collaborate with other communities or higher jurisdictions in order to have any chance of success. Collaboration is also needed in cases where there are several contact centers within close proximity.

That said, 311 can be a bold move toward cross-boundary collaboration and a new form of just-in-time government. The following recommendations are specifically directed to decision makers in government that engage in 311 projects.

A 311 project provides you with the opportunity to create a citizen-centric administrative unit from scratch. During that process, making mistakes is expected—but because you're bringing into being something that did not exist before, you also have the unique opportunity to be truly creative. Therefore:

- Choose the right person to lead your project. The person needs to have not only a broad network throughout government but to be well respected by various agency senior and executive-level representatives.

- Research on public-sector change processes (Kelman 2005) showed that managers prefer surrounding themselves with those who are in favour of new initiatives. I recommend the opposite: spending more time with your critics. It is from them that you can often learn the most helpful things.

- Get support from as many stakeholders as possible. Project teams in the cases studied included representatives from all relevant parties in order to ensure sustainable support. Let those who buy-in strongly take ownership of certain parts of the project.

- Communicate continuously and openly, and set clear objectives—in short, manage expectations. For instance, Miami-Dade County's 311 contact center team did hundreds of tours for departments, municipalities and elected officials, showing them the 311 operations in depth. At the same time and through appropriate channels, create public awareness—it is a powerful driver of support.

- Choose areas that have high exposure politically for your pilot programs so that you can start off with a success story. The more success stories to tell, the more positive support you can win throughout the organization. Organizational units that are already struggling with various problems have usually nothing to lose and might have the greatest potential for improvement and a concommitant openness to radical change.

- Political support is crucial, because turf is the number-one factor in failure. Baltimore and New York City both implemented their contact centers (and Citistat initiative (Baltimore) in times of a budget crisis. But because there were strong mayors and relentless political commitment to achieve the goals, the opposition was not able to stop the projects.

- Look for best practices around you. Many public administrations around the world face the same challenges you do. Some might have found new approaches. Invite them to share their experience and knowledge with the whole organization. This culture of knowledge sharing is the biggest advantage that government has over the private sector. Further, an outside perspective and hands-on results can convince even the strongest of oppositions.

- Think out of the box. Don't accept organizational structures, processes and locations as the way to always do operations. In a cross-boundary environment, legislative process and oversight will be different and will require more openness from everybody if collaboration is to take place. Again, communication is important. Talk to older members of your organization and ask about past reform ideas. In that way you can avoid making mistakes twice. At the same time, you can gain a lot of rich information.

- When making executive-level decisions, always consider the changes that will need to be carried out by the lowest hierarchy level when you estimate the amount of change your organisation will have to endure. The more change, the more opposition you should to expect and the more attention you must give to your communications.

- Do not expect that technology offers you a direct return on investments. Cost-savings opportunities are generated through the transparency and the data products of technology. While technology will shape opportunity and operations, it will only be as successful as the leadership behind it. The environment in which technology exists is all about management and politics, which is the key domain of a public leader.

- Cross-boundary collaboration and technology implementation has many obstacles to overcome. Drawbacks are unavoidable. Be patient and take one step at a time. Incremental change will lead to great change over time.

Appendix A – Case study planning

Document guidelines

(related to CRM/CiRM/311 or citizen orientation)

- List of involved external and internal actors

- Studies (internal, external)

- Project Plans

- Proposals

- Written documentation of meetings

- Emails (i.e. which are a good example of reactions to organizational changes, etc.)

- (Progress) reports, Memos, Policy papers

- Budget plans / calculations

- Citizen Surveys (before/after)

- Citizen preferences analysis or similar

- Other internal documents

Interview guidelines

Executive Level Administrators

Bold questions were the most important ones. In case of time restrictions, the interview focused only on these questions.

Area	Questions
Start	Please describe your involvement in the 311/ CiRM project
	Please describe the role of elected leadership the project?
	Could you summarise some lessons learned so far? (For yourself, government, PA)
	What has changed since the introduction of 311/CiRM
C > PA Rel	What are your plans for a better understanding of the citizens?
C > PA Rel	**How would you describe the relationship between citizen and public administration? (Why manage it)**
C > PA Rel	How would you describe the roles of a. the citizens in terms of PA and b. pa in terms of C?
C > PA Rel	**How does the organization deal with citizen feedback**
C > PA Rel	**What kind of relationship would citizens want to have with their public administration?**
Call Center - 311	**What did you learn from 311 feedback?**
Call Center - 311	How was the reaction of certain divisions or authorities when you announced 311?

Case	What are your current citizen-oriented practices?
Change	What are the biggest barriers to change in your organisation?
CiRM	Who made the decision with respect to CRM?
CiRM	**Did you look at CRM in the private sector? Where are the major differences to public sector use?**
CiRM	**Please define CiRM from your point of view or what you think about the term?**
CiRM	**What would be the goals or vision of CiRM from your point of view?**
CiRM	**Where do you expect the greatest hurdles? Can you recall similar difficulties or experience from other projects?**
CiRM	**What effects do you expect from Citizen Relationship Management/ 311? (C, PA)**
CiRM	What is the effect of ICT and eGovernment on departments, public administration and government?
CiRM	**Does CiRM change the role of PA in society/state (Figure, 3 actors)**
CiRM	**Did you realize a change in citizen behaviour or activities during service delivery since you have information available online?**
CiRM	**For which aspects of CRM did you seek external advice? What was your experience?**
CiRM	**How can you finance a wider channel variety?**
CiRM	What are the challenges of establishing and having a multi channel environment?
CiRM	Which service level is appropriate per channel? (Information, Communication, Transaction)
CiRM	How did or do you plan to implement your CRM project?
CiRM	**How does CRM and eGovernment fit together?**
CiRM	Did the Web channel/ 311 uncover any issue that you were not aware of? (demand, problems, etc.)
CiRM	**Did you redesign processes during your CRM initiatives?**
CiRM	What was your experience when you offered new channels (Web/call) to the citizens?
CiRM	Do you track channel effectiveness (How), that is among others, which channel most effectively serving different customer segments?
CiRM	You did some best practice research before you started. What were the most striking lessons you draw for your own strategy and implementation
CiRM	**What incentives did you offer agency heads or executives to join in sharing?**
Citizen as Customers	**How do you communicate new services, channels and changes to the citizens?**
Participation	**What are your measures of encouraging public participation?**
Citizen-orientation	**What effects of improved customer service on citizens do you expect from citizens in terms of public participation?**
Citizen-orientation	**What is the value for public administration to be more citizen-oriented?**
Citizen-orientation	**Who defines citizen-orientation for the public administration**
Citizen-orientation	**Are citizen needs clearly defined and updated regularly within your organisation?**

Citizen satisfaction	**How do you measure satisfaction at the moment? How often**
Citizen satisfaction	What do you expect from higher citizen satisfaction?
Citizen satisfaction	What are factors for citizen satisfaction (from your own research)?
Citizen satisfaction	From your point of view, would citizens use services more often if there are more satisfied with the way of delivery, the PA in general or are offered a broader service range?
Citizen satisfaction	**How often did you survey customer expectations in the past?**
Citizen satisfaction	Do citizens become less active participants if satisfaction rises
Citizen satisfaction	When do citizens participate?
Collaboration	**Please describe your experience with cross-departmental and multi-jurisdictional collaboration**
Collaboration	**What are the major constraints to agency / multi-jurisdictional collaboration?**
Collaboration	**What are the main incentives for co-operations across agencies?**
Collaboration	**What are you measures to foster cross agency / multi-jurisdictional collaboration?**
Costs and Funding	Can you tell me how many services (combined) you offer to the citizens?
Costs and Funding	**Do you know the costs of each service?**
Costs and Funding	What are the key drivers for costs?
Costs and Funding	Were do you see the greatest opportunity for cost reduction?
Data	Which data do you share with different agencies?
Data	**Which citizen data would you like to store centralized and share across all departments, jurisdictions?**
Data	How can or did you solve data security and privacy issues?
eGov	**What is your understanding of eGovernment and its goals?**
eGov	Did you realize a change in citizen behaviour or activities during service delivery since you put information online?
eGov	Are you satisfied with citizens uptake of eGov?
eGov	**Please describe some of the major challenges in your eGovernment related projects**
eGov	**When comparing with the past, has ICT improved your control of the organisation**
PA > P relationship	**Is there a commitment from politicians to support the citizen service concept (Show my drawing)? Are they aware of the implications?**
PA > P relationship	Did you ever try to approach politics with citizen feedback to change something? How was the reaction?
Performance	Are you measuring performance?
PS improvement	**What is public service improvement (in general) for you? Where is the limit?**
PS improvement	What is public service improvement for the citizens?
PS improvement	**Do you think tasks or new regulations are usually clear enough to create a process/ service / work effectively?**
PS improvement	Do you think they are implemented according to citizens needs?

PS improvement	How would you characterize high quality citizen services?
PS improvement	**Did initiatives lead to loss of resources in other areas? How was reaction by public servants?**
PS improvement	**Where do you see your greatest area of improvement in terms of citizen-orientation?**
Public Services	**Do you have an estimate on how much an average or specific citizen costs the city/county every year?**
Public Services	Do you know how often an average Miami resident has contact with the pa in a year?
Public Services	What is your opinion on offering citizens more choices for one and the same service?
End	How did you initiate change?
	Own comments, questions you would like to get answer from colleagues around the globe on citizen-orientation / citizen relationship / CRM?
	How would you describe the most widely shared aims of your organization?
	If you think about the future, how might 311 and similar activities change the relationship with citizens and EO?
	Is there anything you would like to say regarding anything we discussed?
	Do you have any questions regarding about anything we discussed?

Elected Officials

Area	Questions
Start	Please describe your involvement in the 311/ CiRM project
	Please describe the role of elected leadership the project?
	Could you summarise some lessons learned so far? (For yourself, government, pa)
	What has changed since the introduction of 311/CiRM
C > PA Rel	**How would you describe the relationship between citizen and public administration?**
C > PA Rel	**How do you deal with citizen feedback? (Examples pos/neg)**
C > PA Rel	What kind of relationship would citizens want to have with their public administration?
Call Center - 311	**What did you learn from 311 feedback?**
Change	**What are the biggest constraints to change in public administration**
Change	Did the Internet channel or use of 311 lead to a structural change of public admin?
CiRM	**Please define CiRM from your point of view or what you think about the term?**
CiRM	**What would be the goals or vision of CiRM from your point of view?**
CiRM	**Where do you expect the greatest hurdles? Can you recall similar difficulties or experience from other projects?**
CiRM	**What effects do you expect from Citizen Relationship Management/ 311? (C, PA)**
CiRM	What is the effect of ICT and eGovernment on departments, public administration and government?

CiRM	Does CiRM change the role of PA in society/state (Figure, 3 actors)
CiRM	Did you realize a change in citizen behaviour or activities during service delivery since you have information available online?
Citizen as Customers	What effects of improved customer service on citizens do you expect? (passive)
Citizen-orientation	What is the value for public administration to be more citizen-oriented?
Citizen-orientation	How do you balance the interest of different groups, especially less eloquent groups?
Citizen-orientation	Who defines citizen-orientation in government?
Citizen-orientation	Did you ever change a process/service due to citizen requests/feedback to PA after legislation was passed?
Citizen-orientation	What are your measures of encouraging public participation?
Citizen-orientation	Where do you see your greatest area of improvement in terms of citizen-orientation?
Citizen satisfaction	What are factors for citizen satisfaction (from your own research)?
Citizen satisfaction	When do citizens participate?
Collaboration	Please describe your experience with cross-departmental and jurisdictional collaboration
Collaboration	What are the majors constraints to agency / multi-jurisdictional collaboration?
Collaboration	What are your measures to foster cross agency / multi-jurisdictional collaboration?
Data	What do you think about sharing basic citizen data profiles across agency and jurisdictional boundaries?
eGovernment	What is your understanding of eGovernment, its goals and impact?
PA > P relationship	Do we have to rethink the whole structure and organisation of PA to use the advantages of ICT and be more citizen-oriented?
PA > P relationship	Do you expect any changes in your relationship to PA through 311/CiRM?
PA > P relationship	What do you think about the greater power of PA through citizen knowledge accumulation?
PA > P relationship	What do you think of the possibility that direct citizen contacting to you decreases significantly through 311 and other measures?
PS improvement	What is public service improvement (in general) for you? Where is the limit?
PS improvement	What is public service improvement for the citizens?
PS improvement	Do you think tasks or new regulations are usually clear enough to create a process/ service / work effectively?
PS improvement	Do you think they are implemented according to citizens needs?
PS improvement	How would you characterize high quality citizen services?
End	Are there some questions or things you would like to ask or learn from your colleagues or researchers in the field of CiRM?
	Is there anything you would like to say regarding anything we discussed?

Customer Service Representatives (CSR – 311 call takers)

Area	Questions
Start	Please describe your involvement in the 311/ CiRM project
	Please describe the role of elected leadership the project?
	Could you summarise some lessons learned so far? (For your self, government, pa)
	What has changed since the introduction of 311CiRM
C > PA Rel	How would you describe the relationship between citizen and public administration?
C > PA Rel	How would you describe the roles of a. the citizens in terms of PA and b. pa in terms of C?
C > PA Rel	Please describe some unique experience you had with your callers? (Pos/Neg)
C > PA Rel	How do you analyse citizen input and preferences?
C > PA Rel	Have citizens ever called you with suggestions for improvement of anything gov / PA related?
C > PA Rel	What kind of relationship would citizens want to have with their public administration?
Data	Do you think something like a citizen profile would make your 311 work easier?
Data	Can citizens request a complete erasure of their data?
Collaboration	How often does customer interaction/transaction require cross agency work?
Collaboration	What is your experience with cross-agency work?
Call Center - 311	Why do citizens call 311 (major reasons)?
Call Center - 311	Did you learn something through 311 that you were not aware of of your fellow citizens?
Call Center - 311	When do you support call takers?
Call Center - 312	How often does this happen`?
PS improvement	How would you characterize high quality citizen services?
PS improvement	Where do you see your greatest area of improvement in terms of citizen-orientation?
Public Services	Which service characteristics may be important to your clients/ citizens? (i.e. timeliness, transparency, etc.)
Public Services	What is your experience with citizens as co-producers?
CiRM	How do you like your software solution?
CiRM	Is there anything you would like to improve in future versions?
CiRM	Please describe the role of executives and elected leadership the project?
End	If you think about the future, how might 311 and similar activities change the relationship with citizens and EO?
	Is there anything you would like to say regarding anything we discussed?

311 Manager

Area	Questions
Start	Please describe your involvement in the 311/ CiRM project
	Please describe the role of elected leadership the project?
	Could you summarize some lessons learned so far? (For yourself, government, pa)
	What has changed since the introduction of 311/CiRM
CiRM	You did some best practice research before you started. What were the most striking lessons you draw for your own strategy and implementation
eGov	What is the effect of ICT on organisational and cultural change of departments/ public administration)
eGov	What was or is the impact of eGovernment on your organisation?
eGov	Did you realize a change in citizen behaviour or activities during service delivery since you put information online?
eGov	Are you satisfied with citizens uptake of eGovernment?
eGov	Please describe some of the major difficulties in your eGovernment related projects
eGov	What is your understanding of eGovernment and its goals?
eGov	What are the effects of 311/CiRM and ICT on hierarchy within pa organisation?
eGov	How about control?
C > PA Rel	How would you describe the relationship between citizen and public administration?
C > PA Rel	Please describe some unique experience you had with your callers? Pos/Neg
C > PA Rel	How does the organization deal with citizen feedback
C > PA Rel	What kind of relationship would citizens want to have with their public administration?
C > PA Rel	How much information on citizen feedback do you get at your level in the hierarchy?
Citizen as Customers	What effects of improved customer service on citizens do you expect from citizens in terms of public participation?
Citizen as Customers	How do you communicate new services, channels and changes to the citizens?
Citizen orientation	Can you describe the current state of your organisation on terms of citizen orientation
Citizen orientation	What is the value for public administration to be more citizen oriented?
Citizen orientation	How did you approach the creation of a citizen oriented PA?
Citizen orientation	Are citizen needs clearly defined and updated regularly within your organisation?
Citizen orientation	How do you communicate results from citizen surveys/feedback within your organisation? (also Externally)
Citizen orientation	Did you ever change or a process/service due to citizen requests/feedback to PA?
Data	Which citizen data would you like to store centralized and share across all departments, jurisdictions?
Data	Can citizens request a complete erasure of their data?
Collaboration	Please describe your experience with cross departmental and multijurisdictional collaboration

Collaboration	What are the major constraints to agency / multi-jurisdictional collaboration?
Collaboration	What are the main incentives for cooperation across agencies?
Collaboration	What are you measures to foster cross agency / multi-jurisdictional collaboration?
Collaboration	How often does customer interaction/transaction require cross agency work?
	When you compare Miami/Dade 311 to other 311s you have visited. What is different? What is the same?
Call Center - 311	Why do citizens call 311 (major reasons)?
Call Center - 311	What did you learn from 311 feedback?
Call Center - 311	How do you analyze 311 data and feedback?
Call Center - 311	How was the reaction of certain divisions or authorities when you announced 311? (collaboration)
Call Center - 311	How did you communicate 311?
Call Center - 311	How many citizens are taken care of by public service personell.
Call Center - 311	How often do you train CSR?
Call Center - 311	What are you doing in training?
Call Center - 311	What are your future plans for 311?
PS improvement	What is public service improvement (in general) for you? Where is the limit?
PS improvement	What is public service improvement for the citizens?
Public Services	Can you tell me how many services (combined) you offer to the citizens?
Public Services	Do you know how often each service is used?
Public Services	Do you know the costs of each service?
Public Services	Do you have an estimate on how much an average or specific citizen costs the city/county every year?
PS improvement	Do you think tasks or new regulations are usually clear enough to create a process/ service / work effectively?
PS improvement	Do you think they are implemented according to citizens needs?
PS improvement	How would you characterize high quality citizen services?
PS improvement	Did initiatives lead to loss of resources in other areas? How was reaction by public servants?
PS improvement	Where do you see your greatest area of improvement in terms of citizen orientation?
Public Services	Do you know how often an average Miami resident has contact with the pa in a year?
Public Services	What are the key drivers for costs in current PS?
Public Services	Were do you see the greatest opportunity for cost reduction?
Public Services	How do you want to raise transparency of process?
Public Services	Which customer process involves all state levels?
Public Services	Which product / service characteristics may be important to your clients/ citizens? (i.e. timeliness, transparency, etc.)
Public Services	Which agencies have most citizen contacts?
Public Services	What is your opinion on offering citizens more choices for one and the same service?
Public Services	What is your experience with citizens as coproducers?
CRM	Please describe the role of executives and elected leadership the project?
CRM	Who made the decision with respect to CRM?

CRM	Did you try to request feedback from the citizens before? What was your experience? How did you use the information?
CRM	Please define CRM from your point of view or what you know about the term?
CRM	Describe CRM major goals, impact? Where do you expect the greatest hurdles? Can you recall similar difficulties or experience from former projects?
CRM	What benefits do you expect for the PA from CRM?
CRM	How would staff react to implied changes?
CRM	For which aspects of CRM did you seek external advice? From whome?
CRM - Channels	How can you finance a wider channel variety?
CRM - Channels	What are the challenges of establishing and having a multi channel environment?
CRM - Channels	Which service level is appropriate per channel? (Information, Communication, Transaction)
CRM	How did or do you plan to implement your CRM project?
CRM - Channels	How does CRM and eGovernment fit together?
CRM - Channels	How much will CRM cost you? Estimates?
CRM - Channels	Did the web channel/ 311 uncover latent demand / feedback for certain PS / issues?
CRM	Did you redesign processes during your CRM initiatives?
CRM - Channels	How did you approach the CRM project: One major change or smaller projects?
CRM - Channels	What was your experience when you offered new channels (web/call) to the citizens?
CRM - Channels	Do you track channel effectiveness (How), that is among others, which channel most effectively serving different customer segments?
CRM - Channels	Did you define the role and service level of each channel?
Citizen satisfaction	How do you measure satisfaction at the moment? How often
Performance	Are you measuring performance?
Citizen satisfaction	What do you expect from higher citizen satisfaction?
Citizen satisfaction	What are factors for citizen satisfaction (from your own research)?
Citizen satisfaction	From your point of view, would citizens use services more often if there are more satisfied with the way of delivery, the PA in general or are offered a broader service range?
Citizen satisfaction	How often did you survey customer expectations in the past?
Citizen satisfaction	Do citizens become less active participants if satisfactions rises?
Citizen satisfaction	When do citizens participate?
TQM	Did you have a TQM initiative? What was your experience?
Change	What are the biggest barriers to change in your organisation?
PA > P relationship	Is there a commitment from politicians to support the citizen service concept (Show my drawing)? Are they aware of the implications? Do you think they might misuse it?
PA > P relationship	How much time in the week/day to you spend answering questions?

Jane E. Fountain
Professor of Political Science and Public Policy
Director, National Center for Digital Government
Director, Science, Technology and Society Program

October 26, 2005

To Whom it May Concern

This is to introduce Alexander Schellong and to ask that you support his doctoral dissertation research by making available your time and insights in his research area. Alexander is a highly qualified individual with wide experience in the field of Citizen Relationship Management (CiRM) and eGovernment. He began his studies at a well-known university in Europe, has been a private sector professional and decided to pursue graduate study in public management. Mr. Schellong served with distinction as a Visiting Research Fellow at the National Center for Digital Government (NCDG) which I founded and directed at Harvard's Kennedy School of Government before its recent move with me to the University of Massachusetts at Amherst. His fellowship was based at the Kennedy School of Government from August 2004 to August 2005. He remains a Fellow at Harvard University in the successor program of the NCDG, the Program on Networked Governance.

I have been intrigued by the dissertation research plan developed by Mr. Schellong which concerns the detailed analysis of the Customer Relationship Management concept and technology for public administration and its impact on the citizen government relationship. The project provides a basis for a stream of related studies which, if undertaken, have promise to shape significantly the emerging field of Citizen Relationship Management, which includes a deeper understanding of the citizen as a client of public administration, as well as citizen participation. Alexander will conduct cases studies which include a broad document analysis and in-depth interviews. The knowledge on CiRM/311 and citizen orientation provided through your internal documents and by his interviewees is essential for his dissertation.

This letter is directed towards administrative leaders, public managers, elected officials and other involved actors. I ask you to support Alexander's dissertation research by making available your time and knowledge. Your cooperation is crucial if the case studies are to provide researchers and public managers alike with sound results. Alexander has excellent communicative skills and the professional background to work with managers and employees at all levels within any organization. His approach to case research is to treat data and interviews as confidential material unless reviewed and cleared by the host organization. He approaches his cases with a high degree of professionalism and objectivity. I strongly recommend supporting Alexander Schellong without reservation.

Please do not hesitate to contact me by email at fountain@polsci.umass.edu or by telephone at 413-545-1007 should you have further questions or concerns.

Many thanks and with best regards,

Jane E. Fountain

National Center for Digital Government • Phone: 413-545-1007
fountain@polsci.umass.edu • www.umass.edu/digitalcenter

University of Massachusetts • Thompson Hall • Amherst, MA 01003 • tel: 413·545·3940 • fax: 413·545·1108 • info@pubpol.umass.edu

www.masspolicy.org

164

HARVARD
UNIVERSITY JOHN F. KENNEDY
SCHOOL OF GOVERNMENT

David Lazer
Associate Professor of Public Policy

December 3, 2005

To Whom It May Concern

 I am writing to respectfully ask for your participation or support of the doctoral research entitled "CRM in the Public Sector – Empirical and Theoretical Analysis of the impact of Citizen Relationship Management (CRM) on the citizen government relationship" by Alexander Schellong. There is little academic research on CRM, despite its rapidly emerging importance in local government. Alexander is a Research Fellow at Harvard University, where I have sponsored him in my position as the Director of the Program for Networked Governance.

 Alexander Schellong received his masters in political science and economics from the elite Johann Wolfgang Goethe- University in Germany. He began his PhD studies in winter of 2003 and has been a Research Fellow at Harvard University since August 2004. I have been his sponsor at the Kennedy School, overseeing his research. I am in a good position, therefore, to vouch for him, which I do so with enthusiasm.

 To truly understand the process and challenges in the adoption of CRM in local government, he will need to interview the key decision makers as well as to have access to the documentation regarding CRM in the sites he is studying. Your participation and support of the study is therefore critical to its success.

 In short, I have full confidence in Mr. Schellong's abilities and integrity. He is well qualified to pursue this research. Of course, interviews and other obtained material will not be given to any third parties. Individuals and organizations will not be named unless otherwise requested by participants. Participants may not receive any direct benefit from this study, except to the extent that the study provides general insight into CRM. Mr. Schellong will also personally debrief each organization that has participated in the research regarding his overall findings.

165

Please contact me personally anytime by email (david_lazer@harvard.edu) or telephone (617 384-8319) should you have any questions or concerns.

Sincerely yours,

David Lazer
Associate Professor of Public Policy
Director
Program on Networked Governance
Harvard University

Appendix B - Coding

Open coding (initial pre-coding set: 76 nodes)

311	Cross-/Up-selling
911	Customer Lifetime Value
Baltimore	Customer orientation
BPR / BPA	Customer Satisfaction
Budget	Customer Service
Call Center Implementation	eGovernment
Call Center Operation	Employees feedback/innovation
Call Centers (pre311)	IVR
Challenges	Knowledge Sharing
Challenges (Overcoming, Solving)	Knowledgebase
Change	Latent Demand
Change Management	Leadership
Channels	Marketing
Chicago	Miami-Dade County
CiRM	Multi-channel
CiRM definition	Multi-jurisdictional issues
CiRM Market	New Public Management
CiRM Motivation for	New York City
Citizen Behaviour	One-Stop
Citizen Empowerment	Performance Management
Citizen Insights	Personalization
Citizen Interaction	Privacy
Citizen-oriented organisation	Quality Control
City of Miami	Relationship - EO ◇ C
Closed Loop	Relationship - PA ◇ C
Collaboration	Relationship - PA ◇ EO
Communication (Lack/Importance)	Relationship Pa ◇ Pa
Costs	Segmentation
Counter (Agency)	Self Service
CRM (culture - Lack of)	Services
CRM (culture)	Siebel CRM
CRM (Private vs. Public)	Strategic Planning
CRM analytical	Survey
CRM Europe	Technology
CRM operational	Technology (Issues-Challenges)
CRM other	TQM
CRM Software	Training
CRM Vision	Web: Portal

Open coding (final set: 224 nodes)

211	Citizen Profile
311	Citizen Reaction
411	Citizens Calls
911	City of Miami
Access	Closed Loop
Accountability	Collaboration
Admin 311 perception	Communication (Lack/Importance)
Agreements/ Contracts	Complaint
Backend - Front-end Integration	Complexity
Baltimore	CompStat
Bloomberg	CompStat and 311
Bloomberg, Emma	Conflict of Interest
BPR / BPA	Consultant Influence
Budget	Consultants
Call Center Implementation	Coordination
Call Center Operation	Costs
Call Center/Contact Center front face issue	Counter (Agency)
Call Centers (pre311)	Crime
Call Taker as Advocate/Navigator	Critics
Call takers	CRM (culture - Lack of)
Call Volume	CRM (culture)
Call/Contact Center Manager	CRM (Private vs. Public)
Case Management	CRM analytical
Centralization	CRM operational
Challenges	CRM other
Challenges (Overcoming, Solving)	CRM Software
Change	CRM Vision
Change - 311 impact	Cross-/Up-selling
Change - Loss of resources	Cross-boundary collaboration
Change - Public Servants	Cross-boundary constraints
Change - Role of Leadership	Cross-boundary example
Change (Organizational)	Cross-boundary perception
Change (People)	CSA
Change (Process)	Customer Lifetime Value
Change Management	Customer orientation
Channels	Customer Satisfaction
Chicago	Customer Service
CiRM	Data
CiRM definition	Data analysis and presentation
CiRM Market	Decision Making
CiRM Motivation for	Departments/Agencies
Cities (Exchange for Planning & Impl)	Digital Divide
CitiStat	Efficiency gains
Citizen Behaviour	eGovernment
Citizen Demand	Elected / Re-elected
Citizen Empowerment	Elected Official 311 Perception
Citizen Insights	Elected Officials
Citizen Interaction	Elected Officials - contra
Citizen less important than location/incident	Elected officials - lose contact
Citizen not understanding how gov works	Elected Officials - pro
Citizen-oriented organisation	Emergency Management
Citizen Participation (lack of interest)	Employees feedback/innovation
Citizen Participation/Reintegration	Escalation
Citizen Passive	Executive Power (Lack of)
Citizen Perception (of Gov)	Executive Support/ Decision

Expectations
Failed Projects
Finance
Finance - funding 311
Financial Crisis
Gartner
Getting the buy-in / Buy-in
GIS
Governance Structure
Government perception
Hanson
Hierarchies
Human touch / Contact
Impact- Data
Impact - call takers
Impact - citizens
Impact - elected officials
Impact - government
Implementation
Incentives
Information
Institutionalized
Intangibles
Interviewee Personal Background
IVR
Knowledge - Explicit (Codifiable)
Knowledge - Tacit (non-codifiable)
Knowledge Sharing
Knowledgebase
Knowledgebase Issue
Latent Demand
Leadership
Leadership (Bad)
Legal issues
Legislation / Legislation into Process
Limit to Service Orientation
Management
Marketing
MBO
Miami-Dade County
Mobile
Motorola CSR
Multi-channel
Multi-jurisdictional issues
Municipality
Networked Government
New Public Management
New York City
Non-emergency definitions
One-Stop
Performance Management
Personalization
Personal Relationship influencing project
Philadelphia
Phone/Cell phone Companies
Police role / Police
Policy

Priorities/Conflicts of interest (different)
Privacy
Proactive / Reactive
Process Overlaps
Process Time
PSAP
Public Outreach
Public vs Private differences
Quality Control
Real Time
Reconnecting lower ◇ higher hierarchies
Red Tape
Relationship - EO ◇ C
Relationship - PA ◇ C
Relationship - PA ◇ EO
Relationship Pa ◇ Pa
Resistance
Resource Allocation
Responsiveness
Reverse 911
Savings (Costs)
Secret Shopping
Segmentation
Self Service
Service Level Agreement
Service Request
Services
Servicestat
Shared Services
Siebel CRM
Silo mentality
Situational Awareness
Social Network
Soft launch
Standards
Strategic Planning
Sunk Costs
Survey
Sustainability
System Level Bureaucrat
Taxonomy
Technology
Technology (Issues-Challenges)
Technology (Role)
Technology (Telephony)
Tension between work ethics
Time
TQM
Training
Transparency
Trust
Turf / Territorialism
Unions
Usability
Vendor (Influence, Reliance, etc.)
Voice Options
Web: Portal

Appendix C - TQM

Deming's (1986) 14 points

1. Create constancy of purpose to improve product and service.
2. Adopt new philosophy for new economic age by management learning responsibilities and taking leadership for change.
3. Cease dependence on inspection to achieve quality; eliminate the need for mass inspection by building quality into the product.
4. End awarding business on price, instead minimize total cost and move towards single suppliers for items.
5. Improve constantly and forever the system of production and service to improve quality and productivity and to decrease costs.
6. Institute training on the job.
7. Institute leadership; supervision should be to help to do a better job; overhaul supervision of management and production workers.
8. Drive out fear so that all may work effectively for the organization.
9. Break down barriers between departments; research, design, sales and production must work together to foresee problems in production and use.
10. Eliminate slogans, exhortations, and numerical targets for the workforce, such as zero defects or new productivity levels. Such exhortations are diversory as the bulk of the problems belong to the system and are beyond the power of the workforce.
11. Eliminate quotas or work standards, and management by objectivity or numerical goals; substitute leadership.
12. Remove barriers that rob people of their right to pride workmanship; hourly workers, management and engineering; eliminate annual or merit ratings and management by objective.
13. Institute a vigorous education and self-improvement program.
14. Put everyone in the company to work to accomplish the transformation.

Juran's (1988) quality planning road map

1. Identify who are the customers.
2. Determine the needs of those customers.
3. Translate the needs into language.
4. Develop a product which can respond to those needs.
5. Optimise the product features so as to meet our needs as well as customer needs.
6. Develop a process which is able to produce the product.
7. Optimise the process.
8. Prove that the process can produce the product under operating conditions.
9. Transfer the process to Operations.

Tools of TQM

Archetypes of systems (Senge)

Affinity diagram (Walton)

Arrow diagram (Mizuno)

Benchmarking (Camp)

Brainstorming (de Bono)

Cause – effect diagram (Walton)

Charts and graphs (Walton)

Control charts (Oakland)

Cost – benefit analysis (Oakland)

Five whys (Murgatroyd/ Morgan)

Force field analysis

Histograms (Walton/Oakland)

House of quality (Murgatroyd/Morgan)

Mental mapping (Senge)

Pareto charts (Waltonn)

Process decision program charts (Mizuno)

Process mapping (Murgotroyd/Morgan)

Run charts (Walton)

Sampling (Oakland)

Scatter diagram s(Walton)

Six thinking hats (de Bono)

Six action shoes (de Bono)

Systematic diagram (Mizuno)

Three Mus (Murgatryod/Morgan)

Appendix D – Case data

The City of Baltimore

Abandoned Vehicle Complaint	Illegal Sign Investigation – Public Property
Animal Control – Barking Dog Report	Lot Cleaning (city-owned Lot)
Animal Control – Running at Large	Missed Mixed Refuse Pickup
Animal Control – Stray Animal or Trapped	Missed Recycling Pickup
Animal Control – Unsanitary Conditions	Open Fire Hydrant
Ball Field Maintenance	Park Maintenance
Bulk Trash Pickup	Parking Meter Complaints
City Pool Repair	Playground Maintenance
Construction without Building Permit	Pothole Repair
Dead Animal Pickup	Rat Rubout Request
Debris Hanging From Wires or Poles	Recycling Schedule Request
Dirty Alley Cleaning	Sewer Investigation
Dirty Street Cleaning	Sewer Water in Basement
Food Facility Complaint	Snow or Icy Condition
Footway/ Sidewalk Repair	Steel Plaint Complaint
Forestry Stump Removal	Storm Inlet Choke
Forestry Tree Pruning	Storm Inlet Damage
Forestry Tree Removal	Street Light Out
Forestry Tree Road Hazard	Street Repair
Graffiti Removal	TRP – Truck Restriction Violation
Grass Mowing – Public Property	Traffic Sign – Change Request
HCD Sanitation	Traffic Sign - Missing
Housing Inspection – Animal Issue	Traffic Sign – New Request
Housing Inspection – Fire Protection	Traffic Signal Repair
Housing Inspection – High Grass and Weeds	Traffic/ Parking Sign Damaged
Housing Inspection – Insect Infestation	Water – No Water at Business or Residence
Housing Inspection – Rodent Infestation	Water – Discoloured at Faucet
Housing Inspection – Space and Occupancy	Water – Leak (Exterior)
Housing Inspection – Structural Deficiencies	Water – Low Pressure
Housing Inspection – Trees and Shrubs	Water – Meter Cover Missing/ Damaged
Housing Inspection – Utility Systems	Water – Repair Debris Removal
Housing Inspection – Vacant Residential Property	Water – Repair Surface Repair
Illegal Flyer Investigation – Private Property	Water – in Basement
Illegal Parking Complaint	

Table 6-1: City of Baltimore – Available online service requests

The City of Chicago

1. **Organizational Chart (311)**

2. **Service letter to the citizen**

Organizational Chart (311)

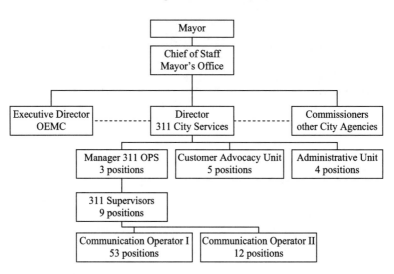

CITY OF CHICAGO
RICHARD M. DALEY
MAYOR

Feb 08, 2006

Gailann Jarocki
3356 W 65th Pl
Chicago, IL 60629

Dear Gailann Jarocki:

We want to thank you for reporting your City service needs to the office of Alderman Thomas. We appreciate your efforts to improve the quality of life in your community and hope that you are satisfied with the level of service received.

Streets and Sanitation records indicate that as of Feb 08, 2006, your request number 06-00179957, concerning a/an Graffiti Removal, has been addressed. If you would like more information regarding the completion of your request, or would like to check the status of other requests, or if you have any questions about the types of services the City provides, please contact the office of Alderman Thomas at 773-778-9609 or call 311 and reference the request number listed above.

This year we anticipate processing some 2.5 million requests for services citywide. We are confident that by working in partnership with you we can expedite the delivery of City services and continue to build a better Chicago. Again, thank you for doing your part. We pledge that we will do our part by providing all residents with the best level of service possible.

Sincerely,

Richard M. Daley
Mayor

Alderman Thomas
Ward 15

Michael Picardi, Commissioner
Streets and Sanitation

The City of New York

1. 311 Privacy Policy

The City of New York
311 Citizen Service Center
Client Information Privacy Policy
("311 Privacy Policy")

The City of New York ("City") is committed to maintaining the confidentiality of the information provided by clients to the 311 Citizen Service Center ("311 Call Center"). This commitment is reflected herein, in the City's 311 Citizen Service Center Client Information Privacy Policy ("311 Privacy Policy"), a formal statement of principles and procedures concerning the protection of client information provided to the 311 Call Center. The objective of the 311 Privacy Policy is the responsible management of 311 client information. It is intended to reflect the high regard which the City views the management of information provided by clients. The City will review the 311 Privacy Policy periodically ensure it is relevant, and remains current with changing laws, technologies and client needs. The City is not responsible for breaches of security by third parties.

Principle 1 - Accountability
The City, through the 311 Call Center, is responsible for personal information under its control and shall designate one or more persons who are accountable for the 311 Call Center's compliance with the 311 Security and Privacy Policy.

1.1 Responsibility for ensuring compliance with the provisions of the 311 Privacy Policy rests with the senior management of 311 Call Center, which shall designate one or more "privacy compliance officers" to be accountable for 311 Call Center compliance with the 311 Privacy Policy. Other individuals within 311 Call Center may be designated to act on behalf of the privacy compliance officers, or to take responsibility for the day-to-day collection and processing of personal information. The 311 Call Center shall make known, upon request, the identity of the privacy compliance officers who oversee the 311 Call Center's compliance with the 311 Privacy Policy.

1.2 The 311 Call Center has implemented policies and procedures to give effect to the 311 Privacy Policy, including:
   a) implementing procedures to protect personal information and to oversee the 311 Call Center's compliance with the 311 Privacy Policy;
   b) training and communicating to staff about the 311 Call Center's policies and practices; and
   c) establishing procedures to receive and respond to inquiries or complaints.

1.3 The 311 Privacy Compliance Officer may be contacted with any questions or comments regarding this policy via mail at

311 Privacy Compliance Officer
NYC DoITT
59 Maiden Lane, 14th Floor Mailroom
New York City, NY 10038.

Principle 2 - Limiting the Collection of Personal Information
The 311 Call Center shall limit the collection of personal information to that which is reasonably necessary to address client needs, to conduct City business, to provide emergency assistance, or as otherwise required by law.

2.1 The 311 Call Center collects personal information only for the following purposes:
   a) to efficiently address client needs;
   b) to conduct and improve City business and/or services;
   c) to help provide emergency assistance, if necessary; and
   d) as otherwise required by law.

2.2 Unless required by law, the 311 Call Center shall not collect personal information for any other purpose without first informing the client.

Principle 3 - Limiting Access and Disclosure of Personal Information
The 311 Call Center shall not use personal information for purposes other than those for which it was provided, except as otherwise disclosed to the client and/or approved by a 311 privacy compliance officer.

3.1 Only those City employees who require access only for the purposes set forth in 2.1 are to be granted access to personal information about clients.

3.2 Personal information is subject to disclosure, without the knowledge and consent of the client, only for the purposes set forth in 2.1.

3.3 The 311 Call Center shall adhere to the Automatic Number Identification ("ANI") Terms and Conditions, as prescribed by New York State's Public Service Commission, which provide:

   a) The City may use or transmit ANI information to third parties for billing and collection, routing, screening, ensuring network performance, and completion of a telephone subscriber's call or transaction, or for performing a service directly related to the telephone subscriber's original call or transaction.
   b) The City is prohibited from utilizing ANI information to establish marketing lists or to conduct outgoing marketing calls, except as permitted by the preceding paragraph, unless the ANI recipient obtains the prior written consent of the telephone subscriber permitting the use of ANI information for such purposes. The City may not utilize ANI information if prohibited elsewhere by law.
   c) The City is prohibited from reselling, or otherwise disclosing ANI information to any other third party for any use other than those listed in subheading a, unless the City obtains the prior written consent of the telephone subscriber permitting such resale or disclosure.

Principle 4 - Limiting the Length of Retention of Personal Information
The 311 Call Center shall retain personal information for the fulfillment of the purposes for which it was collected, except as otherwise provided in 4.3.

4.1 Where personal information is reasonably necessary to provide ongoing assistance to a client, the 311 Call Center shall retain that information that is reasonably sufficient to enable the provision of such service until it is determined that retention is no longer necessary.

4.2 The 311 Call Center shall maintain reasonable and systematic controls and practices for information and records retention and destruction which apply to personal information that is no longer necessary or relevant for the identified purposes or required by law to be retained.

4.3 Voice recordings of phone calls are kept for fourteen days then erased, with several exceptions. First, certain recordings are kept longer than fourteen days for quality assurance purposes. The personal information on these recordings shall be redacted. Second, recordings shall be preserved when subject to subpoena. Third, recordings shall be preserved when subject to Freedom of Information Law requests. Fourth, recordings shall be preserved if they are material to an ongoing law enforcement investigation or proceeding or when otherwise required by law.

Principle 5 - Security Safeguards
The 311 Call Center shall protect personal information by adhering to security safeguards appropriate to the sensitivity of the information.

5.1 The 311 Call Center shall establish commercially reasonable protocols to protect personal information, regardless of the format in which it is held, against such risks as loss or theft, unauthorized access, disclosure, copying, use, modification or destruction, through appropriate security measures.

5.2 Every 311 Call Center employee with access to personal information shall be trained, and required as a condition of employment, to respect the confidentiality of personal information.

5.3 The 311 Call Center shall protect personal information disclosed to third parties affiliated with the 311 Call Center by contractual agreements stipulating the confidentiality of the information and the purposes for which it is to be used.

Principle 6 - Transparency
The 311 Call Center shall make readily available specific information about its policies and practices relating to personal information.

6.1 The 311 Call Center shall make information about its policies and practices available online. Such information will include:
   a) the contact information for the 311 Privacy Compliance Officer; and
   b) the means of gaining access to one's personal information held by the 311 Call Center.

Principle 7 - Client Access to Information
The 311 Call Center shall, upon request, provide individuals with access to information that is being retained about them pursuant to the guidelines that follow. Such individuals shall be able to challenge the accuracy and completeness of the information and to have it amended as appropriate.

7.1 A client can obtain information or seek access to his or her individual record by contacting the 311 Call Center's Privacy Compliance Officer. Information will normally be released to the client only if the client provides the service request number. At the discretion of the Privacy Compliance Officer, status reports may be disclosed to address the purposes set forth in 2.1.

7.2 In certain situations, the 311 Call Center may not be able to provide access to the information it holds about a client that is in a third parties' individual record. For example, the 311 Call Center may not provide access to information if doing so could reasonably be expected to reveal personal information about the third party or could reasonably be expected to compromise the privacy interests of that or any other individual.

7.3 Upon written request to the Privacy Compliance Officer, the 311 Call Center shall review and, if deemed appropriate, correct or complete any information on a client's personal record that is determined to be inaccurate or incomplete.

Principle 8 - Challenging Compliance
Client shall be able to address a challenge concerning compliance with the above principles to the designated person or persons accountable for the 311 Call Center's compliance with the 311 Privacy Policy.

8.1 Complaints or inquiries about the handling of personal information shall be directed to the Privacy Compliance Officer. The Privacy Compliance Officer shall investigate all written complaints concerning compliance with the 311 Privacy Policy.

8.2 If the Privacy Compliance Officer determines that a complaint is justified, the 311 Call Center shall take appropriate measures to resolve the complaint including, if necessary, amending its policies and procedures. A client shall be informed of the outcome of the investigation regarding his or her complaint.

Definitions

311 Call Center – An entity established by the City of New York, and administered by DoITT for the purpose of providing callers with one point of contact from which to obtain information on all non-emergency City services. All rights and obligations herein pertaining to the 311 Call Center apply to the City of New York and DoITT.

Client – Any individual or individuals legitimately seeking to avail themselves of the services provided by and through the 311 Call Center.

Collection – The act of gathering, acquiring, recording or obtaining personal information by the 311 Call Center from a client.

Disclosure – Making personal information available to a third party.

Employee – An employee, consultant or contractor of the 311 Call Center, DoITT, or the City of New York.

Individual record – Information about a specific complaint/report/call that is associated with a unique identifiable number.

Personal information – Information about an identifiable individual that is recorded in any form. Personal information includes a client's name, telephone number, Internet Protocol address, or physical address, as well as the nature of an identifiable client's inquiry, request, and complaints to the 311 Call Center. Personal information is not information that cannot be associated with a specific individual. Aggregated information that cannot be traced to identifiable individuals is not considered "personal information."

Miami-Dade County

1. 311 Technology Diagram
2. Interlocal Agreement

Miami Dade 311 CSR Overview Diagram

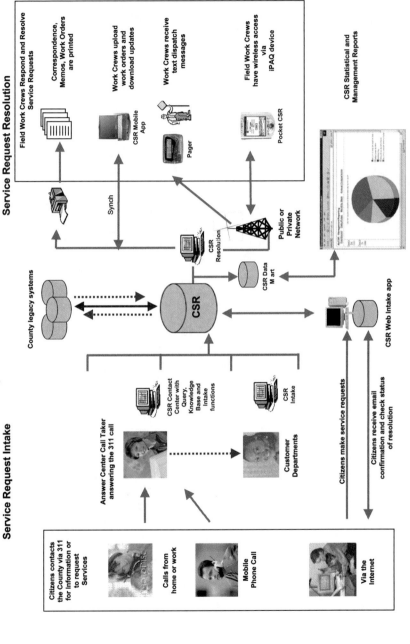

MEMORANDUM

Honorable Chairperson Barbara Carey-Shuler, Ed.D.   DATE: June 8, 2004
and Members, Board of County Commissioners

M: George M. Burgess
       County Manager

SUBJECT: Resolution authorizing
Interlocal Agreement
with the City of Miami
for the 311 Service

RECOMMENDATION

It is recommended that the Board adopt the attached Interlocal Agreement with the City of Miami for the provision of answer center services to the City of Miami and assignment of the 311 telephone number to the County for the establishment of a 311 service. The County and City of Miami mutually agree that the residents of Miami-Dade County would benefit by the use of the 311 telephone number to steer non-emergency calls away from 911, provision of local governmental services and information, and emergency management purposes.

BACKGROUND

The Federal Communications Commission (FCC) directed Bell Communications Research (Bellcore), in its capacity as North American Numbering Plan (NANP) administrator, to set aside 311 telephone number as a code to be used for public citizens to reach non-emergency police and other governmental services. The order does not obligate any entity to adopt 311, but rather it ensures that any local entity that wishes to use 311 has the option to do so. The FCC required that when a provider of telecommunications services receives a request from an entity to use 311, that the provider must take any steps necessary to complete 311 calls from its subscribers to a requesting 311 entity in its service area.

The City of Miami entered into a Special Service Arrangement Agreement with BellSouth Telecommunications, Inc., this Agreement grants the City of Miami exclusive rights to use the 311 telephone number. The County and City have mutually agreed that the residents of Miami-Dade County would benefit by the regional use of the 311 telephone number for local governmental services and emergency management purposes.

The City of Miami Commission approved a different version of a 311 Interlocal agreement in December 2003. At that time the County was in the process of reviewing the draft agreement. This item reflects a revised agreement that both the City Manager and I have agreed to advance. To expeditiously implement the 311 service, I am forwarding this agreement through the Committee process prior to City of Miami Commission review.

The City Commission will review the agreement prior to the Board of County Commissioners final approval.

The original Answer Center plan contemplated locating a limited service Answer Center within the Fire Headquarters. The Fire Headquarters provided no room for future growth possibly necessitating relocation with associated build-out and technology capital costs. I recommended in the adopted 2003-04 fiscal year budget including funding to house the 3-1-1 Answer Center in a portion of the second floor of the building occupied by the Elections Department. The change in location provides a permanent, long-term location. Capital expenditures will be funded through capital financing and pay-as-you-go capital funding.

The Answer Center is scheduled for a soft launch late Fall. Staffing will be phased-in to commensurate with call volumes. The key issues contained in the agreement are:

- The City of Miami will make its best efforts to have the 311 number assigned to Miami-Dade County, including terminating its Special Service Arrangement Agreement with BellSouth Telecommunications, Inc. and making any necessary requests, applications and petitions to BellSouth, the Florida Public Service Commission, and the Federal Communications Commission. This agreement will not become effective until the 311 number is assigned to the County.

- The County will operate and manage the Regional 311 Answer Center. The Regional 311 Answer Center will be capable of routing, managing, recording and reporting on citizen interactions.

- The term of this agreement shall be for a period of ten years and shall automatically renew for three additional periods of ten years each. The County or City of Miami can give either party three hundred sixty (360) days advance written notice of its intention to cancel.

- The City and County will receive the same level of Answer Center case management and call taking services. Over time, we envision offering case management services to all cities as desired and as funds permit.

- The City will indemnify and hold harmless the County and its officers, employees, agents and instrumentalities from any and all liability, losses or damages, which the County or its officers, employees, agents or instrumentalities may incur as a result of claims, demands, suits, causes of actions or proceedings of any kind or nature arising out of, relating to or resulting form the performance of this agreement.

Alex Muñoz
Assistant County Manager

MEMORANDUM
(Revised)

TO: Hon. Chairperson Barbara Carey-Shuler. Ed.D.   DATE: June 8, 2004
      and Members, Board of County Commissioners

FROM: Robert A. Ginsburg   SUBJECT: Agenda Item No. 8(T)(1)(A)
       County Attorney

Please note any items checked.

_____   "4-Day Rule" ("3-Day Rule" for committees) applicable if raised

_____   6 weeks required between first reading and public hearing

_____   4 weeks notification to municipal officials required prior to public
         hearing

_____   Decreases revenues or increases expenditures without balancing budget

_____   Budget required

_____   Statement of fiscal impact required

_____   Bid waiver requiring County Manager's written recommendation

_____   Ordinance creating a new board requires detailed County Manager's
         report for public hearing

_____   Housekeeping item (no policy decision required)

_____   No committee review

3

Approved   _____ Mayor   Agenda Item No.   8(T)(1)(A)

Veto   _____   6-8-04

Override   _____   OFFICIAL FILE COPY

                            CLERK OF THE BOARD

                            OF COUNTY COMMISSIONERS

             R-760-04   DADE COUNTY, FLORIDA

RESOLUTION NO. _____

RESOLUTION APPROVING AN INTERLOCAL AGREEMENT BETWEEN MIAMI-DADE COUNTY AND THE CITY OF MIAMI IN CONNECTION WITH THE REGIONAL 3-1-1 ANSWER CENTER; AUTHORIZING THE COUNTY MANAGER TO EXECUTE THE AGREEMENT AND TAKE ANY ACTION REQUIRED OF THE COUNTY HEREIN

WHEREAS, Miami-Dade County and the City of Miami desire to serve their citizens with a Regional 3-1-1 Answer Center,

NOW, THEREFORE, BE IT RESOLVED BY THE BOARD OF COUNTY COMMISSIONERS OF MIAMI-DADE COUNTY, FLORIDA, that:

Section 1.   The matter contained in the foregoing recital is incorporated by reference in this Resolution.

Section 2.   The Interlocal Agreement between Miami-Dade County and the City of Miami is hereby approved, in substantially the form attached hereto and the County Manager is hereby authorized to execute such agreement after approval from the County Attorney's Office and take any action required of the County herein.

The foregoing resolution was offered by Commissioner Dennis C. Moss   , who moved its adoption. The motion was seconded by Commissioner   Natacha Seijas and upon being put to a vote, the vote was as follows:

Dr. Barbara Carey-Shuler, Chairperson		aye	
Katy Sorenson, Vice-Chairperson		aye	
Bruno A. Barreiro	aye	Jose "Pepe" Diaz	absent
Betty T. Ferguson	aye	Sally A. Heyman	absent
Joe A. Martinez	absent	Jimmy L. Morales	absent
Dennis C. Moss	aye	Dorrin D. Rolle	absent
Natacha Seijas	aye	Rebeca Sosa	aye
Sen. Javier D. Souto	aye		

4

184

The Chairperson thereupon declared the resolution duly passed and adopted this 8th day

of June, 2004. This Resolution and contract, if not vetoed, shall become effective in accordance

with Resolution No. R-377-04.

MIAMI-DADE COUNTY, FLORIDA
BY ITS BOARD OF
COUNTY COMMISSIONERS

HARVEY RUVIN, CLERK

By: **KAY SULLIVAN**
Deputy Clerk

Approved by County Attorney as $\mathcal{T}wL$
to form and legal sufficiency.

Thomas W. Logue

INTERLOCAL AGREEMENT

for

JOINT PARTICIPATION

TO DEVELOP A REGIONAL 311 ANSWER CENTER

Miami-Dade County, Florida, a political subdivision of the State of Florida, (hereinafter "County") and the City of Miami, a municipal corporation organized and existing under the laws of the State of Florida (hereinafter the "City") agree as follows:

1. **OPERATION OF REGIONAL 311 ANSWER CENTER**

1.1 The County and the City agree to cooperate in good faith to establish and operate a Regional 311 Answer Center. The purpose of the Regional 311 Answer Center is to steer non-emergency calls away from 911 and make local governments more user-friendly by providing citizens convenient telephone access to information and service requests regarding their City and County governments. In doing so, the 311 Answer Center will preserve the availability of the emergency 911 systems for those individuals truly in need of emergency response.

1.2 The County will have the responsibility to operate the Regional 311 Answer Center including the responsibility to provide necessary staff and to obtain all equipment, hardware, and software.

1.3 The City will have no responsibility to operate the Regional 311 Answer Center. In this regard the City will have no responsibility to provide staff, equipment, hardware or software for the operation of the Regional 311 Answer Center.

1.4 The County will be responsible to connect the Regional 311 Answer Center network to City's network at the access point designated by the City. The City will remain responsible for City operations on the City's side of the designated access point.

1.5 The City will make reasonable efforts to alert the County in a timely manner to any circumstances or events that may generate excess calls to the Regional 311 Answer Center in order to allow the County to adequately increase staff and resources to receive and handle such calls.

1.6 The County will also undertake certain case management responsibilities regarding calls by the City's residents to the Regional 311 Answer Center for information or services such as routing, recording, and reporting calls regarding certain City Departments. The City will continue to do such case management for calls made directly by residents to the City.

C:\WP\TWL\A259.DOC

1.7   The City and the County will jointly develop an interface to their existing land management and complaint tracking computer systems within 18 months of the date that the Regional 311 Answer Centers begins accepting calls from residents. The City will be responsible to maintain the integrity of the interface between the City's existing system and Regional 311 Answer Center computer system.

1.8   The City will not use automation or automatic means to forward calls to Regional 311 Answer Center except to the extent that the parties may agree in writing. The Regional 311 Answer Center will forward non-emergency police calls to the appropriate non-emergency police telephone number determined by the City.

1.9   The County will be responsible for the reasonable expense of training City personnel on the County's CRS system for the initial launch. After the initial launch, the City will be responsible for training its personnel.

1.10   The County will seek the advice of the City in regards to the campaign to advertise 311 to help make sure the City residents are aware of the service.

1.11   The operations of the Regional 311 Answer Center will include knowledge base, information and referral, and service requests for Miami-Dade County, including the City of Miami. The knowledge base is a collection of information defining the rules, responsibilities and procedures of County and City services, programs, departments and agencies. The City will keep the City's knowledge base current. All City Departments that have supplied knowledge based information to the County will be included in knowledge-based launches.

2.   FUNDING OF REGIONAL 311 ANSWER CENTER

2.1   It is the understanding of the parties that the Regional 311 Answer Center is a regional responsibility of the County. In this regard, the County will be responsible to fund the establishment and operation of the Regional 311 Answer Center. For fiscal year 2003-2004, the County budgeted sixteen million and one hundred eighty-nine thousands dollars ($16.189 million) toward capital costs to acquire necessary infrastructure, hardware and software for the Regional 311 Answer Center.

2.2   The City will not be responsible to fund the establishment or operation of the Regional 311 Answer Center.

2.3   The County will be responsible for the costs associated with connecting the Regional 311 Answer Center network to City's network at the access point designated by the City up to a cost of $500 monthly. The City will assume any access costs in excess of that amount. The City will be responsible for the costs associated with the City's operations on the City's side of the designated access point.

C:\WP\TWL\A259.DOC

7

2.4   The City agrees that it will cooperate and use its best efforts to support any applications by the County to seek grants to establish, enhance, or fund the facilities or operations of the Regional 311 Answer Center.

2.5   In the event that the State authorizes local governments to levy a fee to finance a Regional 311 Answer Center, nothing herein shall prevent the County from levying such fee in the City to the same extent that it levies such fee in the remainder of the County and to apply the proceeds of such fee to finance the Regional 311 Answer Center.

2.6   The County's obligation to operate the Regional 311 Answer Center is subject to the annual budget process of the Board of County Commissioners of Miami-Dade County and nothing in this contract shall be understood to require the County to expend money in excess of the amounts appropriated and budgeted by the Board of County Commissioners.

3.   **PERFORMANCE STANDARDS**

3.1   The County agrees to operate the Regional 311 Answer Center as "State-of-the-Art," which shall mean at least as professional and efficient as any similar Regional 311 Answer Center in any similar community in Florida.   In this regard, the County will utilize five call taking performance standards with maximum and minimum acceptable targets: Average Speed to Answer, Average Abandoned Rate, Average Time in Queue, Percentage of Resolution on First Contact, and a Quality Rating on Calls. The County will set specific numerical targets every budget cycle and will seek advice from the City in doing so. These minimum and maximum targets will conform to the standards of such similar Centers. The County will generate a   monthly report on the performance standards. Upon written request by the City, the County will generate a report explaining why targets are not being met, and setting forth a plan to met or modify the targets. Calls from City residents will be entitled to parity in service as calls from County residents. In particular, Calls from City residents will receive the same level of promptness, professionalism, and service, such as routing, recording, and reporting, as calls from other County residents.   This parity in service will be maintained through staffing, software, or hardware changes.

4   **RE-ASSIGNMENT OF 311 CENTRAL OFFICES**

4.1   The County and the City understand that the Regional 311 Answer Center envisioned by this agreement cannot be established unless the County is assigned the 311 in the relevant area, which includes the entire geographic area of Miami-Dade County. Accordingly, except for sections 4.2 and 4.3, this agreement will have no force and effect unless and until the 311 number is assigned to the County for the 26 current Central Offices outside the City's jurisdiction and the 6 current Central Offices within the City's jurisdiction for the purposes of operating the Regional 311 Answer Center described in this agreement.

4.2   After execution of this agreement, the County will make its best efforts to have the 311 number assigned to the County for the 26 current Central Offices outside the City's jurisdiction and the 6 current Central Offices within the City's jurisdiction for the purposes of operating the Regional 311 Answer Center described in this agreement. The County's efforts will include, but are not limited to making the necessary requests, applications and petitions to BellSouth, the Florida Public Service Commission, and the Federal Communications Commission.

4.3 After execution of this agreement, the City will make its best efforts to have the 311 number assigned to the County for the 26 current Central Offices outside the City's jurisdiction and the 6 current Central Offices within the City's jurisdiction, subject to the provisions in section 5 of this agreement. The City's efforts in this regard will include, but are not limited to, terminating the Special Service Arrangement Agreement, Case no. FL02-N407-02, dated February 21, 2003 and making any necessary requests, applications and petitions to BellSouth, the Florida Public Service Commission, and the Federal Communications Commission and supporting such requests by the County.

5 RE-ASSIGNMENT OF 311 CENTRAL OFFICES IN THE EVENT OF TERMINATION

5.1 In the event that this agreement is terminated, and the City indicates in writing to the County that the City intends to operate a Municipal 311 Answer Center 311 within the City limits, the County will make its best efforts to have the 311 number re-assigned to the City for all Central Offices necessary for the City to offer such service. The County's efforts in this regard will include, but are not limited to, making any necessary requests, applications and petitions to BellSouth, the Florida Public Service Commission, and the Federal Communications Commission and supporting such requests by the City. In the event that the 311 is not allocated on the basis of Central Offices at that time, the County will make its best efforts to ensure the City has all access to the 311 number necessary for the City to operate a Municipal 311 Answer Center within the City's limits.

5.2. In the event that this agreement is terminated, and the County indicates in writing to the City that the County intends to operate the Regional 311 Answer Center 311 outside the City limits, the City will make its best efforts to ensure the County continues to have the 311 number assigned to the County for all Central Offices necessary for the County to offer such service. The City's efforts in this regard will include, but are not limited to, making any necessary requests, applications and petitions to BellSouth, the Florida Public Service Commission, and the Federal Communications Commission and supporting such requests by the County. In the event that the 311 is not allocated on the basis of Central Offices at that time, the City will make its best efforts to ensure the County has all access to the 311 number necessary for the County to operate a Regional 311 Answer Center outside the City limits.

4

6   CITY'S USE OF REGIONAL 311 ANSWER CENTER'S COMPUTER SYSTEM

6.1   The City will be authorized to use the Regional 311 Answer Center's Computer system for purposes of processing service requests to the City generated by the Regional 311 Answer Center or by other sources. The County will not charge the City for such use. When the County initially launches the project, such launch will include the City's departments of Solid Waste, Code Enforcement, Parks and NET. Within six months of the launch, the system shall include the City's departments of Public Works, Building, Planning & Zoning, and CATV. The parties may agree to extend such use to other City departments in the future. To ensure the quality of the City's access in this regard, the County will utilize three system performance standards with maximum and minimum acceptable targets: Average transaction response time, system available for use, and wide area network link ability. The County in consultation with the City shall set specific numerical targets every budget cycle.

6.2   If 311 Regional Answer Center upgrades its computer system, City Departments granted use of the computer system pursuant to this agreement will have use of the upgraded computer system and will not be relegated to any non-upgraded computer system different than the 311 Regional Answer Center computer system used by the corresponding County Department.

7   LENGTH OF AGREEMENT AND RENEWAL PROVISIONS

7.1.   The term of this agreement shall be for a period of ten years from the date that it is executed and shall automatically renew for three additional periods of ten years each unless terminated as provided in section 8 of this agreement.

8   TERMINATION OF AGREEMENT

8.1   Either party can terminate this agreement at any time upon giving 360 days advance written notice of their intent to do so, sent to the other party's Mayor and Manager. Termination of this agreement will not terminate the party's respective responsibilities under section 5 of this agreement which will remain in full force and effect as if this agreement had not been terminated.

8.2   Upon termination, the parties will cooperate in good faith to ensure the return to the City of any City data.

9   INDEMNIFICATION

9.1   The City shall indemnify and hold harmless the County and its officers, employees, agents and instrumentalities from any and all liability, losses or damages, including attorneys' fees and costs of defense, which the County or its officers, employees, agents or instrumentalities may incur as a result of claims, demands, suits, causes of actions or proceedings of any kind or nature arising out of, relating to or resulting from the performance of this agreement by the City or its employees, agents, servants, partners,

5

principals or subcontractors. The City shall pay all claims and losses in connection therewith and shall investigate and defend all claims, suits or actions of any kind or nature in the name of the County, where applicable, including appellate proceedings, and shall pay all costs, judgments, and attorneys' fees which may issue thereon. Provided, however, this indemnification shall only be to the extent and within the limitations of Section 768.28 F. S., subject to the provisions of that statute whereby the City shall not be held liable to pay a personal injury or property damage claim or judgment by any one person which exceeds the sum of $100,000, or any claim or judgment or portions thereof, which, when totaled with all other claims or judgment paid by the government entity arising out of the same incident or occurrence, exceed the sum of $200,000 from any and all personal injury or property damage claims, liabilities, losses or causes of action which may arise as a result of the negligence of the City.

9.2   The County shall indemnify and hold harmless the City and its officers, employees, agents and instrumentalities from any and all liability, losses or damages, including attorneys' fees and costs of defense, which the City or its officers, employees, agents or instrumentalities may incur as a result of claims, demands, suits, causes of actions or proceedings of any kind or nature arising out of, relating to or resulting from the performance of this agreement by the County or its employees, agents, servants, partners, principals or subcontractors. The County shall pay all claims and losses in connection therewith and shall investigate and defend all claims, suits or actions of any kind or nature in the name of the City, where applicable, including appellate proceedings, and shall pay all costs, judgments, and attorneys' fees which may issue thereon. Provided, however, this indemnification shall only be to the extent and within the limitations of Section 768.28 F. S., subject to the provisions of that statute whereby the County shall not be held liable to pay a personal injury or property damage claim or judgment by any one person which exceeds the sum of $100,000, or any claim or judgment or portions thereof, which, when totaled with all other claims or judgment paid by the government entity arising out of the same incident or occurrence, exceed the sum of $200,000 from any and all personal injury or property damage claims, liabilities, losses or causes of action which may arise as a result of the negligence of the County.

10   MERGER AND PRIOR AGREEMENTS

10.1   This document incorporates and includes all prior negotiations, correspondence, conversations, agreements, and understandings applicable to the matters contained herein and the parties agree that there are no commitments, agreements or understandings concerning the subject matter of this Agreement that are not contained in this document. Accordingly, the parties agree that no deviation from the terms hereof shall be predicated upon any prior representations or agreements, whether oral or written.

11   GOVERNMENTAL DISPUTES

11.1   Prior to any party filing suit against the other asserting any claim arising under this Agreement, the procedural options required by the "Florida Governmental Conflict

Resolution Act," sections 164.101 – 164.1061 of Florida Statutes, as amended from time to time, shall be exhausted.

IN WITNESS WHEREOF, the parties hereto have executed these presents this 28ᵀᴴ day of July , 2004.

City of Miami, Florida

By: _____

Name: Joe Arriola, City Manager

Date:

Miami-Dade County, Florida

By: _____

Name: George M. Burgess, County Manager

Date:

4/05 3:45pm

ATTEST:

_____
Priscilla A. Thompson,
CITY CLERK

WITNESS:(If Corporation,
attach Seal and Attest by Secretary)

_____

APPROVED AS TO FORM AND CORRECTNESS:

_____
Maria J. Chiaro,
Interim City Attorney

C:\WP\TWL\A259.DOC

MIAMI-DADE COUNTY, FLORIDA

STEPHEN P. CLARK CENTER

OFFICE OF COUNTY MANAGER
SUITE 2910
111 N.W. 1st STREET
MIAMI, FLORIDA 33128-1994
(305) 375-5311

July 21, 2004

Don Riedel
Director, CitiStat
City of Miami
444 S.W. 2 Avenue, 10th Floor
Miami, FL 33130

VIA Telefax 305-400-5082

Dear Mr. Riedel:

As the Assistant County Manager that oversees the 311 Regional Answer Center project, I can confirm that upon the City's written request, specific recorded data of a City of Miami's citizens interaction with the 311 Regional Answer Center will be provided to the City. The County will work with the City to resolve any identified problems.

Thank you for working with us to resolve this. Should you have further questions, please do not hesitate to contact me.

Sincerely,

Alex Muñoz
Assistant County Manager

Cc: Rafael Suarez-Rivas, Assistant City Attorney
    Harold Concepcion, Team Metro, Miami-Dade County
    Thomas W. Logue, Assistant County Attorney

193

References

6, P. (2001), "E-governance. Do Digital Aids Make a Difference in Policy Making?" in: Prins, J.E.J. (Ed.), "Designing E-Government. On the Crossroads of Technological Innovation and Institutional Change", Kluwer, The Hague, London, Boston, 7-27.

Abbate, J.E. (1994), "From ARPANET to Internet: A history of ARPA-sponsored computer networks, 1966-1988 ", Phd thesis, University of Pennsylvania Philadelphia, PA.

Abbott, J. / Stone, M. / Buttle, F. (2001), "Customer relationship management in practice - A qualitative study", Journal of Database Management, 9, 1, 24-34.

Aberbach, J.D. / Christensen, T. (2003), "Translating Theoretical Ideas Into Modern State Reform", Administration & Society, 35, 5, 491-509.

Abramson, M.A. / Means, G.E. (2001), "E-Government 2001", Rowman&Littlefield, Lanham.

Abramson, M.A. / Morin, T.L. (2003), "E-Government 2003", Rowman&Littlefield, Boulder.

Accenture (2001), "Customer Relationship Management: A Blueprint for Government".

Accenture (2003), "CRM in Government: Bridging the Gaps".

Adler, P.S. / Borys, B. (1996), "Two types of bureaucracy: Enabling and coercive", Administrative Science Quarterly, 41, 1, 61-89.

Agarwal, A. / Harding, D.P. / Schumacher, J.R. (2004), "Organizing for CRM", http://www.mckinseyquarterly.com, 04.09.2004.

Aichholzer, G. / Schmutzer, R. (1999), "E-Government im Aufwind", TA-Datenbank-Nachrichten. 8, 74-79.

Al-Kibsi, G. / Boer, K.d. / Mourshed, M. / Rea, N.P. (2001), "Putting citizens on-line not in line", The McKinsey Quarterly. 2001, 65-73.

Al-Mashari, M. / Zairi, M. (1999), "BPR implementation process: an analysis of key success and failure factors", Business Process Management Journal, 5, 1, 87-112.

Alavi, M. / Leidner, D.E. (2001), "Review: Knowledge management and knowledge management systems: Conceptual foundations and research issues", MIS Quarterly, 25, 1, 107-136.

Albers, S. / Clement, M. / Peters, K. / Skiera, B. (Ed.), (2000), "eCommerce. Einstieg, Strategie und Umsetzung im Unternehmen", F.A.Z.-Institut, Frankfurt am Main.

Albrecht, K. (1993), "Total quality service", Quality Digest, January, 26-28.

Albrecht, K. (2006), "Social intelligence", Jossey-Bass, San Francisco, CA.

Alford, J. (2002a), "Defining the Client in the Public Sector: A Social-Exchange Perspective", Public Administration Review, 62, 3, 337-346.

Alford, J. (2002b), "Why do public-sector clients coproduce?: Toward a contingency theory", Administration & Society, 34, 1, 32-56.

Alkadry, M.G. (2003), "Deliberative discourse between citizens and administrators", Administration & Society, 35, 2, 184-209.

Allan, D.O.J. / Rambajun, N. / Sood, S.P. / Mbarika, V. / Agrawal, R. / Saguib, Z. (2006), "The eGovernment Concept: A Systematic Review of Research and Practitioner Literature", Innovations in Information Technology, 1-5.

Almquist, E. / Bovet, D. / Heaton, C.J. (2003), "What have we learned so Far? Making CRM make Money - Technology alone won't create value", in: Kracklauer, A.H. (Ed.), "Collaborative customer relationship management: taking CRM to the next level", Springer, Berlin, New York, 7-22.

Andersen, P.H. (2001), "Relationship development and marketing communication: an integrative model", Journal of Business & Industrial Marketing, 16, 3, 167-182.

Anderson, E.W. / Fornell, C. / Lehmann, D.R. (1994), "Customer Satisfaction, Market Share, and Profitability: Findings from Sweden", Journal of Marketing, 58, 3, 53-66.

Anderson, E.W. / Fornell, C. / Rust, R.T. (1997), "Customer Satisfaction, Productivity, and Profitability: Differences between Goods and Services", Marketing Science, 16, 2, 129-145.

Anderson, J.C. / Rungtusanatham, M. / Schroeder, R.G. (1994), "A Theory of Quality Management Underlying the Deming Management Method", The Academy of Management Review, 19, 3, 472-509.

Aristotle (1981), "The politics", Penguin, New York.

Arnold, P.E. (1995), "Reform's changing role", Public Administration Review, 55, 5, 407-417.

Ashford, R. / Rowley, J. / Slack, F. (2002), "Electronic Public Service Delivery through Online Kiosks: The User's Perspective", in: Traunmüller, R.L., Klaus (Ed.),

"Electronic Government - First International Conference, EGOV 2002, Aix-en-Provence, France, September 2002, Proceedings", Springer, Berlin, 169-172.

Atlantic Canada Opportunities Agency (2004), "Government on-line", http://www.apeca.gc.ca/e/about/gol.shtml, 1/12/2005.

Atluri, V. / Soon, A.C. / Holowczak, R. / Adam, N.R. (2002), "Automating the De-livery of Governmental Business Services through Workflo Technology", in: McIver, W. / Elmargarmid, A.K. (Ed.), "Advances in Digital Government - Technology, Hu-man Factors and Policy", Kluwer, Boston, 69-83.

Au, G. / Choi, I. (1999), "Facilitating implementation of total quality management through information technology ", Information & Management, 36, 6, 287-299.

Baker, W.H. / Addams, H.L. / Davis, B. (2005), "Critical Factors for Enhancing Municipal Public Hearings", Public Administration Review, 65, 4, 490-99.

Ballantyne, D. / Christopher, M. / Payne, A. (2003), "Relationship marketing: look-ing back, looking forward", Marketing Theory, 3, 1, 159-166.

Bandemer, S. (1998), "Qualitätsmanagement und Controlling in der öffentlichen Verwaltung", in: Behrens, F. (Ed.), "Den Staat neu denken, Modernisierung des öf-fentlichen Sektors", Berlin, 199-228.

Bannister, F. (2001), "Dismantling the silos: extracting new value from IT invest-ments in public administration", Info Systems Journal, 11, 65-84.

Barnes, J.G. (2001), "Secretes of Customer Relationship Management", MacGraw-Hill, New York.

Barnes, M. / Prior, D. (1995), "Spoilt for Choice? How Consumerism can Disem-power Public Service Users", Public Money & Management, July-September, 53-58.

Barnes, M. / Wistow, G. (1992), "Consulting with carers: What do they think?" So-cial Services Research, 20, 1, 9-30.

Barney, J. (1991), "Firm Resources and Sustained Competitive Advantage", Journal of Management, 17, 1, 99-120.

Barzelay, M. (1992), "Breaking through Bureaucracy", University of California Press, Berkley.

Batista, L. / Kawalek, P. (2004), "Translating Customer-Focused Strategic Issues into Operational Processes Through CRM - A Public Sector Approach ", LNCS 3183, Pro-ceedings, EGOV 2004, September 1-3, Zaragoza, Spain, Springer, Berlin, 128-133.

Batley, R. (2004), "The Politics of Service Delivery Reform", Development and Change, 35, 1, 31-56.

Bator, F.M. (1958), "The Anatomy of Market Failure", The Quarterly Journal of Economics, 72, 3, 351-379.

Bauer, H.H. / Grether, M. / Richter, T. (2002), "Customer Relationship Management in der öffentlichen Verwaltung", Management Know-how: 66, Institut für Marktorientierte Unternehmensführung, Mannheim.

Bearing Point (2006), "Kundenmanagement in der Bundesverwaltung", Frankfurt am Main.

Beckett-Camarata, E.J. / Camarata, M.R. / Barker, R.T. (1998), "Integrating Internal and External Customer Relationships through Relationship Management: A Strategic Response to a Changing Global Environment", Journal of Business Research, 41, 71-81.

Behn, R. (1995), "The Big Questions of Public Administration", Public Administration Review, 55, 4, 10-17.

Behn, R. (2002), "The Psychological Barriers to Performance Management: Or why isn't everyone jumping on the Performance-Management bandwagon?" Public Performance and Management Review, 26, 1, 5-25.

Behn, R. (2006), "The Varieties of CitiStat", Public Administration Review, 66, 332-340.

Bekkers, V.J.J.M. (1999), "Electronic service delivery in public administration: some trends and issues", International Review of Administrative Sciences, 65, 6, 183-195.

Bell, D. / Deighton, J. / Reinartz, W.J. / Rust, R.T. / Swartz, G. (2002), "Seven Barriers to Customer Equity Management ", Journal of Service Research, 5, 1, 77-85.

Bendapudi, N. / Berry, L.L. (1997), "Customers` Motivations for Maintaining Relationships with Service Providers", Journal of Retailing, 73, 1, 15-37.

Bennington, L. / Cummane, J. (1997), "The road to privatization: TQM and business planning", International Journal of Public Sector Management, 10, 5, 364-376.

Berger, P.D. / Nasar, N. (1998), "Customer Lifetime Value: Marketing Models and Applications", Journal of Interactive Marketing, 12, 1, 17-30.

Bergeron, B. (2002), "Essentials of CRM", John Wiley & Sons, Hoboken.

Berman, E. (1997), "Dealing with Cynical Citizens", Public Administration Review, 57, 2, 105-112.

Berman, E.M. / West, J.P.W. (1995), "TQM in American Cities: Hypotheses regarding Commitment and Impact", Journal of Public Administration Research and Theory, 5, 2, 213-230.

Berry, L.L. (1983), "Relationship Marketing", in: Berry, L.L., Shostack, G. L., Upah, G. D. (Ed.), "Emerging perspectives on services marketing ", Chicago, 25-28.

Bevir, M. / Rhodes, R.A.W. / Weller, P. (2003), "Traditions of Governance: Interpreting the changing role of the public sector", Public Administration, 81, 1, 1-17.

Bimber, B. (1998), "The Internet and Political Transformation: Populism, Community, and accelerated Pluralism", Polity, 31, 1, 133-60.

Binz-Scharf, M. (2003), "Exploration and Exploitation: Toward a Theory of Knowledge Sharing in Digital Government Projects", Dissertation, No. 2828, Universitaet St. Gallen, St. Gallen.

Bitner, M.J. (1990), "Evaluating service encounters: the effects of physical surroundings and employee responses", Journal of Marketing, 54, 2, 69-82.

Bitran, G.R. / Mondschein, S. (1996), "Mailing Decisions in the Catalogue Sales Industry", Management Science, 42, 9, 1364-1281.

Blanchard, L.A. / Hinnant, C.C. / Wong, W. (1998), "Market-based reforms in government - Toward a social subcontract?" Administration & Society, 30, 5, 483-512.

Blau, P. / Scott, W.R. (2004), "Formal Organizations: A comparative approach", Stanford University Press, Stanford, CA.

Bleyer, M. / Saliterer, I. (2004), "Vom Customer Relationship Management (CRM) zum Public/Citizen Relationship Management", Verwaltung und Management, 10, 6, 1-9.

Bligh, P. / Turk, D. (2004), "CRM Unplugged: releasing CRM's strategic value", John Wiley @ Sons, Hoboken.

Bogumil, J. (1997a), "Implementationsprobleme in fortgeschrittenen Modernisierungsstädten und Schritte zu ihrer Überwindung", in: Kißler, L.B., Jörg (Ed.), "Stillstand auf der "Baustelle"?:Barrieren der kommunalen Verwaltungsmodernisierung und Schritte zur ihrer Überwindung", Nomos, Baden-Baden, 131-150.

Bogumil, J. (1997b), "Vom Untertan zum Kunden? : Möglichkeiten und Grenzen von Kundenorientierung in der Kommunalverwaltung", Edition Sigma, Berlin.

Bogumil, J. / Holtkamp, L. / Kißler, L. (2001), "Verwaltung auf Augenhöhe : Strategie und Praxis kundenorientierter Dienstleistungspolitik", Edition Sigma, Berlin.

Bohmann, J. (1996), "Public Deliberation: Pluralism, Complexity, and Democracy", MIT Press, Cambridge, MA.

Bonin, H.E.G. (2001), "Citizen Relationship Management", Verwaltung und Management, 7, 4, 216-219.

Borins, S. (Ed.), (2002), "The Challenge of Innovating Government", Rowman & Littlefield, Oxford.

Bose, R. (2002), "Customer relationship management: key components for IT success", Industrial Management & Data Systems, 102, 2, 89-97.

Box, R. (1998), "Citizen governance: Leading American communities into the 21st century", Sage, Thousand Oaks, CA.

Box, R. (1999), "Running Government like a Business: Implications for Public Administration Theory", American Review of Public Administration, 29, 1, 19-43.

Box, R. / Gary, S.M. / Reed, B.J. / Reed, C. (2001), "New Public Management and Substantive Democracy", Public Administration Review, 61, 5, 608-619.

Bozeman, B. / Bretschneider, S. (1986), "Public management information systems: Theory and prescription", Public Administration Review, 46, Special Issue, 475-487.

Brewer, G.A. / Selden, S.C. (2000), "Why elephants gallop: Assessing and predicting organizational performance in federal agencies", Journal of Public Administration Research and Theory, 10, 4, 685-712.

Brodie, R.J. / Covielleo, N.E. / Brookes, R.W. / Little, V. (1997), "Towards a paradigm shift in marketing: an examination of current marketing practices", Journal of Marketing Management, 13, 5, 383-406.

Brown, D. (2005), "Electronic government and public administration", International Review of Administrative Sciences, 71, 2, 241-254.

Brown, P. (1992), "Alternative Delivery Systems in the Provisions of Social Services", International Review of Administrative Sciences, 58, 2, 201-214.

Brown, S. / Gulycz, M. (2002), "Performance driven CRM: how to make your customer relationship vision a reality", Wiley Etobicoke, Ontario.

Brudney, J.L. / Hebert, T. / Wright, D.S. (1999), "Reinventing Government in the American States: Measuring and Explaining Administrative Reform", Public Administration Review, 59, 1, 19-30.

Brunner, R.D. (1982), "The Policy Sciences as Science", Policy Sciences, 15, 2, 115-135.

Brustein, J. (2005), "311's Growing Pains", Gotham Gazette. New York, http://www. gothamgazette.com/article/issueoftheweek/20050725/200/1490.

Budäus, D. (2002), "Reform kommunaler Verwaltungen in Deutschland - Entwicklung, Schwerpunkte und Perspektiven", in: Schuster, W. / Murawski, K.-P. (Ed.), "Die regierbare Stadt", Kolhammer, Stuttgart, 15-39.

Bundeskanzleramt Österreich (2005), "E-Government-Strategie", Stabsstelle IKT-Strategie des Bundes, Wien.

Bundesministerium des Innern (2001), "Bund Online 2005- Umsetzungsplan für die eGovernment-Initiative", Bonifatius Druck, Paderborn.

Buntin, J. (1999), "Assertive Policing, Plummeting Crime: the NYPD Takes on Crime in New York City", C-16-99-1530.0, Case Program, John F. Kennedy School of Government, Harvard University, Cambridge, MA.

Burke, B.F. / Wright, D.S. (2002), "Reassessing and reconciling reinvention in the American states: Exploring state administrative performance", State and Local Government Review, 34, 1, 7-17.

Burke, R.R. (2002), "Technology and the Customer Interface: What Consumers Want in the Physical and Virtual Store", Journal of the Academy of Marketing Science, 30, 4, 411-432.

Byrer, T.A. (2006), "Toward a Relevant Agenda for a Responsive Public Administration", Journal of Public Administration Research and Theory Advance Access, published online, August 29,

Cabinet Office (1999), "Modernising Government", London.

Cabinet Office (2000), "e.gov - Electronic Government Services for the 21st Century", London.

Caldow, J. (1999), "The Quest for Electronic Government: A Defining Vision", Institute for Electronic Government, IBM Corp., Washington.

Calista, D.J. (1986), "Reorganization as Reform: The Implementation of Integrated Human Services Agencies", in: Calista, D.J. (Ed.), "Bureaucratic and Governmental Reform", JAI Press, Greenwich, CT, 197-214.

Callahan, R.F. / Gilbert, R.G. (2005), "End-User satisfaction and design features of public agencies", American Review of Public Administration, 35, 1, 57-73.

Campbell, A.J. (2003), "Creating customer knowledge competence: managing customer relationship management programs strategically", Industrial Marketing Management, 32, 375-383.

Campbell, H. / Marshall, R. (2000), "Public Involvement and Planning: Looking Beyond the One to the Many", International Planning Studies, 5, 3, 321-344.

Campbell, K.B. (2005), "Nobody said it was easy Examining the Matryoshka Dolls of Citizen Engagement", Administration & Society, 37, 5, 636-648.

Cap Gemini (2005), "eEurope - Online Availability of Public Services: How is Europe Progressing?" European Commission: Directorate General for Information Society and Media.

Carr, D.K. / Littman, I.D. (1990), "Excellence in Government: Total Quality Management in the 1990s", Coopers & Lybrand, Arlington, VA.

Carroll, J.D. (1995), "The Rethoric of Reform and Political Reality in the National Performance Review"", Public Administration Review, 55, 3, 302-312.

Castells, M. (1996), "Rise of the Network Society: The Information Age: Economy, Society and Culture", Blackwell, Cambridge.

Center for Digital Government (2005), "HELLO, The First Word in Reinvigorating the Relationship between Citizens and their Government: An Introduction to Citizen Service Technologies and 3-1-1", Folsom, CA.

Chen, I.J. / Popovich, K. (2003), "Understanding Customer Relationship Management (CRM) - People, process and technology", Business Process Management Journal, 9, 5, 672-688.

Chen, Q. / Chen, H.-M. (2004), "Exploring the success factors of eCRM strategies in practice", Journal of Database Marketing & Customer Strategy Management, 11, 4, 333-343.

Christensen, C.M. / Verlinden, M. / Westerman, G. (2002), "Disruption, disintegration and the dissipation of differentiability", Industrial and Corporate Change, 11, 5, 955-994.

Christensen, T. / Laegreid, P. (1998), "Administrative reform policy: the case of Norway", International Review of Administrative Sciences, 64, 3, 457-475.

Christensen, T. / Laegreid, P. (Ed.), (2001), "New Public Management: The Transformation of Ideas and Practices", Aldershot, Ashgate.

Christiaens, J. / Windels, P. / Vanslembrouck, S. (2004), "Accounting and Management Reform in Local Authorities: A Tool for Evaluating Empirically the Outcomes", Universiteit Gent, Faculteit Economie, Working Paper 277, Gent.

Ciborra, C.U. (1993), "Teams, Markets and Systems: Business Innovation and Information Technology ", Cambridge University Press, Cambridge.

Ciborra, C.U. (1996), "Improvisation and Information Technology in Organizations", Proceedings of the 17th International Conference on Information Systems, Cleveland, OH, 369-380.

Cleary, R.E. (1992), "Revisiting the Doctoral Dissertation in Public Administration: An Examination of the Dissertations of 1990", Public Administration Review, 52, 1, 55-61.

Cleveland, H. (1975), "How do you get everybody in on the act and still get some action?" Public Management, 57, 3-6.

Coase, R.H. (1976), "Adam Smith` View of Man", Journal of Law and Economics, 19, 529-546.

Cohen, A. / Vigoda, E. (2000), "Do Good Citizens Make Good Organizational Citizens?: An Empirical Examination of the Relationship between General Citizenship and Organizational Citizenship Behavior in Israel", Administration & Society, 32, 595-624.

Cohen, J. (1996), "Procedure and Substance in Deliberative Democracy", in: Benhabib, S. (Ed.), "Democracy and Difference: Contesting the boundaries of the political", Princeton University Press, Princeton, 95-119.

Cohen, S. / Moore, J. (2000), "Today's Buzzword: CRM (Customer Relationship Management)", Public Management, 82, 4, 10-13.

Coleman, J.S. (1988), "Social Capital in the Creation of Human Capital", American Journal of Sociology, 94, 95-120.

Conybeare, J.A.C. (1984), "Public Goods, Prisoners' Dilemmas and the International Political Economy", International Studies Quarterly, 28, 1, 5-22.

Cook, M.E. (2000), "What Citizens Want from E-Government", Center for Technology in Government, SUNY at Albany, Albany.

Cooper, T.L. (2006), "The Responsible Administrator: An Approach to Ethics for the Administrative Role", Jossey-Bass, San Francisco, CA.

Cooper, T.L. / Bryer, T.A. / Meek, J.W. (2006), "Citizen-Centred Collaborative Public Management", Public Administration Review, 66, December, Special Issue, 76-88.

Cooper, T.L. / Gulick, L. (1984), "Citizenship and Professionalism in Public Administration", Public Administration Review, 44, Special Issue: Citizenship and Public, 143-151.

Corner, I. / Hinton, M. (2002), "Customer relationship management systems: implementation risks and relationship dynamics", Qualitative Market Research: An International Journal, 5, 4, 239-251.

Cornes, R. / Sandler, T. (1996), "The Theory of Externalities, Public Goods and Club Goods", Cambridge University Press, Cambridge.

Coulter, P.B. (1988), "Political Voice - Citizen Demand for Urban Public Services", The University of Alabama Press, Tuscaloosa.

Cox, K.R. (1973), "Conflict, Power, and Politics in the City: A Geographic View", McGraw-Hill, New York.

Creswell, J.W. (2003), "Research design: Qualitative, quantitative, and mixed methods approaches", Sage, Thousand Oaks, CA.

Curry, A. / Kkolou (2004), "Evaluating CRM to contribute to TQM improvement - a cross-case comparison", The TQM Magazine, 16, 5, 314-324.

da Silva, R. / Batista, L. (2007), "Boosting government reputation through CRM", International Journal of Public Sector Management, 20, 7, 588-607.

Danziger, J.N. / Andersen, K.V. (2002), "The impacts of Information Technology on Public Administration: An Analysis of Empirical research from the "Golden Age" of Transformation", International Journal of Public Administration, 25, 5, 591-627.

Datamonitor (2005), "CRM in Local Government", London.

Daum, R. (2002), "Integration von Informations- und Kommunikationstechnologien für bürgerorientierte Kommunalverwaltung", Nomos, Baden-Baden.

Dawes, S. (2002a), "Government and Technology: User, Not Regulator", Journal of Public Administration Research and Theory, 4, 627-631.

Dawes, S.S. (2002b), "The Future of eGovernment", Center for Technology in Government, SUNY at Albany, Albany.

Day, D. (1997), "Citizen participation in the planning process: An essentially contested concept?" Journal of Planning Literature, 11, 3, 412-434.

Day, G.S. (2000), "Managing market relationships", Journal of Academy of Marketing Science, 28, 1, 24-30.

de Leon, P. (1992), "The Democratization of the Policy Sciences", Public Administration Review, 52, 2, 125-129.

Dean, J.W. / Bowen, D.E. (1994), "Management Theory and Total Quality: Improving Research and Practice through Theory Development", The Academy of Management Review, 19, 3, 392-418.

deLeon, P. (1997), "Democracy and the policy sciences", SUNY Press, Albany.

deLeon, P. / Steelman, T.A. (2001), "Making Public Policy Programs Effective and Relevant: The Role of the Policy sciences", Journal of Policy Analysis and Management, 20, 1, 163-171.

Deloitte Research (2000), "At the Dawn of e-Government - The Citizen as Customer", New York.

Deloitte Research (2001), "e-Government's next generation - Transforming the Government Enterprise through Customer Service", New York.

Deming, E. (1986), "Out of the crisis", MIT Press, Cambridge.

Denhart, J.V. / Denhart, R.B. (2003), "The new public service: serving, not steering", M.E. Sharpe, Armonk.

Deshpande, R. (2001), "Using Market Knowledge", Sage Publications, Thousand Oaks, CA.

Detlor, B. / Finn, K. (2002), "Towards a Framework for Government Portal Design: The Government, Citizen and Portal perspectives", in: Grönlund, A. (Ed.), "Electronic Government: Design, Applications and Management", Idea Group, London, 99-120.

Dewan, S. / Min, C.K. (1997), "The Substitution of Information Technology for Other Factors of Production: A Firm Level Analysis", Management Science, 43, 12, 1660-1675.

Dewett, T. / Jones, G.R. (2001), "The role of information technology in the organization: a review, model and assessment", Journal of Management, 27, 3, 313-346

Dewey, J. (1927), "The Public and Its Problems", Ohio University Press, Athens, OH.

Dibben, P. (2006), "The 'Socially Excluded' and Local Transport Decision Making: Voice and Responsiveness in a Market Environment", Public Administration Quarterly, 84, 3, 655-672.

DiIulio, J. (1994), "Principal Agents: The Cultural bases of behavior in a Federal Government Bureaucracy", Journal of Public Administration Research and Theory, 4, 277-318.

Douglas, T.J. / Fredendall, L.D. (2004), "Evaluating the Deming Management Model of Total Quality Services", Decision Sciences, 35, 3, 393-422.

Downs, A. (1957), "An Economic Theory of Democracy", Harper & Row, New York.

Dunleavy, P. / Hood, C. (1994), "From old public administration to New Public Management", Public Money and Management, 14, 3, 9-16.

Dunleavy, P. / Margetts, H. / Bastow, S. / Tinkler, J. (2005), "New Public Management is Dead - Long Live Digital-Era Governance", Journal of Public Administration Research and Theory, 16, 3, 467-494.

Dunleavy, P. / Margetts, H. / Bastow, S. / Tinkler, J. (2006), "Digital era governance: IT corporations, the state and e-government", Oxford University Press, Oxford.

Dwyer, F.R. (1997), "Customer Lifetime Valuation of Support Marketing Decision Making", Journal of Direct Marketing, 11, 4, 1-13.

Dwyer, F.R. / Schurr, P.H. / Oh, S. (1987), "Developing buyer-seller relationships", Journal of Marketing, 51, 2, 11-27.

Dyer, J.H. / Singh, H. (1998), "The Relational View: Cooperative Strategy and Sources of Interorganizational Competitive Advantage ", Academy of Management Journal, 23, 4, 660-679.

Ebner, M. / Hu, A. / Levitt, D. / McCrory, J. (2002), "How to rescue CRM", The McKinsey Quarterly, 4, Special Edition: Technology, 49-57.

Ehrenberg, R.H. / Stupak, R.J. (1994), "Total Quality Management: Its relationship to administrative theory and organizational behavior in the public sector", Public Administration Quarterly, 18, 1, 75-98.

Ehret, M. (2004), "Managing the trade-off between relationships and value networks. Towards a value-based approach of customer relationship management in business-to-business markets", Industrial Marketing Management, 33, 465-473.

Eisfeld, D. (1973), "Die Stadt der Stadtbewohner. Neue Formen städtischer Demokratie", Deutsche Verlags-Anstalt, Stuttgart.

Eisinger, P.K. (1972), "The Pattern of Citizen Contacts with Urban Officials", in: Hahn, H. (Ed.), "People and Politics in Urban Society", Sage, Beverly Hills, CA, 43-69.

Eriksson, K. / Mattsson, J. (2002), "Manager's perception of relationship management in heterogenous markets", Industrial Marketing Management, 31, 6, 535-543.

Eschenfelder, K.R. (2004), "Behind the Web site: An inside look at the production of Web-based textual government information", Government Information Quartlerly, 21, 337-459.

Etzioni, A. (1958), "Administration and the Consumer", Administrative Science Quarterly, 3, 2, 251-264.

Evans, K.G. (2000), "Reclaiming John Dewey: Democracy, Inquiry, Pragmatism and Public Management", Administration & Society, 32, 3, 308-328.

Fama, E.F. (1980), "Agency Problems and the Theory of the Firm", Journal of Political Economy, 88, 2, 288-307.

Ferlie, E. / Lynn, A. / Fitzgerald, L. (1996), "The New Public Management in Action", Oxford University Press, Oxford.

Finer, H. (1931), "Officials and the Public", Public Administration, 9, 1, 23-35.

Finer, H. ([1941] 1972), "Administrative responsibility in democratic government", in: Rourke, F.E. (Ed.), "Bureaucratic Power in National Politics", Little, Brown, Boston, 326-337.

Finlayson, A. (2003), "Public choice theory: enemy of democracy", Soundings, 24, 25-40.

Fishkin, J. (1995a), "Voice of the People: Public Opinion and Democracy", Yale University Press, New Haven.

Fishkin, J.S. (1995b), "The Voice of the People: Public Opinion and Democracy", Yale University Press, New Haven, CT.

Flathman, R. (1981), "Citizenship and Authority: A Chastened View of Citizenship", News for Teachers of Political Science, 30, 9-19.

Ford, D. (1980), "Understanding Business Markets: Interaction, Relationships and Networks", Academic Press, London.

Fountain, J.E. (2001a), "Building the Virtual State - Information Technology and Institutional Change", The Brookings Institution, Washington.

Fountain, J.E. (2001b), "Paradoxes of Public Sector Customer Service", Governance: An International Journal of Policy and Administration, 14, 1, 55-73.

Fountain, J.E. (2003), "Information, Institutions and Governance: Advancing a Basic Social Science Research Program for Digital Government", Faculty Research Working Paper Series, KSG, Harvard University, Cambridge, MA.

Fountain, J.E. (2004), "Prospects of the Virtual State", Occasional Paper, University o Tokyo 21st Century COE program "Invention of Policy Systems in Advanced Countries", Tokyo.

Fountain, J.E. / Osiro-Urzua, C.A. (2001), "Public Sector: First Stage of a Deep Transformation", in: Litan, R. / Rivlin, A. (Ed.), "The Economic Payoff from the Internet Revolution", Brookings, Washington, 235-268.

Fournier, S. / Dobscha, S. / Mick, D. (1998), "Preventing the premature death of relationship marketing", Harvard Business Review, 76, 1, 42-48.

Fowler, H.W. / Fowler, F.G. / Pearsall, J. (Ed.), (2004), "Concise Oxford English Dictionary ", Oxford University Press, Cambridge.

Fox, C. / Miller, H.T. (1995), "Postmodern Public Administration: Towards a discourse", Sage, Thousand Oaks, CA.

Frederickson, G. (1991), "Toward a Theory of the Public for Public Administration", Administration & Society, 22, 2, 395-417.

Frederickson, G. (1996), "Comparing the Reinventing Government Movement with the New Public Administration", Public Administration Review, 56, 2, 263-70.

Frederickson, H.G. / Smith, K.B. (2003), "The Public Administration Theory Primer", Westview, Boulder.

Freeland, J. (2002), "The ultimate CRM handbook: strategies and concepts for building enduring customer loyalty and profitability", McGraw-Hill, New York.

Friedrich, C.J. ([1941] 1972), "Public policy and the nature of administrative responsibility", in: Rourke, F.E. (Ed.), "Bureaucratic Power in National Politics", Little, Brown, Boston, 316-326.

Frissen, P.H.A. (1998), "Public Administration in Cyberspace", in: Snellen, I. / van de Donk, W.B.H.J. (Ed.), "Public Administration in an information age", IOS Press, Amsterdam, 33-46.

Fung, A. (2006), "Varieties of Participation in Complex Governance", Public Administration Review, 66, December, Special Issue, 66-75.

Galbreath, J. / Rogers, T. (1999), "Customer Relationship Management", TQM Magazine, 11, 3, 161-171.

Galitz, W.O. / Cirillo, D.J. (1983), "The electronic office: how to make it user friendly", Management Review, 72, 4, 24-38.

Garbarino, E. / Johnson, M.S. (1999), "The Different Roles of Satisfaction, Trust, and Commitment in Customer Relationships", Journal of Marketing, 63, 2, 70-87.

Garthrop, L.C. / Waldo, D. (1984), "Civis, civitas, and civilitas: A new focus for the year 2000", Public Administration Review, 44, Special Issue: Citizenship and Public Administration, 101-106.

Gartner (2004), "Reaping Business Rewards from CRM - From Charting the Vision to Measuring the Benefits", Stamford, CT.

Gentle, M. (2002), "The CRM Project Management Handbook", Kogan Page, London.

Gibbert, M. / Leibold, M. / Probst, G. (2002), "Five Styles of Customer Knowledge Management, and How Smart Companies Use Them to Create Value", European Management Journal, 20, 5, 459-469.

Giddens, A. (1984), "The constitution of society. Outline of the theory of structuration", University of California Press, Berkeley (CA).

Gil-Garcia, J.R. / Pardo, T. (2005), "E-Government success factors: Mapping practical tools to theoretical foundations", Government Information Quartlerly, 22, 187-216.

Gilbert, G.R. / Nicholls, J.A.F. / Roslow, S. (1998), "Measuring public sector customer service satisfaction", Public Manager, 26, 4, 21-25.

Gisler, M. / Spahni, D. (2001), "eGovernment - Eine Standortbestimmung", Paul Haupt, Bern, Stuttgart, Wien.

Glaser, B. / Strauss, A. (1967), "The Discovery of Grounded Theory", Aldine, Chicago (IL).

Godfrey, A.B. (1993), "Ten areas for future research in total quality management", Quality Management Journal, 1, 47-70.

Godin, S. (1999), "Permission marketing : turning strangers into friends, and friends into customers", Simon & Schuster, New York.

Goldsmith, S. / Eggers, W.D. (2004), "Governing by Network", Brookings, Washington.

Goldstein, H. (2005), "Who Killed the Virtual Case File?" http://www.spectrum. ieee.org/sep05/1455, 12/9.

Goode, W.J. / Hatt, P.K. (Ed.), (1952), "The case study", McGraw Hill, New York.

Goodsell, C.T. (Ed.), (1981), "The Public Encounter: Where State and Citizen Meet", Indiana University Press, Bloomington.

Goodsell, C.T. (2004), "The Case for Bureaucracy", CQ Press, Washington, DC.

Gore, A. (1993), "Creating a Government That Works Better and Costs Less: Report of the National Performance Review", Random House, New York.

Gradstein, M. (1993), "Rent Seeking and the Provision of Public Goods", The Economic Journal, 103, 420, 1236-1243.

Grafton, C. (2003), ""Shadow Theories" in Fountain´s Theory of Technology Enactment", Social Science Computer Review, 21, 4, 411-416.

Grant, R. (1995), "AMR Captures TQM - Essence Escapes", The Academy of Management Review, 20, 1, 11-15.

Greco, A.J. / Ragins, E.J. (2003), "Customer Relationship Management and E-Business: More Than a Software Solution", Review of Business, 24, Winter, 25-30.

Green, D.P. / Shapiro, I. (1994), "Pathologies of Rational Choice Theory: A Critique of Applications in Political Science", Yale University Press, New Haven, CT.

Greenhill, A. (1998), " Blurring The Boundaries: Disentangling The Implications Of Virtual Space", Proceedings of the IFIP WG8.2 and 8.6 Joint Working Conference on Information Systems, December 10-13, Hesinki, Finland,

Gregory, B. (2003), "All the King's Horses and All the King's Men: Putting New Zealand's Public Sector Back Together Again", International Public Management Review, 4, 2, 41-58.

Griffin, A. / Hauser, J.R. (1993), "The Voice of the Customer", Marketing Science, 12, 1, 1-27.

Grönlund, A. (Ed.), (2002), "Electronic Government: Design, Applications and Management", Idea Group Publishing, London.

Grönroos, C. (1990a), "Relationship Approach to Marketing in Service Contexts: The Marketing and Organizational Behavior Interface", Journal of Business Research, 20, 1, 3-11.

Grönroos, C. (1990b), "Service Management and Marketing: Managing the Moments of Truth in Service Competition", Lexington Books, Lexington, MA.

Grönroos, C. (1994), "From Scientific Management to Service Management: A Management Perspective for the Age of Service Competition", International Journal of Service Industry Management, 5, 1, 5-20.

Grunow, D. (1987), "Das Forschungsdesign in der empirischen Verwaltungsforschung", in: Koch, R. (Ed.), "Verwaltungsforschung in Perspektive", Nomos, Baden-Baden, 27-38.

Grunow, D. (1988), "Bürgernahe Verwaltung", Campus, Frankfurt, New York.

GSA (2004), "Citizen Relationship Management", Newsletter, 14, January, Washington.

Gummesson, E. (1987), "The New Marketing - Developing Long-Term Interactive Relationships", Long Range Planning, 20, 4, 10-20.

Gwinner, K.P. / Gremler, D.D. / Bitner, M.J. (1998), "Relational Benefits in Service Industries: The Consumer's Perspective", Journal of the Academy of Marketing Science, 26, 2, 101-114.

Habermas, J. (1992), "Further reflections on the public sphere", in: Calhoun, C. (Ed.), "Habermas and the Public Sphere", MIT Press, Cambridge, MA, 421-61.

Habermas, J. (1996), "Three Normative Models of Democracy", in: Benhabib, S. (Ed.), "Democracy and Difference: Contesting the boundaries of the political", Princeton University Press, Princeton, 21-30.

Hagen, M. (2000), "One Stop Government in Germany", http://infosoc2.informatik. uni-bremen.de/egovernment/cost/one-stop-government/ main2.html, 26.04.

Håkansson, H. (1975), "Industrial Marketing - An Organizational Problem?" Industrial Marketing Management, 4, 113-123.

Halachmie, A. (1995), "Re-engineering and public management: Some issues and considerations", International Review of Administrative Sciences, 61, 3, 329-341.

Halstead, D. / Page, J. (1992), "The Effects of Satisfaction and Complaining Behavior: The Differential Role of Brand and Category Expectations", Marketing letters, 7, 3, 114-129.

Hammer, M. (1990), "Reengineering work: don't automate, obliterate", Harvard Business Review, 68 4, 104-112.

Hammer, M. / Champy, J. (1993), "Reeingineering the Corporation", Harper Business, New York.

Han-yuh, L. / Lai, P. (2004), "Managing process centred e-Government in Taiwan: a customer relationship management approach", Electronic Government, an International Journal, 1, 4, 398-419.

Hansen, K.M. / Ejersbo, N. (2002), "The relationship between politicians and administrators - a logic of disharmony", Public Administration, 80, 4, 733-750.

Haque, M.S. (1999), "Relationship between citizenship and public administration: a reconfiguration", International Review of Administrative Sciences, 65, 3, 309-325.

Hart, D.K. (1972), "Theories of Government Related to Decentralization and Citizen Participation", Public Administration Review, 32, October, Special Issue, 603-621.

Hart, D.K. (1984), "The virtuous citizen, the honorable bureaucrat, and "public administration", Public Administration Review, 44, Special Issue: Citizenship and Public Administration, 111-120.

Hart, S. / Hogg, G. / Banerjee, M. (2004), "Does the level of experience have an effect on CRM programs? Exploratory research findings", Industrial Marketing Management, 33, 549-560.

Hartley, J. (2004), "Case Study Research", in: Cassell, C. / Symon, G. (Ed.), "Essential Guide to Qualitative Methods in Orgnizational Research", Sage, London, Thousands Oaks, New Delhi, 323-333.

Hasan, M. (2003), "Ensure success of CRM with a change in mindest", Marketing Management, 37, 8, 16.

Hayes, B.E. (1998), "Measuring Customer Satisfaction: Survey Design, Use, and Statistical Analysis Methods", ASQ Quality Press, Milwaukee, WI.

Hedlund, G. / Nonaka, I. (1993), "Models of knowledge management in the west and in Japan", in: Lorange, P. / Chakravarthy, B. / Roos, J. / Van de Ven, A. (Ed.), "Implementing strategic processes : change, learning, and co-operation", Blackwell Business, Cambridge, MA, 117-144.

Heeks, R. (2003), "Most eGovernment-for-Development Projects Fail: How Can Risks be Reduced", 14, iGovernment Working Paper Series, University of Manchester, Manchester.

Heeks, R. / Bailur, S. (2006), "Analyzing e-government research: Perspectives, philosophies, theories, methods, and practice", Government Information Quartlerly, doi:10.1016/j.giq.2006.06.005, 243-265.

Heeks, R. / Bailur, S. (2007), "Analyzing e-government research: Perspectives, philosophies, theories, methods, and practice", Government Information Quartlerly, 24, 2,

Heikkila, T. / Isett, K.R. (2007), "Citizen Involvement and Performance Management in Special-Purpose Governments", Public Administration Review, 67, 2, 238-248.

Heinrich, B. (2005), "Transforming strategic goals of CRM into process goals and activities ", Business Process Management Journal, 11, 6, 709-723.

Heintze, T. / Bretschneider, S. (2000), "Information technology and restructuring in public organizations: Does adoption of information technology affect organizational structures", Journal of Public Administration Research and Theory, 10, 4, 801-830.

Henderson, L.J. (2003), "The Baltimore CitiStat Program: Performance and Accountability", Center for Public Policy, The University of Baltimore, Baltimore.

Herbert, A.W. (1972), "Management under conditions of decentralization and citizen participation", Public Administration Review, 32, Special Issue: Curriculum Essays on Citizens, Politics, and Administration in Urban Neighborhoods, 622-637.

Hero, R.E. / Durand, R. (1985), "Explaining Citizen Evaluation of Urban Services: A Comparison of Some Alternative Models", Urban Affairs Quarterly, 20, 3, 344-54.

Herring, E.P. (1936), "Public Administration and the public interest", McGrawHill, New York.

Herriot, R.E. / Firestone, W.A. (1983), "Multisite qualitative policy research: Optimizing description and generalizability", Educational Researcher, 12, 14-19.

Hewson Group (2002), "Customer Relationship Management in the Public Sector", http://:www.hewson.co.uk/public_sector/crm_public_sector_more.htm, 10.05.2002.

Hewson Group (2004), "Towards a Citizen-Centric Authority", Hewson Group,

Hiller, J.S. / Bèlanger, F. (2001), "Privacy Strategies for Electronic Government", in: Abramson, M.A. / Means, G.E. (Ed.), "E-Government 2001", Rowman & Littlefield, Lanham, Boulder, New York, Oxford, 162-198.

Hirschfelder, R. (1998), "Verwaltungsreform mit Total Quality Management in Saarbrücken - Zwischenbericht und Ausblick", in: Kißler, L.B., Jörg (Ed.), "Stillstand auf der "Baustelle"?:Barrieren der kommunalen Verwaltungsmodernisierung und Schritte zur ihrer Überwindung", Nomos, Baden-Baden, 69-85.

Hirschmann, A. (1970), "Exit, Voice, and Loyalty", Harvard University Press, Cambridge, MA.

Hirschmann, D. (1999), "Customer Service in the United States Agency for International Development", Administration & Society, 31, 1, 95-119.

Ho, A.T. (2002), "E-Government: Reinventing Local Governments and the E-Government Initative", Public Administration Review, 62, 4, 434-444.

Hobbes, T. (1998), "On the Citizen", Cambridge University Press, Cambridge.

Hobbes, T. (2004), "The Leviathan", Kessinger Publishing, Whitefish, MT.

Hohn, S. (1997), "Der Reformprozeß in der öffentlichen Verwaltung vor dem Hintergrund der Informationsgesellschaft: dargestellt am Beispiel von Bürgerinformationsystemen in Online-Medien als Weiterentwicklung des Bürgeramtkonzeptes", Universitätsverlag Trauner, Linz.

Holliday, I. (2000), "Is the British State Hollowing Out?" The Political Quarterly, 71, 2, 167-176.

Homburg , C. (2003), "Kundenzufriedenheit: Konzepte - Methode - Erfahrungen", Wiesbaden, Gabler.

Homburg, C. / Stock, R. (2003), "Theoretische Perspektiven zur Kundenzufriedenheit", in: Homburg, C. (Ed.), "Kundenzufriedenheit - Konzepte - Methoden - Erfahrungen", Wiesbaden, Gabler, 17-52.

Hood, C. (1995), "Contemporary public management: a new global paradigm?" Public Policy and Administration, 10, 2, 104-117.

Hood, C. (1996), "Exploring Variations in Public Management Reform of the 1980s", in: Bekke, A. / Perry, J.L. / Toonen, T. (Ed.), "Civil Service Systems in Comparative Perspective", Indiana University Press, Bloomington, IN, 268-287.

Hood, C. / Peters, G. (2004), "The middle Aging of New Public Management: Into the Age of Paradox?" Journal of Public Administration Research and Theory, 14, 3, 267-282.

Hosmer, L.T. (1995), "Trust: The Connecting Link between organizational theory and philosophical ethics", Academy of Management Review, 20, 2, 379-403.

Howe, J. (2006), "The rise of crowdsourcing", Wired.

Hu, W. (2006), "Keeping a Running Count of New York's Complaints", The New York Times. New York, 6/24.

Huber, G.P. (1990), "A Theory of the Effects of Advanced Information Technologies on Organizational Design, Intelligence, and Decision Making", Academy of Management Review, 15, 1, 47-71.

Ingelstam, L. / Palmlund, I. (1991), "Computers and People in the Welfare State: Information Technology and Social Security in Sweden", Informatization and the Public Sector, 1, 2, 5-20.

Irani, Z. / Al-Sebie, M. / Elliman, T. (2006), "Transaction Stage of e-Government Systems: Identification of Its Location and Importance", Proceedings of HICSS 39th, 04-07 Jan, Hawaii, IEEE, 82c.

Ishikawa, K. (1982), "Guide to Quality Control", Asian Productivity Organization, White Plains, NY.

Jacobs, J. (1961), "The death and life of great American cities", Random House, New York.

Jain, D. / Singh, S.S. (2002), "Customer Lifetime Value Research in Marketing: A review and future directions", Journal of Interactive Marketing, 16, 2, 34-46.

Janowitz, M. / Delany, W. (1957), "The Bureaucrat and the Public: A Study of Informational Perspective", Administrative Science Quarterly, 2, 2, 141-162.

Janssen, M. / Wagenaar, R. (2002), "Customer Relationship Management in E-government: A Dutch survey", European Conference on E-Government, St Catherine's College Oxford, UK, 1-2 October, 227-238.

Jensen, J.L. / Rodgers, R. (2001), "Cumulating the Intellectual Gold of Case Study Research", Public Administration Review, 61, 2, 235-246.

Jones, B.D. / Greenberg, S. / Drew, J. (1980), "Service Delivery in the City: Citizen Demand and Bureaucratic Rules", Longman, New York.

Jones, B.D. / Greenberg, S. / Kaufman, C. / Drew, J. (1977), "Bureaucratic response to citizen initiated contacts: Environmental enforcement in Detroit", American Political Science Review, 72, 1, 148-65.

Jupp, V. (2003), "Realizing the Vision of eGovernment", in: Curtin, G.G. / Sommer, M.K. / Vis-Sommer, V. (Ed.), "The World of E-Government", Haworth Press, New York, 129-145.

Kalu, K.N. (2003a), "Entrepreneurs or conservators?" Administration & Society, 35, 5, 539-563.

Kalu, K.N. (2003b), "Of Citizenship, Virtue, and the Administrative Imperative: Deconstructing Aristotelian Civic Republicanism", Public Administration Review, 63, 4, 418-427.

Kamarck, E.C. (2002), "The End of Government as We Know it", in: Donahue, J.D. / Nye, J.S.J. (Ed.), "Market-Based Government", Brookings Institution Press, Washington D.C., 227-263.

Kathi, P.C. / Cooper, T.L. (2005), "Democratizing the administrative state: Connecting neighborhood councils and city agencies", Public Administration Review, 65, 5, 559-67.

Kavanagh, S. (2001), "Constituent Relationship Management Systems: A Primer for Public Managers", Government Finance Review, April, 1-5.

Kavanagh, S. (Ed.), (2007), "Revolutionizing Constituent Relationships: The Promise of CRM Systems for Public Sector", Government Finance Officers Association, Chicago.

Kearney, R.C. / Feldman, B.M. / Scavo, C.P.F. (2000), "Reinventing Government: City Manager Attitudes and Actions", Public Administration Review, 60, 6, 610-620.

Keeton, K.B. (1982), "Residents' characteristics and satisfaction with city service delivery", Dissertation, University of Delaware, Newark, DE.

Kelemen, M. (2000), "Too much or too little ambiguity: the language of total quality management", Journal of Management Studies, 37, 4, 483-498.

Keller, K.L. (1993), "Conceptualizing, Measuring, and Managing Customer-Based Brand Equity", Journal of Marketing, 57, 1, 1-22.

Kelly, J.M. (2005), "The Dilemma of the Unsatisfied Customer in a Market Model of Public Administration", Public Administration Review, 65, 1, 76-84.

Kelly, J.M. / Swindell, D. (2003), "The case of the inexperienced user: Rethinking filter questions in citizen satisfaction surveys", The American Review of Public Administration, 33, 1, 91-108.

Kelly, R.M. (1998), "An inclusive Democratic Polity, Representative Bureaucracies, and the New Public Management", Public Administration Review, 58, 3, 201-208.

Kettl, D. (1998), "Reinventing Government: A Fifth-Year Report Card", Brookings, Washington D.C.

Kettl, D. / Milward, H.B. (Ed.), (1996), "The State of Public Management", John Hopkins University Press, Baltimore, MD.

KGSt (1974), "Bürgerberatungsstellen", 10/1974, Köln.

Kickert, W.J.M. (2000), "Public management reforms in the Netherlands: Social reconstruction of reform ideas and underlying frames of reference", Eburon, Delft.

Kindleberger, C.P. (1986), "The World in Depression 1929-1939", University of California Press, Berkeley.

King, C.S. / Feltey, K.M. / Susel, B.O.N. (1998), "The Question of Participation: Toward Authentic Public Participation in Public Administration", Public Administration Review, 58, 4, 317-326.

King, S.F. (2007), "Citizen as Customers: Exploring the Future of CRM in UK Local Government", Government Information Quarterly, 24, 1, 47-63.

King, S.F. / Burgess, T.F. (2005), "Citizen Relationship Management: the Rocky Road from Transactions to Empowerment", Proceedings of the 10th UK Academy for Information Systems Conference, March, Newcastle.

King, S.F. / Cotterill, S. (2007), "Transformational Government? The Role of Information Technology in Delivering Citizen-Centric Local Public Services", Local Government Studies, 33, 3, 333-354.

Kirlin, J.J. (1996), "The big questions of public administration in a democracy", Public Administration Review, 56, 5, 416-423.

Kißler, L. / Bogumil, J. / Greifenstein, R. / Wiechmann, E. (1997), "Moderne Zeiten im Rathaus?" Edition Sigma, Berlin.

Klages, H. (1982), "Das Verhältnis zwischen Staat und Bürgern in der Bundesrepublik Deutschland", in: Buschmann, H. / Buse, M.J. (Ed.), "Bürgernahe Verwaltung in der Verwaltungsausbildung. Vorträge, Protokolle und Materialien zu einem Fachkongress der Fachhochschule des Bundes für öffentliche Verwaltung am 1./2. Oktober 1981 in Berlin ", Nomos, Baden-Baden, 1982-I.

Klages, H. / Löffler, E. (1998), "New public management in Germany: the implementation process of the New Steering Model", International Review of Administrative Sciences, 64, 41-54.

König, K. (2003), "On the typology of public administration", International Review of Administrative Sciences, 69, 4, 449-462.

König, K. / Adam, M. (2001), "Governance als entwicklungspolitischer Ansatz", 219, Speyerer Forschungsberichte, Deutsche Hochschule für Verwaltungswissenschaften Speyer, Speyer.

Kontzer, T. / Chabrow, E. (2002), "Portals do their civic duty", http://www.informationweek.com/story/IWK20024040S0013, 27.04.

Kotler, P. / Bliemel, F. (2001), "Marketing Management", Schäffer-Poeschel, Stuttgart.

Kotorov, R. (2003), "Customer relationship management: strategic lessons and future directions", Business Process Management Journal, 9, 5, 556-571.

Kracklauer, A.H. (Ed.), (2003), "Collaborative customer relationship management: taking CRM to the next level", Springer, Berlin, New York.

Kraemer, K.L. / King, J.L. (1986), "Computing and public organizations", Public Administration Review, 46, 488-496.

Krutilla, J.V. (1967), "Conservation Reconsidered", The American Economic Review, 57, 4, 777-786.

Kubicek, H. (2001), "Die digitale Spaltung der Gesellschaft. Herausforderungen und Strategien", http://www.ifib.de/publikationsdateien/ddivide_siemens.pdf, 10/6.

Kumar, V. / Ramani, G. / Bohling, T. (2004), "Customer Lifetime Value", Journal of Interactive Marketing, 18, 3, 60-72.

Laing, A. (2003), "Marketing in the public sector: Towards a typology of public services", Marketing Theory, 3, 4, 427-445.

Lake, D.A. / Baum, M.A. (2001), "The Invisible Hand of Democracy - Political Control and the Provision of Public Services", Comparative Political Studies, 34, 6, 587-621.

Lance, D. (2002), "eGovernment - Creating Tools for Trade", eGov Präsenz, 2, 1, 9-11.

Lane, J.-E. (2000), "New Public Management", Routledge, London.

Larsen, B. / Milakovich, M. (2005), "Citizen Relationship Management and E-Government", Proceedings of Electronic Government, 4th International Conference, EGOV 2005, Copenhagen, Denmark, August 22-26, LNCS 3591, Springer, 57-68.

Lawrence, P. (1989), "Why Organizations Change?" in: Mohrman, A.M. / Mohrman, S.A. / Ledford, G.F. / Cummings, T.G. / Lawler, E.E. (Ed.), "Large Scale Organizational Change", Jossey-Bass, San Francisco, 48-61.

Lawrence, P. / Dyer, D. (1983), "Renewing American Industry", Free Press, New York.

Lawton, R.L. (1993), "Creating a Customer-Centered Culture", ASQC Quality Press, Milwaukee, WI.

Layne, K. / Lee, J. (2001), "Developing fully functional E-government: A four stage model", Government Information Quartlerly, 18, 122-136.

Le Grand, J. / Bartlett, W. (Ed.), (1993), "Quasi Markets and Social Policy", Macmillan, London.

Leighley, J.E. (1995), "Attitudes, Opportunities and Incentives: A Field Essay on Political Participation ", Political Research Quarterly, 48, 1, 181-209.

Lenaghan, J.B.N. / Mitchell, E. (1996), "Setting priorities: Is there a role for citizens juries?" British Medical Journal, 312, 7046, 1591-1593.

Lengnick-Hall, C.A. (1996), "Customer Contributions to Quality: A Different View of the Customer-Oriented Firm", The Academy of Management Review, 21, 3, 791-823.

Lenk, K. (1990), "Neue Informationsdienste im Verhältnis von Bürger und Verwaltung", Decker & Müller, Heidelberg.

Lenk, K. (1994), "Information systems in public administration: from research to design", Informatization in the Public Sector, 3, 4, 307-324.

Lenk, K. / Traunmüller, R. (2002), "Electronic Government: Where Are We Heading?" Proceedings EGOV 2002, Aix-en-Provence, LNCS 2456, Springer, 1-9.

Levine, C.H. / Fisher, G. (1984), "Citizenship and Service Delivery: The Promise of Coproduction", Public Administration Review, 44, March, Special Issue, 178-189.

Lewis, G.B. (1990), "In Search of the Machiavellian Milquetoasts: Comparing Attitudes of Bureaucrats and Ordinary People", Public Administration Review, 50, 2, 220-227.

Lichtenstein, S. / Slovic, P. (Ed.), (2006), "The Construction of Preference", Cambridge University Press, Cambridge.

Light, B. (2003), "CRM packaged software: a study of organisational experiences", Business Process Management, 8, 5, 603-616.

Lin, B. / Ogunyemi, F. (1996), "Implications of total quality management in federal services: the US experience", International Journal of Public Sector Management, 9, 4, 4-11.

Lindsay, W.M. / Petrick, J.A. (1997), "Total quality and organization development", Delreay Beach, FL.

Lipsky, M. (1980), "Street-Level Bureaucracy", Russell Sage, New York.

Locke, J. (1988), "Two treatises of Government", Cambridge University Press, Cambridge.

Lovelock, C.H. (1992), "Designing and Managing the Customer-Service Function", in: Lovelock, C.H. (Ed.), "Managing Services", Prentice Hall, New Jersey, 285-297.

Lowenthal, J.N. (1994), "Reengineering the Organization: A Step-by-Step Approach to Corporate Revitalization", ASQC Quality Press, Milwaukee, WI.

Lowery, D. (1998), "Consumer Sovereignty and Quasi-market Failure", Journal of Public Administration Research and Theory, 8, 2, 137-72.

Lowry, T. (2007), "The CEO Mayor", BusinessWeek.

Lucke von, J. (2003), "Regieren und Verwalten im Informationszeitalter : Abschlussbericht des Forschungsprojektes "Regieren und Verwalten im Informationszeitalter" am Forschungsinstitut für Öffentliche Verwaltung bei der Deutschen Hochschule für Verwaltungswissenschaften Speyer", Duncker & Humblot, Berlin.

Lueck, T. (2007), "Ready or Not (for Many, It's 'Not'), New Noie Code is Taking Efect", The New York Times. New York, 6/30.

Lumpkin, J.R. / Caballero, M.J. / Chonko, L.B. (1989), "Direct marketing, direct selling, and the mature consumer : a research study", New York, Quorum Books.

Lynn, L.E. (1996), "Public Management as Art, Science and Profession", Chatham House, Chatham, NJ.

Lynn, L.E. (1998), "The New Public Management: How to Transform a Theme into a Legacy", Public Administration Review, 58, 3, 231-237.

Mahrer, H. / Krimmer, R. (2005), "Towards the enhancement of e-democracy: identifying the notion of the "middleman paradox"", Info Systems Journal, 15, 27-42.

Malthouse, E.C. / Blattberg, R.C. (2005), "Can we predict customer lifetime value", Journal of Interactive Marketing, 19, 1, 2-52.

Mani, B., G. (1995), "Old Wine in New Bottles Tastes Better: A Case Study of TQM Implementation in the IRS", Public Administration Review, 55, 2, 147-158.

Maor, M. (1999), "The paradox of managerialism", Public Administration Review, 59, 1, 5-18.

March, J. / Olsen, J. (1989), "Rediscovering Institutions: The Organizational Basis of Politics", The Free Press, New York.

Marche, S. / McNiven, J.D. (2003), "E-Government and E-Governance: The Future Isn´t What It Used To Be", Canadian Journal of Administrative Sciences, 20, 1, 74-86.

Marguand, D. / Altena, J.V. (2004), "Decline of the Public: The Hollowing Out of Citizenship ", Polity Press, Cambridge.

Marsh, D. / Rhodes, R.A.W. (1992), "Policy networks in British government", Oxford University Press, Oxford.

Marshall, D. (1990), "The restorative qualities of citizenship", Public Administration Review, 50, 1, 21-25.

Martin, W.J. (1995), "The global information society", Aslib Gower, Hampshire.

May, R. (1995), "Lean Politics", Knaur, München.

Mayer-Schoenberger, V. (2007), "Useful Void: The Art of Forgetting in the Age of Ubiquitous Computing", RWP07-022, Faculty Research Working Paper Series, John F. Kennedy School of Government, Harvard University, Cambridge, MA.

Mazerolle, L. / Rogan, D. / Frank, J. / Famega, C. / Eck, J.E. (2003), "Managing Citizen Calls to the Police: An Assessment of Non-Emergency Call Systems", 199060, National Institute of Justice, Washington, D.C.

McIver, W. / Elmargarmid, A.K. (2002), "Advances in Digital Government: Technology, Human Factors, and Policy", Kluwer International, Boston.

McIvor, R. / McHugh, M. / Cadden, C. (2002), "Internet technologies: supporting transparency in the public sector", The International Journal of Public Sector Management, 15, 3, 170-187.

McKean, J. (2004), "Customers Are People... The Human Touch", John Wiley &Sons, Hoboken, NJ.

McSwite, O.C. (2005), "Taking public administration seriously: Beyond humanism and bureaucrat bashing", Administration & Society, 37, 1, 116-125.

Mele, C. (2007), "The synergic relationship between TQM and marketing in creating customer value", Managing Service Quality, 17, 3, 240-258.

Melitski, J. (2003), "Capacity and e-government performance: An analysis based on early adopters o internet technologies in New Jersey", Public Performance and Management Review, 26, 4, 376-390.

Melkers, J. / Thomas, J.C. (1998), "What Do Administrators Think Citizens Think? Administrator Predictions as an Adjunct to Citizen Surveys", Public Administration Review, 58, 4, 327-334.

Merton, R.K. (1938), "The unanticipated consequences of purposive social actions", American Sociological Review, 1, 894-904.

Meyer, W.W. (2004), "The growth of public and private bureaucracies", Theory and Society, 16, 2, 215-235.

Michel, H. (2005), "e-Administration, e-Government, e-Governance and the Learning City: A typology of Citizenship management using ICTs ", Electronic Journal of e-Government, 3, 4, http://www.ejeg.com/volume-3/vol3-iss4/v3-i4-art7.htm.

Milakovich, M.E. (2003), "Balancing customer service, empowerment and performance with citizenship, repsonsiveness and political accountability", International Journal of Public Management Review, 4, 1, 61-82.

Miles, M. / Huberman, A. (1994), "Qualitative Data Analysis", Sage, Thousand Oaks, CA.

Miller, B. (1992), "Collective Action and Rational Choice: Place, Community, and the Limits to Individual Self-Interest", Economic Geography, 68, 1, 22-42.

Mills, P.K. / Chase, R.B. (1983), "Motivating the client/employee system as a service production strategy", Academy of Management Review, 8, 2, 301-310.

Milward, H.B. / Provan, K.G. (2000), "Governing the Hollow State", Journal of Public Administration Research and Theory, 10, 2, 359-380.

Milward, H.B. / Provan, K.G. (2003), "Managing the hollow state - Collaboration and contracting", Public Management Review, 5, 1, 1-18.

Milward, H.B. / Provan, K.G. / Else, B.A. (1993), "What does the "hollow state" look like?" in: Bozeman, B. (Ed.), "Public Management: The State of the Art", Jossey-Bass, San Francisco, 309-322.

Ministerio de Administraciones Publicas (2003), "Plane de Choque para el impulso de la administratción electrónice en Espana", Madrid.

Ministro per L'innovazione e le Tecnologie (2002), "Linee guida del Governo per lo sviluppo della Società dell'Informazione nella legislature", Roma.

Minsky, M. (1986), "The society of mind", Simon and Schuster, New York.

Mintrom, M. (2003), "Market Organizations and Deliberative Democracy", Administration & Society, 35, 1, 52-81.

Mintzberg, H. (1975), "The manager's job: Folklore and fact", Harvard Business Review, 53, 4, 49-61.

Miranda, A.d. (2003), "Total Quality Management and Inequality: The Triple Helix in Global Historical Perspective", Science, Technology & Human Values, 28, 1, 34-51.

Mithas, S. / Almirall, D. / Krishnan, M.S. (2006), "Do CRM Systems Cause One-to-One Marketing Effectiveness", Statistical Science, 21, 2, 223-233.

Mittal, V. / Kamakura, W.A. (2001), "Satisfaction, Repurchase Intent, and Repurchase Behavior: Investigating the Moderating Effect of Customer characteristics", Journal of Marketing, 38, 1, 131-142.

Miyake, N. (1986), "Constructive interaction and the iterative process of understanding ", Cognitive Science, 10, 2, 151-177.

Moe, R.C. / Gilmour, R.S. (1995), "Rediscovering the principle of public administration: The neglected foundation of public law", Public Administration Review, 55, 2, 135-146.

Möller, K. / Halinen, A. (2000), "Relationship marketing theory: its roots and direction", Journal of Marketing Management, 16, 29-54.

Moon, M.J. (2002), "The Evolution of E-Government among Municipalities: Rethoric or Reality?" Public Administration Review, 62, 4, 424-434.

Moore, M.H. (1995), "Creating Public Value", Harvard University Press, Cambridge, MA.

Moorman, C. / Deshpande, R. / Zaltman, G. (1993), "Factors Affecting Trust in Market Research Relationships", Journal of Marketing, 57, 1, 81-101.

Morone, J. (1990), "The Democratic Wish: Popular Participation and the Limits of American Government." Basic Books, New York.

Mosse, B. / Whitley, E.A. (2007), "Critically Classifying: UK E-Government Website Benchmarking and the Recasting of the Citizen as Customer", Working Paper, Department of Management, Information Systems Group, London School of Economics and Political Science, London.

Myers, J.B. / Pickersgill, A.D. / van Metre, E.S. (2004), "Steering customers to the right channels", McKinsey Quarterly, 4,

Myron, D. (2004), "CRM.GOV", Customer Relationship Management. 8, 26-29.

Nairn, A. (2002), "CRM: Helpful or full of hype?" Journal of Database Management, 9, 4, 376-382.

Naschold, F. / Watt, A. / Arnkill, R. (1996), "New Frontiers in Public Sector Management: trends and issues in state and local government in Europe", Walter de Gruyter, Berlin, New York.

Nash, E.L. (1993), "Database marketing : the ultimate marketing tool", McGraw-Hill, New York.

Naßmacher, H. / Naßmacher, K.-H. (1998), "Kommunalpolitik in Deutschland", Leske+Budrich, Opladen.

National Audit Office (2003), "Difficult forms - How government agencies interact with citizens", HC 1145, Session 2002-2003, London.

National Office for the Information Economy (2000), "Government Online: A Strategy for the Future", Canberra.

Neumann, W.L. (1997), "Social Research Methods: Qualitative and Quantitative Approaches", Allan & Bacon, Needham Heights.

Newell, F. (2003), "Why CRM Doesn't Work", Bloomberg, Princeton.

Niskanen, W.A. (1968), "The Peculiar Economics of Bureaucracy", The American Economic Review, 58, 2, 293-305.

Nonaka, I. / Takeuchi, H. (1995), "The knowledge-creating company. How Japanese companies create the dynamics of innovation", Oxford University Press, New York.

Norman, R. / Ramirez, R. (1993), "From value chain to value constellation: designing interactive strategy", Harvard Business Review, 71, 4, 65-77.

Norris, D.F. (2003), "Building the Virtual State...or Not?" Social Science Computer Review, 21, 4, 417-424.

Northern Ireland eGovernment Unit (2000), "A Digital Inclusion Strategy", Dublin.

Nyborg, K. (2000), "Homo Economicus and Homo Politicus: Interpretation and Aggregation of Environmental Values", Journal of Economic Behavior & Organization, 42, 3, 305-322.

O'Looney, J. (2002), "Wiring governments: challenges and possibilities for public managers", Quorum, Westport.

OECD (2000), "Government of the Future", Paris.

OECD (2001), "Understanding the Digital Divide", OECD Publications, Paris.

OECD (2003), "The e-Government Imperative", Paris.

OECD (2005), "OECD e-Government Studies - Mexico", Paris.

Olsen, S.O. (2002), "Comparative Evaluation and the Relationship between Quality, Satisfaction, and Repurchase Loyalty", Journal of the Academy of Marketing Science, 30, 3, 240-249.

Osborne, D. / Gaebler, T. (1992), "Reinventing Government: How the Entrepreneurial Spirit is Transforming the Public Sector", Addison-Wesley, Reading, MA.

Oviatt, B. / McDougall, P. (1995), "Global start-ups: Entrepreneurs on a worldwide stage", Academy of Management Executive, 92, 30-43.

Pan, S.-L. / Tan, C.-W. / Lim, E.T.K. (2006), "Customer relationship management (CRM) in e-government: a relational perspective", DECISION SUPPORT SYSTEMS, 42, 1, 237-250.

Pang, L.M.G. / Norris, R. (2002), "Applying customer relationship management (CRM) to government", The Journal of Government Financial Management, 51, 1, 41-45.

Parkhe, A. / Miller, S.R. (2000), "The Structure of Optimal Trust: A Comment and Some Extensions", Academy of Management Review, 25, 1, 10-11.

Patterson, P. (1998), "Market Metaphors and Political Vocabularies", Public Productivity and Management Review, 22, 2, 220-231.

Payne, A. / Frow, P. (2004), "The role of multichannel integration in customer relationship management", Industrial Marketing Management, 33, 527-538.

Pegnato, J. (1997), "Is a Citizen a Customer? Public Productivity and Management Review", 20, 4, 387-394,

Peled, A. (2000), "Do computers cut red tape?" American Review of Public Administration, 31, 4, 414-435.

Peoplesoft (2002), "Creating a Constituent-Focused Government", Pleasanton.

Peppard, J. (2000), "Customer relationship management (CRM) in financial services", European Management Journal, 18, 3, 312-327.

Peppers, D. / Rogers, M. (1993), "The One to One Future: Building relationships one customer at a time", Currency / Doubleday, New York.

Peppers, D. / Rogers, M. (2004), "Managing Customer Relationships", John Wiley & Sons, Hoboken.

Peppers, D. / Rogers, M. / Dorf, B. (1999), "Is your company ready for one-to-one marketing?" Harvard Business Review, 77, 1, 101-119.

Perry, C. / Wong, S.M. / Bernhardt, S. (1995), "Relationship between TQM, marketing and strategic management", Asia Pacific Journal of Quality Management, 4, 3, 16-29.

Perry, J.L. / Katula, M.C. (2001), "Does Service affect citizenship?" Administration & Society, 33, 3, 330-365.

Perry, J.L. / Kraemer, K.L. (1986), "Research Methodology in the "Public Administration Review"", Public Administration Review, 46, 3, 215-226.

Peters, B. / Pierre, J. (1998), "Governance without Government? Rethinking Public Administration", Journal of Public Administration Research and Theory, 8, 2, 223-43.

Petts, J. / Leach, B. (2000), "Evaluating Methods for Public Participation: Literature Review", Environment Agency, Bristol.

Phillips, A. (1996), "Why does local democracy matter?" in: Pratchett, L. / Wilson, D. (Ed.), "Local democracy and local government", McMillan, London, 20-37.

Piccoli, G. / O'Connor, P. / Capaccioli, C. / Alvarez, R. (2003), "Customer Relationship Management - A Driver for Change in the Structure of the U.S. Lodging Industry", Cornell Hotel and Restaurant Administration Quarterly, 61-73.

Pino, E.d. (2002), "Spanish Citizens and Public Administration: Stereotypes, Expectations and Perceptions in a Federalising System", Paper prepared for EGPA Conference, Potsdam, Germany, 4.-7. September, 2002, Madrid.

Pippke, W. (1990), "Beratungsgestaltung bei computergestützer Sachbearbeitung", in: Lenk, K. (Ed.), "Neue Informationsdienste im Verhältnis von Bürger und Verwaltung", Decker & Müller, Heidelberg, 79-95.

Pippke, W. (1998), "Umgang mit Publikum: Kommunikation der Kommunalverwaltung mit dem Bürger", Link, Kronach.

PITAC (1998), "Interim Report to the President", President's Information Technology Advisory Committee (PITAC), National Coordination Office for Computing, Information and Communication, Arlington, VA.

Poister, T.H. / Gary, T.H. (1994), "Citizen ratings of public and private service quality: a comparative perspective", Public Administration Review, 54, 2, 155-160.

Poister, T.H. / Thomas, J.C. (2007), "The Wisdom of Crowds: Learning from Administrators' Predicitions of Citizen Perceptions", Public Administration Review, March/April, 279-289.

Pollitt, C. (1993), "Managerialism and the Public Services: Cuts or cultural change in the 1990s?" Blackwell, Oxford.

Pollitt, C. / Bouckaert, G. (2000), "Public Management Reform", Oxford University Press, Oxford.

Porter, M.E. (1985), "Competitive advantage: creating and sustaining superior performance", Free Press, New York.

Powell, T.C. (1995), "Total Quality Management as Competitive Advantage: A Review and Empirical Study", Strategic Management Journal, 16, 1, 15-37.

Price, L.L. / Arnould, E.J. / Tierney, P. (1995), "Going to extremes: Managing service encounters and assessing provider performance", Journal of Marketing, 59, 2, 83-97.

Proeller, I. / Zwahlen, T. (2003), "Kundenmanagement in der öffentlichen Verwaltung", Mummert Consulting, Zürich.

Pröhl, M. / Plamper, H. (2000), "Von der Mißtrauens - zur Vertrauenskultur: Erfolgsbedingungen des Neuen Steuerungsmodells", in: Töpfer, A. (Ed.), "Die erfolgreiche Steuerung öffentlicher Verwaltungen", Gabler, Wiesbaden, 113-124.

Punch, K.F. (2000), "Introduction to Social Research - Quantitative and Qualitative Approaches", Sage, London, Thousand Oaks, New Delhi.

Putnam, R. (1993), "Making Democracy Work: Civic Traditions in Modern Italy", Princeton University Press, Princeton.

Raaij, E.M.v. / Verooij, M.J.A. / Triest, S.v. (2003), "The implementation of customer profitability analysis: A case study", Industrial Marketing Management, 32, 573- 583.

Rago, W.V. (1994), "Adapting Total Quality Management (TQM) to Government: Another Point of View", Public Administration Review. 54, 61-64.

Rahman, S. (2004), "The Future of TQM is Part. Can TQM be Resurrected?" Total Quality Management, 15, 4, 411-422.

Rawls, J. (1971), "A Theory of Justice", Harvard University Press, Cambridge, MA.

Reddick, C.G. (2005), "Citizen interaction with e-government: From the streets to the servers?" Government Information Quartlerly, 22, 38-47.

Redman, T. (1995), "Is quality management working in the UK?" Journal of General Management, 20, 3, 44-59.

Reed, R. / Lemak, D.J. / Montgomery, J.C. (1996), "Beyond Process: TQM Content and Firm Performance", The Academy of Management Review, 21, 1, 173-202.

Reger, R.K. / Gustafson, L.T. (1994), "Reframing the organization: why implementing total quality is easier said than done", Academy of Management Review, 19, 565-584.

Reichheld, F.F. / Teal, T. (1996), "The Loyalty Effect", HBS Press, Cambridge, MA.

Reinartz, W.J. / Krafft, M. / Hoyer, W.D. (2004), "The Customer Relationship Management Process: Its Measurement and Impact on Performance", Journal of Marketing Research, 41, 3, 293-305.

Reinartz, W.J. / Kumar, V. (2000), "On the Profitability of Long Lifetime Customers: An Empirical Investigation and Implications for Marketing", Journal of Marketing, 64, 4, 17-35.

Reinermann, H. (2003), "Verwaltungsmodernisierung mit New Public Management und Electronic Government", http://www.hfv-speyer.de/rei/PUBLICA/online/Duwen dag.pdf, 05.01.

Reinermann, H. / Fiedler, H. / Grimmer, K. / Lenk, K. (Ed.), (1988), "Neue Informationstechniken. Neue Verwaltungsstrukturen", v. Decker und Müller, Heidelberg.

Reinermann, H. / Ridley, F.F. / Thoenig, J.-C. (1998), "Neues Politik- und Verwaltungsmanagement in der kommunalen Praxis - ein internationaler Vergleich", Interne Studie, Konrad-Adenauer-Stiftung, Sankt Augustin.

Reinermann, H. / von Lucke, J. (2002), "Portale in der öffentlichen Verwaltung", Forschungsinstitut für öffentliche Verwaltung, Forschungsberichte, 205, Speyer.

Riccucci, N.M. (2001), "The "Old" Public Management versus the "New" Public Management: Where does Public Administration Fit in?" Public Administration Review, 61, 2, 172-175.

Richter, P. / Cornford, J. / McLoughlin, I. (2005), "The e-Citizen as talk, as text and as technology: CRM and e-Government", Electronic Journal of e-Government, 2, 3, 207-218.

Ridley, F.F. (1996), "The New Public Management in Europe: Comparative Perspectives", Public Policy and Administration, 11, 1, 16-29.

Rigby, D.K. / Reichheld, F.F. / Schefter, P. (2002), "Avoid the four perils of CRM", Harvard Business Review, 80, 4, 101-109.

Riker, W.H. (1982), "Liberalism against Populism: A Confrontation between the Theory of Democracy and the Theory of Social Choice", Waveland Press, Prospect, IL.

Riley, P. (1973), "On Kant as the Most Adequate of the Social Contract Theorists", Political Theory, 1, 4, 450-471.

Rivera, R. (2007), "311 Expands With Scouts to Patrol the Streets ", The New York Times. New York, 8/17.

Roberts, C. (2002), "Keeping Public Officials Accountable through Dialogue: Resolving the Accountability Paradox", Public Administration Review, 62, 6, 658-669.

Roberts, N. (2004), "Public Deliberation in an age of Direct Citizen Participation", American Review of Public Administration, 34, 4, 315-353.

Rocheleau, B. (1997), "Governmental information system problems and failures: A preliminary preview", Public Administration and Management: An Interactive Journal, 2, 3, online.

Rocheleau, B. (2000), "Prescriptions for Public-Sector Information Management", American Review of Public Administration, 30, 4, 414-435.

Rocheleau, B. / Wu, L. (2002), "Public versus Private Information Systems - Do They Differ in Important Ways? A Review and Empirical Test", American Review of Public Administration, 2002, 32, 4.

Rogers, E.M. (1983), "Diffusion of Innovation", Free Press, New York.

Rohr, J.A. (1986), "To run a constitution: The legitimacy of the administrative state. Law", University of Kansas Press, Lawrence.

Rosegrant, S. (1992), "The Toxics Release Inventory: Sharing Government Information with the Public", Case Study, C16-92-1154.0, John F. Kennedy School of Government, Harvard University, Cambridge, MA.

Rosenbaum, W.A. (1978), "Public Involvement as Reform and Ritual", in: Langton, S. (Ed.), "Citizen Participation in America", Lexington Books, Lexington, MA, 81-96.

Rosenbloom, D.H. (1993), "Have an Administrative Rx? Don't forget the politics", Public Administration Review, 53, 6, 503-506.

Rosener, J. (1978), "Citizen Participation: Can We Measure Its Effectiveness?" Public Administration Review, 38, 5, 457-463.

Rousseau, J.-J. (1999), "The Social Contract", Oxford University Press, Oxford.

Rowe, G. / Frewer, L.J. (2000), "Public Participation Methods: A Framework for Evaluation", Science, Technology, & Human Values, 25, 1, 3-29.

Rubin, H.J. / Rubin, I.S. (1995), "Qualitative Interviewing - The Art of Hearing Data", Sage, Thousand Oaks, CA.

Ryan, N. (2001), "Reconstructing Citizens as Consumers: Implications for New Modes of Governance", Australian Journal of Public Administration, 60, 3, 104-109.

Sasaki, T. / Watanabe, Y.A. / Minamino, K. (2007), "An Empirical Study on Citizen Relationship Management in Japan", PICMET, Portland, August 5-9, Portland International Center for Management of Engineering and Technology, 2820-2823.

Saueressig, G. (1999), "Internetbasierte Self-Service-Systeme für kundenorientierte Dienstleistungsprozesse in öffentlichen Verwaltungen", dissertation.de, Berlin.

Sawhney, M. / Zabin, J. (2002), "Managing and Measuring Relational Equity in the Network Economy", Journal of the Academy of Marketing Science, 30, 3, 313-332.

Schachter, H.L. (1997), "Reinventing Government or Reinventing Ourselves: The Role of Citizen Owners in Making a Better Government", SUNY Press, New York.

Scharitzer, D. / Korunka, C. (2000), "New public management: evaluating the success of total quality management and change management interventions in public services from the employees' and customers' perspective", Total Quality Management, 11, 7, 941-953.

Schedler, K. (2003), "Local and Regional Public Management Reforms in Switzerland", Public Administration, 81, 2, 325-344.

Schedler, K. / Summermatter, L. (2002), "Was treibt eGovernment?" in: Spahni, D. (Ed.), "eGovernment 2 - Perspektiven und Prognosen", Haupt, Bern, 106-122.

Schedler, K. / Summermatter, L. (2006), "Customer orientation in electronic government: Motives and effects", Government Information Quartlerly, 24, 2, 291-311.

Schelin, S.H. (2003), "E-Government: An overview", in: Garson, G.D. (Ed.), "Public information technology: Policy and management issues", Idea Group, Hershey, PA, 120-137.

Schellong, A. (2005), "CRM in the Public Sector - Towards a conceptual research framework", 6th Annual International Conference on Digital Government Research, DG.O, Atlanta, GA,

Schellong, A. (2006), "Citizen Relationship Management", in: Anttiroiko, A.-V. / Malkia, M. (Ed.), "Encyclopedia of Digital Government", Idea Group, Hershey, PA, 174-182.

Schellong, A. / Langenberg, T. (2007), "Managing Citizen Relationships in Disasters: Hurricane Wilma, 311 and Miami-Dade County", System Sciences, HICSS 2007, Waikoloa, HI, 10.1109/HICSS.2007.331.

Schellong, A. / Mans, D. (2004), "Citizens preferences towards One-Stop Government", DG.O 2004 - The National Conference on Digital Government Research, Seattle, 24.-26. May.

Schmitt, H.E. (2003), "CRM-Systeme in der öffentlichen Verwaltung: eine Analyse von Einsatzpotentialen mit Schwerpunkt A2C", WiKu, Berlin.

Schmittlein, D. / Morrison, D.G. / Colombo, R. (1987), "Counting Your Customers: Who are they and what will they do Next", Management Science, 33, January, 1-24.

Schmittlein, D. / Peterson, R.A. (1994), "Customer base analysis: an industrial purchase process application", Marketing Science, 13, 1, 41-67.

Schröter, E. / Wollmann, H. (Ed.), (1998), "Der Staats-, Markt- und Zivilbürger und seine Muskeln in der Verwaltungsmodernisierung. Oder: vom Fliegen- zum Schwergewicht?" Brinkhäuser, Boston, Basel.

Schumacher, J. / Meyer, M. (2004), "Customer Relationship Management strukturiert dargestellt: Prozesse, Systeme, Technologien", Springer, Berlin.

Schumpeter, J.A. (1942), "Capitalism, Socialism and Democracy", Harper & Row, New York.

Schwetz, W. (2001), "Customer Relationship Management - Mit dem richtigen CRM System Kundenbeziehungen erfolgreich gestalten", Gabler, Wiesbaden.

Secan, M.A. (1996), "Quality Management in Public Organizations: The United States and Germany", Dissertation, University of Nebraska, Lincoln.

Seifert, J.W. / Petersen, R.E. (2001), "The Promise of all Things E? Expectations and Implications of Electronic Government", 97th Annual Meeting of the American Political Science Association, Information Technology and Politics Section, 30.08 - 02.09, San Francisco,

Serra, G. (1995), "Citizen-initiated contact and satisfaction with bureaucracy: A multi-variate analysis", Public Administration Research and Theory, 5, 2, 175-188.

Sharp, B. / Sharp, A. (1997), "Loyalty programs and their impact on repeat-purchase loyalty patterns", International Journal of Research in Marketing, 14, 5, 473-486.

Sharp, E.B. (1986), "Citizen demand making in the urban context", University of Alabama Press, Tuscaloosa.

Sharpe, R. (2000), "Citizens´ Preferences - Measuring the acceptability of E-channels", Kable Ltd., London.

Shepppard, J.E. / Mintz-Roth, J.O. (2004), "District Managers Rate 311: Citizen Service Center Needs Improvement", Public Advocate for the City of New York, New York City, NY.

Shine, S. / Cornelius, C.B. (2003), "Government: Giving the People what they want", in: Freeland, J. (Ed.), "The Ultimate CRM Handbook", McGraw-Hill, New York, 269-279.

Shoemaker, M.E. (2001), "A framework for examining IT-enabled market relationships", Journal of Personal Selling and Sales Management, 21, 2, 177-185.

Siew Siew, L. / Leng, L.Y. (2003), "E-Government in Action: Singapore Case Study", Journal of Political Marketing, 2, 3/4, 19-30.

Simon, H. (1947), "Administrative behavior", Macmillan, New York.

Simon, H. (1955), "A behavioral model of rational choice", Quarterly Journal of Economics, 69, 99-118.

Singh, J. / Siredeshmukh, D. (2000), "Agency and Trust Mechanisms in Consumer Satisfaction and Loyalty Judgments", Journal of Academy of Marketing Science, 28, 1, 150-167.

Singh, S.S. (2003), "Customer Lifetime Value Analysis", Dissertation, Northwestern University, Evanston, IL.

Skalen, P. (2004), "New public management reform and the construction of organizational identities", International Journal of Public Sector Management, 17, 3, 251-63.

Skelcher, C. (1992), "Improving the quality of local public services", The Service Industry Journal, 12, 4, 463-477.

Smith, G.E. / Huntsman, C.A. (1997), "Reframing the Metaphor of the Citizen-Government Relationship: A Value-Centered Perspective", Public Administration Review, 57, 4, 309-318.

Smith, J. (2005), "Migrating citizens to e-government channels in Hong Kong", http://www.pstm.net/article/index.php?articleid=511, 15th of April 2006.

Smith, M.R. / Marx, L. (1994), "Does Technology Drive History? The Dilemma of Technological Determinism", MIT Press, Cambridge, MA.

Smith, S.R. / Lipsky, M. (1999), "Nonprofits for hire: The welfare state in the age of contracting", Harvard University Press, Cambridge, MA.

Snellen, I. (1994), "Automation of Policy Implementation", Informatization and the Public Sector, 3, 2, 135-148.

Souder, D. (2001), "CRM Improves Citizen Service in Fairfax County", Public Management, 83, 4, 14-17.

Spencer, B.A. (1994), "Models of Organization and Total Quality Management: A Comparison and Critical Evaluation", The Academy of Management Review, 19, 3, 446-471.

Srivastava, R.K. / Shervani, T.A. / Fahey, L. (1999), "Marketing, business process and shareholder value: An organizationally embedded view of marketing activities and the discipline of marketing", Journal of Marketing (Special Issue), 63, 168-179.

Stake, R.E. (1994), "Case Studies", in: Denzin, N.K. / Lincoln, Y.S. (Ed.), "Handbook of Qualitative Research", Sage, London, Thousands Oaks, New Delhi, 236-247.

Stallings, R.A. / Ferris, J.M. (1988), "Public Administration Research: Work in PAR, 1940-1984", Public Administration Review, 48, 1, 580-587.

Stark, A. (2002), "What is the New Public Management?" Journal of Public Administration Research and Theory, 12, 1, 137-151.

Steenkamp, J. (1989), "Product quality: An investigation into the concept and how it is perceived by consumers", Van Gorcum, Maastricht.

Steingard, D.S. / Fitzgibbons, D.E. (1993), "A postmodern deconstruction of total quality management (TQM)", Journal of Organisational Change Management, 6, 5, 27-42.

Stewart, J. (1992), "The rebuilding of public accountability", in: Stewart, J. / Lewis, N. / Longley, D. (Ed.), "Accountability to the Public", European Policy Forum, London, 3-13.

Stewart, J. (1993), "The Limitations of Government by Contract", Public Money and Management, 13, 3, 7-12.

Stewart, J. / Ranson, S. (1988), "Management in the public domain", Public Money and Management, 8, 13-19.

Steyaert, J. (2000), "Local Governments Online and the Role of the Resident", Social Science Computer Review, 18, 1, 3-16.

Stipak, B. (1979), "Citizen Satisfaction with Urban Services: Potential Misuse as a Performance Indicator", Public Administration Review, 39, 1, 46-52.

Stipak, B. (1980), "Local Governments' Use of Citizen Surveys", Public Administration Review, 40, 5, 521-525.

Stivers, C. (1990), "The Public Agency as Polis: Active Citizenship in the Administrative State", Administration & Society, 22, 1, 86-105.

Stoker, G. (1998), "British Local Government: Under New Management", in: Grunow, D.W., Helmut (Ed.), "Lokale Verwaltungsforschung in Aktion: Fortschritte und Fallstricke", Brinkhäuser, Basel, Boston, 372-385.

Stoltzfus, K. (2005), "Motivations for Implementing E-Government: An Investigation of the Global Phenomenon", dg.O2005, Atlanta, GA, May 15-18, 333-338.

Stone, M. / Bond, A. / Clarkson, R. / Hayes, P. / Lavers, P. / Traynor, C. / Williams, D. / Woodcock, N. (2003), "Managing public sector customers", in: Foss, B. / Stone, M. / Woodcock, N. (Ed.), "Customer management scorecard", Kogan Page, London and Sterling, VA, 255-280.

Strang, D. / Soule, S.A. (1998), "Diffusion in Organizations and Social Movements: From Hybrid Corn to Poison Pills", Annual Review of Sociology, 24, 265-290.

Strauss, A. (1987), "Qualitative analysis for social scientists", Cambridge University Press, Cambridge.

Strauss, A.L. / Corbin, J.M. (1998), "Basics of Qualitative Research: Grounded Theory Procedures and Techniques", Sage, Newbury Park.

Streib, G. / Slotkin, B.J. / Rivera, M. (2001), "Public Administration Research from a Practitioner Perspective", Public Administration Review, 61, 5, 515-525.

Swindell, D. / Kelly, J.M. (2002), "A multiple-indicator approach to municipal service evaluation: Correlating performance measurement and citizen satisfaction across jurisdictions", Public Administration Review, 62, 5, 610-620.

Swiss, J.E. (1992), "Adapting Total Quality Management (TQM) to Government", Public Administration Review, 52, 4, 356-362.

Symonds, M. (2000), "Government and the internet: no gain without pain", The Economist. 355, 9-14.

Szymanski, D.M. / Henard, D.H. (2001), "Customer Satisfaction: A Meta-Analysis of the Empirical Evidence", Journal of the Academy of Marketing Science, 29, 1, 16-35.

Tapscott, D. (2004), "Citizen Relationship Management", Intelligence Enterprise, 7, 13, 16-17.

Taylor, F.W. (1911), "The principles of scientific management", Harper & Brothers, New York.

Taylor, S. / Baker, T. (1994), "An Assessment of the Relationship Between Service Quality and Customer Satisfaction in the Formation of Consumers' Purchase Intentions", Journal of Retailing, 70, 2, 163-178.

Terry, L.D. (1995), "Leadership of Public Bureaucracies: The Administrator as Conservator", Sage, Thousand Oaks.

Terry, L.D. (1998), "Administrative leadership, neo-managerialism, and the public management movement", Public Administration Review, 58, 3, 194-200.

Tesch, R. (1990), "Qualitative Research: Analysis Types and Software Tools", Falmer Press, New York.

The Royal Academy of Engineering (2004), "The Challenges of Complex IT Projects", London.

Thomas, J.C. (1982), "Citizen-Initiated Contacts with Government Agencies: A Test of Three Theories", American Journal of Political Science, 26, August, 504-522.

Thomas, J.C. (1999), "Bringing the Public into Public Administration: The Struggle Continues", Public Administration Review, 59, 1, 83-88.

Thomas, J.C. / Melkers, J. (1999), "Explaining citizen-initiated contact with municipal bureaucrats: Lessons from the Atlanta experience", Urban Affairs Review, 34, 5, 667-690.

Thomas, J.C. / Streib, G. (2003), "The New Face of Government: Citizens-Initiated Contacts in the Era of E-Government", Journal of Public Administration Research and Theory, 13, 1, 83-102.

Thompson, F.J. (1976), "Sources of Responsiveness By A Government Monopoly - The Case of a People Processor", Administration & Society, 7, 4, 387-418.

Torgerson, D. (1985), "Contextual orientation in policy analysis: The contribution of Harold D. Lasswell", Policy Sciences, 18, 3, 241-261.

Traunmüller, R. / Lenk, K. (2002), "Electronic Government", Springer, Berlin.

Troitzsch, K.G. / Kaiser, S. / Mayer, A. / Meyer, U. (2003), "E-Government - Forschungsfragen, State-of-the-Art und Perspektiven", 37, Arbeitsberichte, Institut für Wirtschaftsinformatik- und Verwaltungsinformatik, Universität Koblenz, Koblenz.

Trostmann, T. / Lewy, S. (2002), "CERM - Citizen Encounter and Relationship Management", eGov Präsenz, 2, 2, 32-35.

Tullock, G. (1967), "The Welfare Costs of Tariffs, Monopolies and Theft", Western Economic Journal, 5, 3, 224-232.

United Nations (2001), "Benchmarking E-government: A global Perspective", New York.

United Nations (2003), "World Public Sector Report 2003 - eGovernment at the crossroads", ST/ESA/PAD/SER.E/49, New York.

United Nations (2004), "UN Global E-Government Readiness Report 2004 - Towards Access for opportunity", UNPAN/2004/11, New York.

United Nations (2005), "UN Global E-Government Readiness Report 2005 - From e-Government to e-Inclusion", UNPAN/2005/14, New York.

US Department of Defense (1990), "Total Quality Management Guide", Government Printing Office, Washington.

Van Dijk, J. / Hacker, K. (2003), "The Digital Divide as a Complex and Dynamic Phenomenon", The Information Society, 19, 315-326.

van Ryzin, G.G. (2004), "Expectations, performance, and citizen satisfaction with urban services", Journal of Policy Analysis and Management, 23, 3, 433-448.

van Ryzin, G.G. / Muzzio, D. / Immerwahr, S. / Gulick, L. / Martinez, E. (2004), "Drivers and consequences of citizen satisfaction: An application of the American customer satisfaction index model to New York City", Public Administration Review, 64, 3, 331-341.

van Sylke, D.M. / Roch, C.H. (2004), "What do they know, and whom do they hold accountable? Citizens in the Government-Nonprofit Contracting Relationship", Journal of Public Administration Research and Theory, 14, 2, 191-209.

Vardon, S. (2000), "We're from the Government and We're Here to Help - Centrelink's Story", Australian Journal of Public Administration, 28, 3, 63-71.

Vaughan, D. (1992), "Theory elaboration: the heuristics of case analysis", in: Ragin, C.C. / Becker, H.S. (Ed.), "What is a Case? Exploring the Foundations of Social Inquiry", Cambridge University Press, Cambridge, 173-202.

Velditz, A. / Dyer, J.A. / Durand, R. (1980), "Citizen Contacts with Local Governments: A comparative View", American Journal of Political Science, 24, February, 50-67.

Verba, S. / Nie, N.H. (1972), "Participation in America", Harper & Row, New York.

Verba, S. / Schlozman, K.L. / Brady, H.E. (1995), "Voice and Equality: Civic voluntarism in American Politics", Harvard University Press, Cambride, MA.

Verhoef, P.C. / Donkers, B. (2001), "Predicting customer potential value: An application in the insurance industry", Decision Support System, 32, 2, 189-199.

Verhoef, P.C. / Langerak, F. (2002), "Eleven misconceptions about customer relationship management", Business Strategy Review, 13, 4, 70-76.

Verhoef, P.C. / Langerak, F. (2003), "Strategically embedding CRM", Business Strategy Review, 14, 4, 75-80.

Vigoda, E. (2000), "Are you being served? The Responsiveness of Public Administration to Citizens' Demands: An Empirical Examination in Israel", Public Administration, 78, 1, 91-165.

Vigoda, E. (2002a), "Administrative agents of democracy? A structural equation modeling of the relationship between public-sector performance and citizenship involvement", Journal of Public Administration Research and Theory, 12, 2, 241-272.

Vigoda, E. (2002b), "From Responsiveness to Collaboration: Governance, Citizens, and the Next Generation of Public Administration", Public Administration Review, 62, 5, 527-540.

Vigoda, E. / Golembiewski, R.T. (2001), "Citizenship behavior and the spirit of new managerialism - A Theoretical Framework and Challenge for Governance", American Review of Public Administration, 31, 3, 273-295.

Vigoda, E. / Shoham, A. / Schwabsky, N. / A., R. (2005), "Public Sector Innovation for the managerial and the post-managerial era: promises and realities in a globalizing public administration", International Journal of Public Management, 8, 1, 57-81.

von Hippel, E. (2005), "Democratizing Innovation", The MIT Press, Cambridge, MA.

von Lucke, J. (2003a), "Citizen-Relationship-Management über Hochleistungsportale der öffentlichen Verwaltung", in: Uhr, W. / Esswein, W. / Schoop, E. (Ed.), "Wirtschaftsinformatik 2003 - Medien - Märkte - Mobilität", Physica, Heidelberg, 901-915.

von Lucke, J. (2003b), "Regieren und Verwalten im Informationszeitalter : Abschlussbericht des Forschungsprojektes "Regieren und Verwalten im Informationszeitalter" am Forschungsinstitut für Öffentliche Verwaltung bei der Deutschen Hochschule für Verwaltungswissenschaften Speyer", Duncker & Humblot, Berlin.

Waldo, D. (1984), "The administrative state: A study of the political theory of american public administration", Holmes & Meier, New York.

Walsh, J.P. / Ungson, G.R. (1991), "Organizational Memory", The Academy of Management Review, 16, 1, 57-91.

Walsh, K. (1991), "Citizens and consumers: marketing and public sector management", Public Money and Management, 11, 2, 9-16.

Watson, D.J. / Juster, R.J. / Johnson, G.W. (1991), "Institutionalized Uses of Citizen Surveys in Budgetary and Policy-Making Process", Public Administration Review, 51, 3, 232-239.

Weber, M. (1922), "Wirtschaft und Gesellschaft", Tübingen.

Weiss, R.S. (1994), "Learning From Strangers: The Art and Method of Qualitative Interview Studies", The Free Press, New York.

Werner, K. / Wind, M. (1997), "Verwaltung und Vernetzung", Leske+Budrich, Opladen.

West, D.M. (2004), "Global E-Government, 2004", Center for Public Policy, Brown University, Providence.

West, D.M. (2005a), "Digital Government. Technology and Public Sector Performance", Princeton University Press, Princeton, Oxford.

West, D.M. (2005b), "Global E-Government, 2005", Center for Public Policy, Brown University, Providence.

Whitehouse, C. / Spencer, R.E. / Payne, M. (2002), "Customer Strategy: Whom do you want to reach?" in: Freeland, J. (Ed.), "The Ultimate CRM Handbook", McGraw Hill, New York, London, 18-29.

Whitley, R.C. (1991), "The Customer Driven Company", Addison-Wesley, Reading.

Wicks, A.C. / Berman, S.L. / Jones, T.M. (1999), "The structure of optimal trust: Moral and strategic implications", Academy of Management Review, 24, 1, 99-116.

Wilkinson, A. / Willmott, H. (1995), "Making Quality Critical: New Perspectives on Organizational Change", Routledge, London.

Wilson, J.Q. (1989), "Bureaucracy", Basic Books, New York.

Wilson, L. / Durant, R. (1993), "Evaluating TQM: The Case for a Theory Driven Approach", Public Administration Review, 23, 3, 137-146.

Wilson, W. ([1887] 1987), "The Study of Administration", in: Shafritz, J.M. / Hyde, A., C. (Ed.), "Classics of Public Administration", Dorsey Press, Chicago, 10-25.

Wimmer, M. / Krenner, J. (2001), "An Integrated Online One-stop Government Plattform: The "eGov" Project", in: Hofer, C. (Ed.), "IDIMIT- 9th Interdisciplinary Information Management Talks: Proceedings", Universitätsverlag Trauner, Linz, 329-337.

Wimmer, M.A. (2002), "Integrated Service Modelling for Online One-stop Government", Electronic Markets, 12, 3, 149-156.

Wimmer, M.A. / Traunmüller, R. / Lenk, K. (2001), "Electronic business invading the public sector: considerations on change and design", System Sciences, HICSS 2001, Waikoloa, HI, 0-7695-0981-9, 10.

Windhoff-Héretier, A. (1983), "Partizipation und Politikinhalte", in: Gabriel, O.W. (Ed.), "Bürgerbeteiligung und kommunale Demokratie", München, 305-338.

Wisniewski, M. (2001), "Using SERVQUAL to assess customer satisfaction with public sector services", Managing Service Quality, 11, 6, 380-388.

Worcester Regional Research Bureau (2003), "Compstat and Citistat: Should Worcester adopt these management techniques?" 03-01, Worcester, MA.

Wruck, K.H. / Jensen, M.C. (1998), "The two key principles behing effective TQM programs", European Financial Management, 4, 3, 401-423.

Wustinger, J. / Jakisch, G. / Wohlmannstetter, R. / Riedl, R. (2002), "vCRM - Vienna Citizen Request Management", EGOV 2002, Aix-en-Provence, France, September 2-5, Springer, 191-194.

Xu, Y. / Yen, D.C. / Lin, B. / Chou, D.C. (2002), "Adopting customer relationship management technology", Industrial Marketing Management & Data Systems, 102, 8, 442-452.

Yamamoto, H. (2003), "New Public Management: Japan's practice", Institute for International Policy Studies, IIPS Policy Paper, 293e, Tokyo.

Yang, K. (2005), "Public Administrators' Trust in Citizens: A Missing Link in Citizen Involvement Efforts", Public Administration Review, 65, 3, 273-285.

Yin, R.K. (2003), "Case Study Research, Design and Methods", Sage, London.

Zablah, A.R. / Bellenger, D.N. / Johnston, W.J. (2004), "An evaluation of divergent perspectives on customer relationship management: Towards a common understanding of an emerging phenomenon", Industrial Marketing Management, 33, 475-489.

Zaltman, G. (2003), "How customers think. Essential Insights into the mind of the Market", HBS Press, Cambridge, MA.

Zhou, X. (2004), "E-Government in China: a content analysis of national and provincial web sites", Journal of Computer Mediated Communication, 9, 4, doi:10.1111/j.1083-6101.2004.tb00297.x.

Zimmermann, K.W. / Just, T. (2000), "Interest Groups, Referenda, and the Political Process: On the Efficiency of Direct Democracy", Constitutional Political Economy, 11, 2, 147-163.

Zito, J. (2003), "From good to excellent - A case for service and change @ Miami-Dade County", Miami-Dade County.

Zmud, R.W. (1983), "Information systems in organizations", Scott & Foresman, Glenview, IL.

Zuurmond, A. (1994), "From Bureaucracy to Infocracy: A Tale of Two Cities", Information Infrastructure and Policy, 3, 3/4, 189-204.

Index

Peter Lang · Internationaler Verlag der Wissenschaften

Rainer Pitschas

Trusted Governance due to Public Value Management

Public Governance in Europe between Economization and Common Weal: A Value-Based Concept of Public Administration

Frankfurt am Main, Berlin, Bern, Bruxelles, New York, Oxford, Wien, 2006.
VII, 137 pp.
Speyerer Schriften zur Verwaltungswissenschaft. Edited by Rainer Pitschas.
Vol. 1
ISBN 978-3-631-55490-6 · pb. € 36.20*

Reinventing Government and modernizing public administration is an important issue in public policy. There is a variety of reform strategies for achieving sustainable development and efficiency of public authorities, but until now, the proposed reforms have not been very successful. It is not surprising that meanwhile, trust in New Public Management partially vanished. Instead of having faith in the "economization" of public management, the question of values arises. In this book, the necessary change towards a Public Value Management (as a counter-movement in Europe against the merely economical way of modernizing public administration) is explained and reflected.

Contents: Values in public administration · Professionalization of public servants, integrity and honesty · Responsibility for public property, money, power and the interests of a social state under the rule of law

Frankfurt am Main · Berlin · Bern · Bruxelles · New York · Oxford · Wien
Distribution: Verlag Peter Lang AG
Moosstr. 1, CH-2542 Pieterlen
Telefax 00 41 (0) 32 / 376 17 27

*The €-price includes German tax rate
Prices are subject to change without notice
Homepage http://www.peterlang.de